MAKE ROOM FOR *Sentiment*

A Physician's Story

by
Theodore E. Woodward, M.D., M.A.C.P.
*In collaboration with the Medical Alumni Association
of the University of Maryland and
The Historical Society of Carroll County*

Medical Alumni Association of the University of Maryland, Inc.
522 West Lombard Street
Baltimore, Maryland 21201

Copyright © 1998 by Medical Alumni Association of the
University of Maryland, Inc.

Printed in the United States of America.

ISBN 0-9619119-1-3

With love and affection
to my dear Celeste, Bill, Craig, and Sis,
and in loving memory of
Lewis, Mother, and Father.
Without them not much would have been worthwhile.

CONTENTS

PREFACE

$\mathcal{T}$his record of personal glimpses was written for my family, friends, and others who might be interested. From time to time, Celeste and a few close to us have said: "Ted, you ought to write a book." With the realization that memory soon fails, often rapidly, I decided to try, not fully expecting to complete the job! Stimulus has come from encouragement of those close to me and help from a diary kept during all the time spent overseas in the military service, from rather detailed letters written to Celeste, and from a fair recall of old events.

It is a simple and honest portrayal of a happy life which has been blessed with a wonderful boyhood, an affectionate and loving family, and a wealth of friends. These have provided me many rewarding experiences and enriched me beyond measure.

An attempt is made to pay tribute where it belongs, without exaggeration and, hopefully, without serious omission, whenever possible.

Perhaps the message is to emphasize the importance of the family and how a loving and devoted couple can be happy, raise affectionate children, work and live with them, nurture and cultivate friendship, and try to contribute something of benefit to others. Conceivably, the result will be a sense of commitment and contentment.

ACKNOWLEDGMENTS

There are numerous persons to whom I am sincerely indebted. They are: Mrs. Peggy Riley, Mrs. Celeste Marousek, Mrs. Wanda Johnson, Ms. Molly Lutz, and Mrs. Shirley Taylor who handled the job remarkably well in preparation of various sections of this manuscript. The initial draft was completed by my longtime secretary, Mrs. Carol Young. I am indebted to all of them and grateful for their unstinting help. Many of the old photographs were prepared for publication by the Medical Media Department of the Veterans Affairs Medical Center and the Department of Illustrative Services of the University of Maryland School of Medicine. Grateful thanks are expressed to Mr. Stephen A. Johnston and his staff at Brushwood Graphics, Inc. They, in collaboration with Ms. Betsy Winship of Stony Run Publishing Services, carefully edited the manuscript and expertly arranged descriptive material and photographs. They congenially accepted last-minute additions and changes. Jay Graybeal, Curator of The Carroll County Historical Association, and Larry Pitrof, Executive Director of the Maryland Medical Alumni Association, gave much assistance with administrative and editorial details. Philip Mackowiak, my friend and long-standing colleague, kindly prepared the copy for the book jacket. My wife, Celeste, in addition to her strong support, carefully corrected and edited my many misspellings and inaccurate dates of events.

$Chapter$ 1

EARLY DAYS

A strange event occurred soon after I was born in a general practitioner's home in Westminster, Maryland, the youngest of four sons of Dr. and Mrs. Lewis K. Woodward. Baptism in the Reformed Church was often celebrated in private residences. When the balding minister, Reverend Slagle, was about to anoint my equally bald head with water, he was promptly hit on the occiput with a marble. My brother, John, age 4, reasoned that a premature drowning was transpiring and took steps to offer support for his newest playmate. The service then proceeded without further incident and introduction to the Christian faith was consummated.

One of my early recollections involved an event that occurred in November 1918, when the German Imperial Army capitulated to the Allied Forces. Vivid in my memory, even now, is a huge bonfire at the highest point in Westminster on the athletic field at Western Maryland College. I sat on the shoulder of our dearest family friend, Walter H. Davis, and watched Kaiser Wilhelm burn in effigy. This was a huge fire and practically all of the town's population attended. From early childhood, I remember

1

threatening dreams that a German soldier might whisk me from my family nest at night. These were the concerns of the day; now children have other visions and fears.

Early tutoring began at home which was a needed advantage. Miss Alice Miller, later Mrs. Frank Mather, tutored me in my father's waiting room when it was available for lessons. She was a most kind and patient woman in spite of her restless charge and never ceased to be amazed at my ability to spell "hardware," "lumber," and "Westminster." Directly across the street, printed in large letters, was the WESTMINSTER HARDWARE STORE AND SMITH AND REIFSNIDER LUMBER YARD—unfair advantage, but undoubtedly she surmised the obvious subterfuge.

I had a happy childhood. No one ever had a more loving or understanding mother. Mother was one of those very special persons who shared her love and care equally for each of her sons— William, the oldest, then Lewis, John, and her baby, Theodore. We were expected to be neat and courteous, but she tolerated a considerable level of noise and general commotion. Father, on the other hand, was a little short on patience, particularly when patients were being examined in his first-floor office and the second floor sounded like it contained a small riot. Once, when several of us were noisily rearranging things upstairs, he shouted up the hallway, "What are you doing?" "Nothing," we answered. "Then quit it," was the reply.

Just behind my family's barn was the village blacksmith whose shop provided many interesting hours. He always kept a hot fire fanned by a bellows. He shoed horses, made or repaired rims for wheels of buggies or wagons, and made odd things such as metal braces or hooks. It was fun to watch him rasp the cartilage of the hoof of a horse with a file, shape the shoe after heating it red hot, then cooling it and measuring it to fit properly. It was then nailed to the horse's hoof, without pain since the cartilage lacks a nerve supply.

On one very important occasion, the blacksmith saved my hide and much more. While still in short pants, I discovered the mystery of fire and attempted to start a small one against the barn door which backed onto the alley. When it took hold, I quickly recognized the need for some water and ran to the kitchen for a can full. Happily, the smithy across the alley witnessed the action and put out the blaze. Naturally, my father heard about this event and disciplined me accordingly.

I remembered being spanked a few times by Mother for such routine mischief as returning home too late, taking something which belonged to someone else, and telling a few fibs. Father knew how to properly "lay on the hands" which usually transpired in his office, with my bottom bared.

Mother was the one who sensed when her boys became homesick at camp, who wrote frequently, or who arranged for a watermelon or cake to be delivered in person. She was the one who quietly, but firmly, had us write a thank-you note after a special visit or treat by a family friend.

Mother was kind to everyone and, in turn, was loved by all. Never one to complain, she accepted life and its problems as the grand lady she was. There were disappointments, major ones. My brother Bill was seldom well. He spent most of his adult life in a mental institution. Bill was the brightest of us all and had a tough time as the oldest boy during the very difficult years of the depression. Yet, he was the one who taught me baseball, football, and the like. He was a fine track man and tennis player. I recall so vividly a Mother's Day when my mother received a lovely bouquet of flowers from Bill. She knew the affection which prompted the gift and cried.

Never do I recall a harsh or unkind word from my mother about other people. Perhaps she was too kind and uncritical, but I don't recall that trait ever having hurt anyone. These traits she inherited after her father, my grandfather Neidig. Her younger sister, my Aunt Grace Neidig, was made from the same mold. They were two fine ladies. We had the great pleasure of Aunt Grace's presence for many years after Mother's death. Aunt Grace's love and affection reminded me much of Mother, which softened the loss. Celeste, my dear wife, could not have been nicer or more sensitive to Aunt Grace. She took her into our home as if she were her own mother or favorite aunt. Aunt Grace was just as proud of Celeste and our children as was Mother.

Someone, perhaps Mother, decided that I might become the first musician in the family. In any event, a violin was purchased and Philip Royer, a very talented violinist, was subjected to the dubious task of making a violinist out of a Woodward. Lessons were about twice weekly at his studio on West Main Street near the Forks of Main Street and it was most painful for student and probably for the teacher. Perhaps there was progress to a point when "O Solo Mio" could be played by ear. This sort of thing cut into important matters such as sandlot football, baseball, and raising a rumpus in general. Finally, it was determined I had progressed to the point that a better violin was warranted. My great uncle, Theodore E. Englar, whose name I bear with pride, generously stepped in and had a special violin purchased. Its tone was much different, although I carry the reputation of not knowing the nature of any tone. One day, while practicing on the "john," a rather unorthodox setting for such a performance, a prophetic thing happened. On leaning too far to one side, I slipped, fell on the floor, and smashed the violin into little pieces. This omen allowed me to convince my Mother, and everyone else concerned, that there was little future to this line of endeavor.

Walking to school was routine and lunches consisted largely of peanut butter and jelly sandwiches, which usually made a gooey mess, plus an apple. From West End School, just behind Himler's Store, I attended grade school and later the Westminster Elementary School. Classes were small, coeducational, and all pupils knew one another, played together, and agonized when teachers taught by asking questions. Recesses were happy events with marbles, dodge ball, football, and baseball dominating the boys' events. Usually, the West End boys and East End boys competed on afternoons and weekends, particularly in football. The West End boys' practice field was either Park Place or Reifsnider's field on the hill. King Gehr, Ed Dorsey, John Reifsnider, Tim Babylon, Nevin Strine, Milton Katz, Richard Myers, Babs Thomas, Everett Jones, Milton Rosenberg, and George Bare were some of the combatants.

One incident, which could have ended in a serious mishap, should be told. Father hunted occasionally and agreed for me to use his Winchester pump gun (12-gauge) for rabbit hunting with my friends. In his office, he showed me how to put a 12-gauge shell in the chamber and gently let the hammer down by holding it with the thumb and slowly pull the trigger. The live shell was then ejected. I tried this a few times until it suited him. Then I proceeded to the kitchen to demonstrate my newfound prowess. Mother was seated at the kitchen cabinet along with Tim Babylon and King Gehr and Beatrice, our maid. Proudly, I put a live shell in the chamber, while bragging: a "big hunter." In letting down the hammer, it slipped and the gun discharged. Beatrice jumped the whole length of the kitchen. Fortunately, the gun was aimed at the floor, and when the dust settled, there was a huge hole in the floor, the shot going down to the furnace below. Father, then in his office, was naturally terrified by the sound and was horrified by what might have happened in the kitchen—

fortunately, only a hole in the floor. I did not go hunting that day, nor for many to come. No sooner had my audience left the kitchen than my dear friend, Tim, blasted up and down Main Street, "You ought to see what Theodore did!" For several years, I was known as "the big game hunter."

Since leaving home, there is one dish I have never again sampled, namely oatmeal. Mother decided that this was a daily need and I consumed it until the day of leaving for college. I have not eaten it since, although I am very aware that this is a unique, nourishing, all-purpose food. Another dish, equally unnecessary, is mush and milk, usually a breakfast staple. I could handle fried mush, which came that evening or a day later, provided it was smothered in butter and molasses. Other meals at home were just great and fully appreciated all the more in later years when college and army life were encountered. One of the best combinations known to me is beef kidney stew and french fried potatoes. This, along with griddle cakes, were usually the principal treat for Christmas morning breakfast.

Father well fulfilled his role as a general practitioner as had his father, Lewis Woodward, who died of nephritis in 1882, at the age of 33. A letter written in 1881 by my grandfather to his brother well describes medical life and conditions in Westminster late in the nineteenth century.

Lewis K. Woodward, Father

Phoebe Helen (Neidig) Woodward, Mother

Westminster, Maryland
April 11, 1881

My Dear Brother:
      Your silence being so protracted, I thought I would not wait longer for a reply to my last [letter]. I just don't remember when. We are all in the enjoyment of very good health and in a general way this is the condition for our locality. I am not very busy, slight catarrhs only prevailing at this time. This is a beautiful and pleasant morning though the weather has been cool and wet and spring backward, if there is as much grumbling about the weather with you and everywhere as there is here, we certainly are a discontented people. Business is opening here briskly and but few idle workmen, suppose it is the same with you if I may judge by the amount of the late railroad talk; there has been so much pro and con I have been anxious to know what you have to say about it. We had talked somewhat of coming up this spring, but have concluded otherwise and will give you folks an opportunity to come down once. If nothing prevents I expect to go in to New York in June, 14th to 17th so don't set that time for coming. Our Institute of Homeopathy meets there and then it is necessary a physician keeps up with the times so if nothing intervenes, I wish to meet with four or five hundred other M.D.'s.
      Retrospective: I suppose you are busy at your daily work and not think of me nor that this is the tenth anniversary of my "setting" or "settling down" here in Maryland. Ten years ago this evening after a long and dreary drive found us entering this town as strangers, a place now so familiar to me; time passes quickly and the ten years though short has seemed even shorter than it really is, though changes have been brought about to make it appear longer, as an instance of the changes. I might yet add that the old Dr. S. Shipley has died, his family have sold out and moved away. I have found a better location and the old office is now occupied as a green grocery and meat store; similar changes have gone on all over town and I know of but one family in our old square where they have not removed or that death has not entered. This day is commemorative too of our marriage just five years ago. While the time is just evenly divided between my unmarried and married life here the contrast has been very great, with the first no one but myself to see after everything as the saying is free and easy, but still very unsettled. I think now I could hardly endure it again; in the latter five years the responsibility great, wife and little ones to see after and care for, a couple of servants to over-see and often work men here arranging and re-arranging, all takes care and little patience, yet, with all this my life is a very happy one and would not exchange it for any one else in this or any other town or country. The greatest share of all this happiness results from the noble qualities of her who promised to share the cares and trials of life till death doth part. Some may have thought it an ill omen

when you and me had to return after getting as far as J.J. Flimes on our first day's journey here (suppose you haven't forgotten) but fortune has smiled on me through-out and I often think I enjoy so much more than I deserve. With all the pleasures of <u>home</u> life, the ups and downs of a physician's life partly counterbalances it and no one but a physician knows the mental worry they have to endure, some one has said that if a physician hasn't a good practice, he is not of much account, and when he has, he has more than his share of trouble, and so it is. I came here determined to succeed and I believe I have; have generally plenty to do, of course a good deal of it not very remunerative having to take care my share of charity patients with the rest, the very low rate of charges here is a drawback to anyone desiring to become very rich, but as my inclination is not in that direction, that does not worry me. I suppose one of my greatest sources of worry since I have been here was my co-partnership with Dr. S. and I have resolved (the resolution might be broken) that I will never enter with another unless it should be one in my own family. I will give my reasons some other time. I hear from Dr. S. directly every few weeks and is doing right well. During my settlement here, I have lost one hundred and fifty patients; of those seventy were under five years of age and nineteen were over seventy years of age. During the last few years I lose on an average twenty-two patients a year. Have had I suppose over two hundred patients under treatment at one time; prescribed for twenty today which is little less than average.

Although it has taken a good while (longer than I expected) I am getting well out of debt, will give Aaron a check for two hundred and seventy-five dollars which will leave a balance due him of sixty. Take your own time but when you are ready you may pass the interest over to him and then I will be free. I have about filled my paper so close. Accept the love of us all to yourselves all and <u>come down</u>. Write oftener to your brother.

Lewis W.

My father finished Hahnemann Medical College in 1898, at age 20. He promptly entered practice in Westminster. His associates, for whom he had great respect, were Drs. Henry Fitzhugh, Charles Froutz, Luther Bare, Charles L. Billingslea, W. C. Jeannette, Thomas Coonan, James T. Marsh, and others to come later. He had a busy general practice and possessed good clinical judgment when it came to transferring patients to hospitals either in Hanover, Baltimore, or Frederick. No hospital facilities were available in Carroll County. On a regular basis, he ordered many thousands of all types of pills—aspirin, cascara sagrada, coryza pills, ergot, and others. Aspirin came in green, pink, and white versions. It was my chore to count them into separate bottles for distribution to various physicians. Doctors dispensed medicines night and day since there was no means for the patient to reach the drugstore at odd hours. By ordering in bulk, physicians purchased medicines much more cheaply and were able to render less expensive care.

One anecdote about a practicing country doctor remains fixed in my memory. It was related to me by Father about a doctor well north of Westminster near the Mason–Dixon line. A farmer ambled up the stairs to his office and was asked by the doctor whether he had come for "some more of those pills." The response was, "No. I found out that you can buy a whole bottle of those same pills for ten cents in the drugstore." The quick response was, "Now, let me tell you how they make pills. The medicine is mixed like one mixes dough which is spread over a die and the pills are pressed out. All of the pills with the most medicine are in the center of the die and are distributed to the doctors, while the pills with the least medicine go to the outside; these are sent to the drugstores." This is convenient reasoning!

Being raised in a physician's family, with my father's office in our house, gave us the chance to see all kinds of people at all hours of the day and night. Minor injuries were common, with the necessary suturing and injection of tetanus toxoid performed in the back office. Most skin conditions were covered with a type of salve which, for wounds, is now inappropriate because it held no antiseptic value and prevented oxygen from penetrating the wound. When Father was short-tempered and had red mercurochrome on his hands at breakfast, I knew that he had been involved in an all-night obstetrical case. Of course now we know that mercurochrome has no other function than to color the skin. Yet, it was then widely used as an antiseptic. Staphylococci are known to grow in this formerly commonly used solution.

Throughout his busy life, Father liked banking as much as he did medicine. Often, Father left Westminster and its First National Bank to travel to Baltimore to Baker Watts, the First National Bank, or another of the bonding or banking institutions there. Carrying his black bag prompted others to remark about Father's conscientiousness and dedication to medicine. Little did they know that the bag contained negotiable securities!

Father ate like a bird and was slim most of his life. He was most meticulous in his diet; in fact, he was a very finicky eater whose daily bread would have proved monotonous to most. Poached eggs, soft boiled eggs, milk, mashed potatoes, breast of chicken, custard, and occasionally, Postum, were all that he required or wanted. One long night, Father assisted a Hanover county physician with a difficult delivery since Father had a special talent for obstetrics and was often called upon for his expertise. For breakfast, my Father was served a Pennsylvania Dutch-style meal of eggs, cereal, ham, scrapple, bacon, and hot biscuits to start. The physician's wife, Mrs. Wetzel, placed a tray at my Father's place with two pieces of cake and a large portion of pie. Diplomatically, Father took the smallest piece of cake which prompted: "No, Doctor, that is all for you." On another occasion, Father, Mother, and their friends, Mr. and Mrs. Walter Davis, visited New Orleans. The ladies were eager to sample the fare at Antoine's, one of the nicest restaurants of that unique city. After the others had placed their orders, the waiter asked Father for his choice: "A bowl of split pea soup and two soft boiled eggs." It is said that the waiter was never revived!

In those days, bills were sent to patients once or twice a year, in June and in December. Often payment was in kind since many patients could not afford dollars which were often scarce. The office would be filled with sacks of potatoes, apples, turnips, live turkeys, chickens, guineas, and household goods. Even today, I continue payment on a small life insurance policy, the initial premium having been defrayed by the agent who paid his many doctor's bills in this way.

Beginning in grade school and continuing into high school, I was involved in a family enterprise which, upon reflection, was a slick maneuver. Father recorded births and deaths for the county. Certificates of births and deaths were completed by the responsible physician and sent to him, the Registrar, at 31 West Main Street, where we lived. It was then I learned that doctors neither wrote legibly nor spelled correctly. Even up to 1930, the cause of death for heart attacks was often noted as "acute indigestion" or "acute dilation of the heart." This was well before the understanding and general knowledge of coronary artery disease and heart attacks which resulted from coronary artery thrombosis.

The electrocardiogram was just not used. Father, as Registrar, received ten cents for recording each certificate in a ledger which was then filed in the county courthouse. He was too busy to do this so he farmed out the chore to my older brother, Lewis, then in Prep School at Western Maryland College. He was paid five cents. Because of Lewis' too many obligations, I actually did the work and was paid one cent per certificate, a flagrant display of child abuse with nine cents taken off the top.

Chapter 2

ADOLESCENCE AND
HIGH SCHOOL DAYS

*N*othing beats being raised in a small town where most everyone is friendly and congenial. School classes were not a drudgery and most pupils took their assignments seriously. There was a splendid mix of boys and girls from town and country. All pulled together. Football was only for college men so we had to be content with soccer in the fall and track in the spring and early summer. Pickup teams for playing dodge ball, basketball, or football kept us occupied.

Winters were hard with a lot of snow and ice. King's field, off Bond Street, West Main Street, College Hill, starting at the college, and West Green Street were favorite sledding sites. Sleds and horse-drawn sleighs provided transportation throughout town. It was great fun to latch onto the rear runner of a horse-drawn sled to be transported uphill. Snow kicked up from the horse's shoes did not matter. Jumping a stream after coming down a hill on a crust of ice was the height of excitement. A broken rib here or there was of little importance.

Scouting activities took place year-round. Usually a school teacher served as Scout Master and to become a tenderfoot was just as important, at the time, as being admitted to college or graduate school. The chance to make bread from dough twisted on a stick, to fry eggs over a fire beside a stream, to sleep out under canvas, and to be scared stiff of night creatures, in addition to hiking and learning about insects, plants, and rocks, were all maturing experiences. The twelve-mile hike up to Taneytown and beyond was a requirement for the hiking merit badge. There was a nice stream with an overhanging cliff which made it a great site. John Reifsnider and I accomplished this together refusing many rides during this long walk.

Smoking cornsilk by putting it in paper rolls was never a good idea because mothers could always smell much better than boys could. Wrapping paper around punk and smoking it like a cigarette was another adult habit we mimicked which usually led to grief and a sick stomach. These days and experiences were very important to me because they formed lifetime friendships and taught me the importance of working and playing together.

When summer came, two working opportunities were available for growing boys. Carroll County is very fertile and its farms are among the most productive anywhere. Sweet pea season came in June, tomatoes next, followed by corn. Shrivers and the Smith and Yingling Company were the major canners for the county. Once peas were cut in the field, they had to be promptly processed lest they spoil. Harvesting the peas by machine, grading according to various sizes, 1 to 5, cleaning, cooking, canning, sealing, cooling, labeling, boxing, and stacking in warehouses was the whole process. The factory might run twenty-four hours at a time. Pay at the end of the week, at the low rate of seventeen cents per hour, for some, was money well-earned. Men performed the heavier work and were naturally paid more.

Working on a farm provided me with many new experiences. For two summers, I worked sunup to sundown for Mr. John Warehime. Hay was made in June and it was a tough job to spread it in the barn loft when the temperature under the tin roof hit 110 degrees. Manning the blowers was not the choicest of jobs. Thinning corn was a back-breaker. It consisted of walking up row per row, stalk by stalk, bending over and removing the extra shoot. By so doing, the remaining stalk and ear of corn would be fuller. Cutting corn with a machete-like blade demanded care and attention lest your ankle get cut. Stacking corn took energy and muscle. Breakfast was served at sunup, and dinner, at mid-day. The walk home at night was usually followed by an early to bed evening.

On one occasion, when I had reached 16 and obtained a driver's license, Father permitted me to use his new Buick car to ride not far from town with Tim, George, and King along. I was prompted to show off my prowess. Bond Street Extended was a dirt road and I hit a ditch filled with water. The expedient maneuver would have been to slow to a stop and then ease through—not I. It occurred to me to accelerate and at the same time avoid the fault in the road. There was a jolt; no one was hurt, but the right rear window was shattered. Things were very chilly at home that evening and it became my appropriate obligation to have the window replaced. The cost was $17.00, a full week's salary from the canning factory. Later, after this event was over, Big Dav (Walter Davis), owner of the automobile company, said, "Theodore, we thought your Father was paying the bill; had we known, it would have been done at cost." Growing up involves a lot of maturing experiences.

Parties in various homes always included boys and girls and a general good time was had by all. Two games got the risqué activity of the evening into action. "Musical Chairs" or "Winkem" was very popular. Boys stood behind the chair of a particular girl. The boy's hands were required to rest by his side. One had an empty chair and the game plan for him was to wink unobtrusively at the girl whom he wished to reach his chair. If she succeeded in escaping the grasp of the boy behind her, the new master was entitled to a kiss. This usually took place in the outside hall with a prompt return to resume the game.

"Spin the Bottle" provided more action for smaller groups. The boy spun a bottle in the center of a circle of girls. When the bottle stopped at a particular girl, she was made to pay with a kiss. Some fellows learned to aim the bottle very well and were adept at having it stop at the same place each time. The competitive spirit helped make our country great!

Fun with the opposite sex was sufficiently open to be relatively harmless. Necking and petting on the back porch, on the sofa, or in the rumble seat were spirited enough to satisfy both parties. Most of us were too afraid of pregnancy or infection to go any further.

High school was a great time of life. During the spring, the track and field events, under the auspices of the Maryland Scholastic Association (MAS), took precedence over many other outside activities. Never fast in the dashes, I tried for longer distances and a few field events. The standing hop, skip, and jump caught my fancy which enabled me to set a county and state record—which lasted only a short time—of about 27 feet.

Baseball and softball were popular and our team in Westminster won the county championship in softball. During the championship game in 1930, the bat left my grip, flew on a straight line and beaned Sterling Fowble (the sheriff's son, whom we all called Sheriff) squarely on the forehead. He fell to the ground, temporarily stunned, a large gash on his head. We left the game, I being the most scared, and went to Father's office. He sutured the gap and I was relieved when all came out well. Much later, "Sheriff" moved to Baltimore to coach baseball at Southern High School. One of his proteges was Al Kaline, later with the Detroit Tigers who managed to make quite a name for himself and who always took pains to pay tribute to his old coach who had a distinguished coaching career.

During elementary and high school, we were asked to participate in school or Sunday school plays around Christmas or Easter time which were unwanted activities. They could seldom be refused because of parental discipline. Practice sessions were more fun when it was possible to "horse around." When it came time for the main event, the instructors turned very serious. My memory span and lack of any artistic talent whatsoever relegated me to very minor parts. Francis Bowers, who lived nearby at Park Square, took his acting seriously and always made a good showing, Miss Gwendolyn (Gwen) Williams (later Gwen Dunn), who taught history, was one of the teachers in high school who had a dramatic flair.

My father was the physician for male students at Western Maryland College. Often, a football celebrity would come to the office for an individual examination or injury. During the mid and late 1920s, the "Green Terrors" had national ranking among small college football teams. On several occasions, at the end of a successful season, the whole football team was invited to our home for supper. As a boy, imagine my excitement to see, fully dressed in their Sunday clothes, stars such as George Ekatitis, Bill Shepard, Frank Sillen, Paul Bates, Paul Havens, Tiny Pincura, and Nate Weinstock.

I spent several summers in the late 1920s at Camp Red Cloud, a Friends School-sponsored camp on Silver Lake near Binghamton, New York. Here, camp life was under canvas; there were daily inspections commanding military precision and cleanliness, since a number of counselors were West Point men. It offered all kinds of activities and the competition was keen. I recall being tossed off the thirty-foot diving tower by a Point man named (Tiny) Hewitt, a football star. My older brother Lewis once shared a tent with General John J. Pershing, who came to the camp to visit his son. We enjoyed canoe trips down the Susquehanna River, cross-country runs, and other sporting events.

Later, I attended Camp Conoy, the Baltimore YMCA camp on the South River not far from Annapolis, first as a camper and later as a counselor. The counselors decided to have a social weekend and invite girls. Having no date, I was left dangling. One of the campers in my tent had a sister at the YWCA camp not far away and volunteered to call on my behalf. The conversation evolved as follows: "Sis, the counselors at Conoy are having a dinner and dance. My counselor couldn't think of anyone else so he thought he would ask you"! A rather negative approach. I never met this young lady though I am sure she was most attractive.

Lewis had the happy facility of always doing the right thing. He was a good student whose scholastic record was a proper display of his knowledge. Once while in college preparatory school his semester grade card indicated A's in every subject. Naturally, mother and father were pleased, yet father remarked "get pluses the next time"!

Depression years made things difficult and after college graduation Lewis worked for the Bethlehem Steel Company. He later entered Maryland Medical School and there he achieved an enviable record; everyone liked and respected him, he was a people person, always obliging, never complaining.

As a freshman medical student beginning in 1934, I lived with Lewis and his wife Fannie Mae, who had a small flat on Saratoga Street in Baltimore, just next door to Marconi's restaurant.

After his graduation Lewis progressed through the house officer ranks and became chief surgical resident under Dr. Arthur Shipley. He had a distinguished World War II record as a U.S. Marine medical officer with active combat service in the South West Pacific. He engaged in surgical practice in Woodstock, Virginia, and ultimately became medical director of the U.S. Department of State. Among his many global experiences for the State Department, his visit and work with Dr. Albert Schweitzer in Gabon, Belgian Congo, Africa, was the most memorable. Martha Frances, his daughter, was the "apple of his eye." His later life was marked by partial invalidism caused by Parkinson's Disease. We were the best of friends.

One of my fondest childhood memories is of my Uncle Theo. Theodore F. Englar was born in 1844 at Wakefield, Carroll County, Maryland. I have always enjoyed the company of older people and Uncle Theo was among my favorites, not merely because my parents named me after him.

He started out in farm country, since his parents acquired land known as the Englar Farm, which was several hundred acres just east of Westminster. Later, he moved into town and took his residence on Park Place. He, along with Mr. Sponseller, took over the mill on Liberty Street just off Main Street on a railroad siding which made transport of flour along the Western Maryland Railroad quite accessible. Originally, it was the Roop–Roberts mill. The name of their brand was Meadowbrook flour.

His wife, Aunt Renie, was a Roop, the sister of my father's mother who lived at Meadowbrook, a farm several miles northwest of College Hill. We lived next door to Uncle Theo since Father bought the old Matthews home at 1 Park Place from him in 1928. Living next to Uncle Theo gave me ready access to their home and great opportunities to listen.

Uncle Theo was 19 at the time of the Gettysburg battle, a major turning point of the Civil War. An initial skirmish took place in Westminster. The guns of Gettysburg were heard in Westminster and Uncle Theo, as a boy, was on the battlefield the day after Picketts' charge. His memory was sharp and his stories

Theodore F. Englar and Irene Roop
Englar wedding picture

Theodore and Irene Englar with William
E. Woodward, 1939

Theodore F. Englar and Theodore E.
Woodward, 1914

William C. Neidig (Maternal Grandfather)

of the blood, horror, and stench remain fixed. He heard Lincoln's address in the Memorial Cemetery and saw the President lead the parade through Gettysburg's dirt streets. People snickered when they saw this very tall, bearded, rather awkward man, dressed all in black, wearing a stovepipe hat, riding a donkey leading the parade to the cemetery. His legs were so long that his feet dragged

The Meadowbrook Family
50th Anniversary of Theo and Irene Englar, 1917

Meadowbrook, 1984

along the ground. Uncle Theo heard his famous address after sitting through Senator Edward Everett's oration. Always there has been controversy over whether Lincoln's speech was appreciated and applauded. Uncle Theo's version to me was that at first everyone was completely captivated by Lincoln's brief impressive words, which were then followed by solid applause. Lincoln was not the invited orator that day, nor was he regarded then as an appealing speaker, yet, he uttered one of history's greatest speeches.

At the end of the nineteenth century, after his presidency, General Grant traveled from town to town. On several occasions, Uncle Theo had drinks with this memorable military man.

My uncle's equanimity, humor, and practical sense were very impressive to me as a boy. At his flour mill, he had a safe. The door was not locked and there was a sign: "this is a safe and it is not locked." It cost several hundred dollars, I suppose, and he figured it was better to avoid destruction of the safe in that way. Money was never taken from it. One evening during his twilight years, I sat with him on his front porch for company. The mayor of the town came to talk to him, which was a practice many enjoyed. The man gave Uncle Theo about a half hour of purity. "Now, Mr. Englar, I never drank, I never smoked, I never ran around with the ladies, I never did this or that." After this dissertation, he got up to leave. Uncle Theo let him get to the steps, tapped me on the leg and said sufficiently loudly to be heard: "Dorey, there is a man who never lived!"

He loved to hunt and traveled over much of the United States to fulfill this hobby. He was a very good shot and used a 10-gauge double barrel shotgun which I now treasure. I took up hunting more seriously years later, mostly for wild fowl. Samuel (Sam) Revell, my associate as a medical student and house officer, enticed me to hunt during our early hospital days in 1938. We went to Middle River to use a blind of one of his friends off a small island and hit a bluebird day. Nothing was flying. At the end of that boring day, three large white birds bigger than a Canada goose, flew over. Out of frustration more than anything else, we pulled the trigger and one fell to the beach and hit like a ton bomb. This was a silly thing to do and soon all of the other frustrated hunters around came out: "Where is it? Where is it?" We pleaded ignorance and by that time had it in a sack, hidden in the brush. We waited until very dark, put the bag under the rear seat of the boat, and headed for land, thence rapidly to the University Hospital. Here we lived, breathed, worked, ate, and everything else. In those days, the house doctors and everyone else knew the cook and there was a good, general, close congeniality. The cook not only cleaned but dressed that big white bird, which we had advertised as a Canada goose. I sent it to Westminster to Mother, posing it as a Canada goose. Agnes fixed the dinner, "Canada goose, several guineas, and all the trimmings." The hardworking young doctors who made the trip were Sam Revell, William (Bill) Long, Edward (Ed) Cotter, John Bowers, and Ephraim (Eph) Lisansky. Uncle Theo came from next door to be with the boys. There was a preprandial drink and then the dinner which everyone enjoyed. After dinner, we went into the living room for port; Uncle Theo grabbed me by the arm and said, "Dorey, that was no goose."

So many things could be said about this remarkable everyday man. As a boy, in late June of each year, he would call me down to the mill and slip $5.00 into my hand, a considerable sum then. The family always congregated at Meadowbrook for celebration of the Fourth of July. With the money that he gave me, he said, "Dorey, do you think that you could arrange for things not to be so quiet at Meadowbrook on the Fourth?" Five dollars bought a great deal of fireworks of all types, the noisy kind, two inchers, three inchers, five inchers, torpedoes, snakes, roman candles, and sky rockets for the night display.

Another memorable incident with Uncle Theo was a fishing trip to Solomon's Island, a favorite site. I remember all four of the boys sleeping crosswise in the bed which afforded a little more breathing space. Whether the feet stuck out did not matter to boys. My Father and Uncle Ray Fogle had special fishing gear with rod and reel. Yet, there sat Uncle Theo quietly on the gunnel with a hand line fishing on the bottom. He pulled up nice large trout, twice as many as anyone. He knew that this fish has a soft mouth, took the hook lightly, and needed a gentle and steady pull to land safely in the boat. This type of care is not as necessary for rock or bluefish which strike harder and usually sink the hook firmly.

Aunt Renie, Uncle Theo's wife and my father's aunt, died in 1939 of gastric cancer for which we physicians could do nothing. She was a delightfully kind person and they were an ideal couple for seventy years. Several things she said to me have stuck in my memory. "Theodore, pennies make dollars." Her gallbladder was diseased and bothered her from time to time. She would say, "My

Lewis K. Woodward, Jr. (Brother) and his daughter Martha Frances

gallbladder is sluggish, I think that I will drink a glass of warm olive oil." This was not bad reasoning for a sleepy gallbladder. Also, Aunt Renie would say, "It's going to rain soon, my joints hurt." All of this was good, solid, practical advice for a young boy who might consider medicine as a career. During the summer, she kept me supplied with iced cold watermelon. Also, Uncle Theo taught me how to get a melon in late September, shellac it all over to keep the air out, and take it down to the Koontz icehouse. It would keep until Christmas and made a unique dessert. Uncle Theo lived several years more and died quietly in 1941.

During his lingering years, we put him on an ounce or so of whiskey at the end of the day which sparked his appetite and served as a good expectorant. Once, when in his nineties, I caught him with his glasses on the end of his nose, reading the newspaper. "Uncle Theo," I said, "why do you wear glasses?" He replied, "Dorey, don't you think I ought to look my age?"

In an editorial memorial tribute (written by Mr. Peyton Gorsuch) on August 21, 1942, it was said of him:

Mr. Englar was one of the youngest men for his age known to me. He loved and enjoyed life and was one of the few who accepted it as it came, the good and the bad, the sunshine and the clouds, and did not worry or complain. If clouds came, he spent no time in self-pity or moaning over his hard luck, but found some anti-worry temperament which probably contributed in no small way to his long life of 98 years.

He was kind, courteous and considerate for his business associates, employees and all he came in contact with and made friends, not enemies, and if he had a temper it was under perfect control. He disliked publicity especially of his many acts of kindness and charity and his liberal contributions to movements he deemed worthy of support. He had a fine sense of humor and his conversation was cheerful, entertaining and helpful.

A little more of his type of genetic material would serve us all well today.

Chapter 3

EDUCATION AT A SMALL LIBERAL ARTS COLLEGE

I experienced something of a shock in the transition from a small-town high school to a liberal arts college with a high academic standing. My grounding in the physical sciences and mathematics had its gaps, not because of the instruction I received in Westminster, but because I had the antithesis of a mathematical mind.

On entering my assigned dormitory room, the first thing I noticed was an empty bed and a hulk of a man sound asleep. His huge rump covered by shorts was about all that could be seen. Since football players came early, I assumed that he was one of these stalwarts, which was a correct conclusion. I puttered around quietly taking care not to disturb this Goliath. After awhile he awoke, ignored me completely, walked around a bit, looked over his desk and dresser, and said, "I can't find me pen." Then I fully understood that this was Pennsylvania Dutch country and I had better learn the language. John Wentzel, from Sunbury, and I roomed together for several months and became friends. Since it was prearranged that he would room with another Sunbury upper classman when such room assignments could be made, I later transferred to another room in the same dormitory with Paul Sanner, from Johnstown, Pennsylvania.

Franklin and Marshall is a small liberal arts college situated in Lancaster, Pennsylvania, a typical college town. My choice of program aimed toward the Bachelor of Science degree with a major in chemistry. As expected, math gave me the most trouble since my mind was not geared that way. The math professor was excellent and frequently taught by interrogation of students while they performed at the blackboard. Early in the course, I was caught in this exercise, a system I had not experienced before during those happy high school years. The professor asked me the solution to a problem which stumped me completely. From this, he worked down to some simple equations. By this time, I was so flustered, I couldn't solve a simple fraction. He became rightfully annoyed and gave me a simpler equation with the comment: "Solve the equation or leave the room." Promptly, I left the classroom with the thought that most of my career, whatever it was meant to be, had terminated. For about a week or more, I attended all my classes but math. One evening, I answered a knock on my dormitory door. The math professor, Walter Murray, came in, asked how I was, talked to me like a father, and suggested I return to class. Often I have wondered in how many other colleges would this act of kindness have happened. A little extra counseling with his mature advice as to how and what to study, in order to catch up, straightened things out. That frightening experience as a young freshman in college made a profound impression upon me regarding the important functions of teachers.

There were no easy courses for me during that first year. General biology was made interesting because of Professor Frederick Foster whom, as I recall, had some medical school exposure. His lectures were always sparked with practical information. He would add ten points to your final grade if you successfully dissected, intact, the entire brain and spinal cord of an earthworm. This was a tedious job because the brain forked at the point where it coursed around the esophagus. He was very adept at picking up the very fine silk thread we used to repair the break at the critical junction. I failed in my quest for ten points. Professor Foster stressed the need to be broadly informed. On every examination, you could count on a question such as

"Name six justices of the Supreme Court," "Who is president of the Pennsylvania Railroad," or "How many steps are there in this laboratory from the first to third floor." He believed in developing our powers of observation.

My various courses in religion were also broadening for me. The teachings of Confucius, Buddha, and Lao Tse, and the Tao or Nirvana, had never entered my mind. It seemed amusing to accept the concept of reincarnation, but after visiting India years later, it was easier to accept that this fanciful belief was the only way out of an impossible life situation.

Chemistry was more difficult for me than the biological sciences because of its greater requirement for mathematic ability. Making simple chemicals made it much easier to understand what those damned formulae meant on the blackboard. Most anyone with a simple brain could make cobalt and feel that something real had been accomplished. Organic chemistry was the most fun. Our organic chemistry professor Herbert Beck was departmental chairman and took great delight in making sure that things were tidy and learned well. Indeed, it took him five minutes to be sure that the blackboards were clean and the window shades all set at a proper level. At least this meant five fewer minutes that some of us, unprepared, might be made to look the dummy. He enjoyed teaching and took pains to introduce his students to something beyond academic matters. A few of us were privileged to visit his home and partake of a gentleman's sport called fox hunting. The lovely countryside of Lancaster County equaled that of Maryland's Green Spring Valley and Virginia's Shenandoah Valley. I managed to stay on the horse but in a less than graceful manner, in spite of my earlier farm experiences.

Physics was tough and took a lot of work, again because of the mathematical requirement. Some of that material just did not seem to apply to someday helping people recover from their medical illness. My naive stupidity was realized repeatedly not much later.

There was a language requirement for a baccalaureate degree. This is a very good idea and it is a shame that most medical schools no longer require this for admission. Study of a foreign language helps considerably in learning one's native language. My high school studies had provided this elementary knowledge of French plus the college experience served me very well during later years and may, inadvertently, have influenced my career for better or worse.

After landing with the invasion forces in North Africa in December 1942, we were dumped on Morocco where the basic tongue is French. After the noise and confusion died down, I went with Lt. Col. George Banton, Chief Preventive Medicine Officer of the USA Fifth Army, to the Pasteur Institute in Casablanca where it was possible for me to speak in garbled French understandably to Dr. Marcel Baltazard, Acting Director, who spoke not a word of English. My rudimentary facility with French, along with a few other capabilities, led to an invitation for me to work on typhus fever at the Pasteur Institute. My career change from a general practitioner to something else possibly had its partial beginnings in this way. My point is that most Americans should learn another language which will help them speak English better in the process.

Perhaps the college course that most reshaped my thinking was the one in philosophy taught by Professor Elijah Kresge. He was a kind, gracious gentleman in every sense. Just observing him as a model went a long way toward learning manners and courteous behavior. Professor Kresge was near retirement which in no way lessened his influence upon us. The works, writings, and beliefs of the world's great thinkers were interpreted for us and we were all expected to express our own points of view on reading assignments. In hinting about the pressures and tensions of adult life, Professor Kresge said that every person needs a room where he can go, ruminate, and give the world the sphinx sign (thumb to nose with outstretched fingers). This was quite daring advice in 1933! (When Professor Kresge's son was killed suddenly in an automobile accident while I was a student, I learned the essence of courage from his quiet demeanor.)

In no sense was college all study—far from it! Sports were a favorite outlet for me, which was rather challenging since most of my classmates were older, stronger, and much more sophisticated. The first mistake I made was trying out for football, which pitted me against brawny, older men from places like Scranton, Pittsburgh, Johnstown, and Wilkes-Barre. These fellows were born with muscle and began using it in high school. Sandlot football in Westminster was no match. In any event, I put the football uniform on for the first time. Trying out for an end position nearly crushed me into pieces too small to chew. This lasted about a week until better judgment prevailed. Who ever heard of a 115-pound end?

Immediately, I switched to soccer and cross-country for fall, sports that called for slender fellows with reasonably long and strong legs and a desire to compete. Swimming became my winter outlet and here came another mistake. I chose diving over straight swimming, although it would have been wiser to have chosen distance swimming because of my long legs and good endurance. Nevertheless, soccer and swimming broadened my cadre of friends. Fellows who play together, sweat together, and get along well together tend, in my mind, to make concerned and good physicians.

Spring brought a new set of choices which for me included track and tennis. There was no lacrosse at Franklin and Marshall, somewhat of a disappointment for a Maryland boy. My track events were the two-mile and one-mile run which took a lot of practice. My game of tennis was sufficiently satisfactory to make the team, primarily because of my pesky ability to get the ball back, no matter how, and a fair serve. The opportunity to earn five varsity letters during my junior and senior years plus a few sweaters with appropriate stripes engendered a little silent pride.

My brother, Bill, taught me a very important lesson which was about at the time of his worsening health. Perhaps it was the sophomore year, 1932, when I came home with a few varsity letters. I had wanted Mother to sew one of the blue and white Franklin and Marshall insignia on a sweater. Bill said, "Why do you want to do that? Put them in the trunk; you will know who earned them and that they are always there." I never thanked him enough for this.

My classroom and athletic associations brought me in contact with a great group of fellows. Franklin and Marshall was not a co-educational college until much later. With these contacts came an invitation to become a pledge and later join a fraternity. It was a rather intense and an eye-opening experience to have a whole week (pledge week) of being invited to houses for social functions. To gain an invitation required your best sophisticated behavior. Somehow, Sigma Pi made me an offer, accepted in part because some of my new college friends were leaning that way.

This was a good choice since the fellows comprised all types of interests. It made a good, solid, and small community.

My closest friends became Gordon (Slim) Chalmers from Shorthills, New Jersey, John Moore and Paul Sanner from Johnstown, Pennsylvania, Richard (Dick) Bastian from Wellesboro, Pennsylvania, Fred Jones from Stroudsburg, Pennsylvania, and Joseph (Joe) Apple from Frederick, Maryland. Slim was a year behind and a star athlete, having competed in backstroke with the 1932 Olympic Swimming Team. He was a business major, as was Johnny Moore, one of the most sophisticated and best looking men in the class. John had natural ability which we all admired. Practicing for track events was a matter of his putting on and taking off his track shoes to see whether they fit, on the Friday just before the meet competition held on Saturdays. He did manage to practice starts and stops; John also smoked more than was good for him. Yet, he ran a 10-second 100-yard and 22-second 220-yard dash which was enough to beat most competition.

Dick Bastian was a good organizer with a great sense of humor. Frederick (Fred) Jones knew all along that he was to become a doctor, indeed a surgeon. We studied anatomy and chemistry together for many long hours, along with John Wentzel. Many times we smelled up the dormitory room with cats taken from the laboratory to brush up on anatomy. This knowledge of anatomy was a great help because this mammal's structure is much like that of humans.

Engaging in competitive sports provided the opportunity to visit many interesting places and to learn to work as part of a team. These kind of experiences were great stimuli for bringing fellows together and fostering concern for the other fellow. Years later, during World War II, it fell my lot to view combat fitness films for young men in battle. It was so clear to me then that many of the lessons on agility, endurance, and courage shown by our troops were learned on the athletic field and the enthusiasm engendered by competing for something. Educators should not lose sight of this in evaluating character and judgment: medical competence is not only a sequel of scholastic attainments.

During my junior and senior years I was elected class vice president. Roy Phillips was always the president and a good one. He was a first-class wrestler; later he became athletic director of

Wenzel, John

Jones, Fred

Moore, John

Bastian, Dick

Swimming Team, F & M, 1933

Cross Coutnry Team, F & M, 1932

R. Taylor (left), Co-Captain, Soccer, with author, 1933

the college. I was not elected to Phi Beta Kappa, which disappointed Father to some extent. My first year and a half at college were spent in trying to learn how to learn. Good marks came later, but a little late for honorary distinction.

As early as 1933, it was my intention to pursue a career in chemistry. Father had not encouraged a medical career, probably because he knew it to be tedious and he never fully relished dealing with seriously ill people. Yet, encouraged by others to apply to medical school, I really had no idea of what other direction to take. The University of Maryland School of Medicine was my only overture and I was accepted there as a student in 1934 with the intent to become another general practitioner.

Three of my college summers were spent at a Citizens Military Training Camp (CMTC). The first one selected was Fort Eustis, Virginia, and next Fort Monroe at Hampton Roads. The camp program was free and we received a few dollars from the government for travel expenses. The program attracted fellows from Maryland, the District of Columbia, Pennsylvania, and New Jersey. We received classroom exercises, drilling instructions, learned the Manual of Arms, and enjoyed all kinds of competitive sports. We also received training in how to fire Long Tom (155 mm) and 16-inch disappearing land guns which projected a missile thirty-six miles.

My three years of summer experiences were aimed at earning a commission as a second lieutenant in the Coast Artillery Reserve Corps. Many completed the various exercises and achieved this commission. It was good training for young men and seemed to inculcate a genuine interest in national affairs and the importance of maintaining a strong defense.

This military training at a rather young and receptive age served to impress me with the importance of a certain degree of regimentation, national pride, and physical fitness. Most everyone entered the camp training programs on an equal basis and the freedom to compete to the extent of their abilities. This was the fair competitive basis upon which our country was founded. Although that goal has not been fully achieved for all races, our country leads the world in freedom and opportunity in spite of our intense compulsion for self-criticism.

Chapter 4

MEDICAL SCHOOL DAYS

*H*ardly any experience in scholarly attainment compares with the shock of transition from college, and its attendant comforts, to medical school. Practically everyone was scared stiff from day one until the first semester was successfully maneuvered. Were I given the chance to turn the clock back and travel the same road, it would not begin again until the end of the first semester in January of my freshman medical school year.

Our class of about ninety had the advantage of attending lectures in Davidge Hall which is an old and handsome building of great historical interest. Seats were tiered and numbered with each student assigned in alphabetical order to a specific seat. It was unnecessary to call the roll because an empty seat was obvious. Lectures were attended—or else.

The entire first semester consisted of anatomy, gross anatomy learned by lecture, dissection of the human body, and organized study. The class was split into groups of four, each group being assigned to a dissection table on which lay an intact cadaver. Our first exposure to our cadaver was somewhat shock-

33

ing when its canvas covering was removed. That was enough for a few of my new classmates who took one look and departed permanently through the door. Perhaps this was because of the idea of cadaver dissection itself or the odor which is characteristically bad, to put it mildly.

The Anatomy Department was well organized under a taskmaster, Dr. Eduard Uhlenhuth. He, along with Dr. Frank Figge and Dr. Monte Edwards, was particularly lucid and most helpful in integrating the details gleaned from the dissection exercises with the dissecting manuals. The mere presence of Dr. Uhlenhuth spread chilling apprehension over the entire class. Usually, he entered the lecture hall from a small door and walkway to confront the class firmly seated in place. With finger already pointed, he would ask, "Mr. Miniszek, tell me the branches of the otic ganglion." Failing to receive the correct answer, he would jump from student to student until satisfied. Once he decided to demonstrate to the class the various reflections of the peritoneum, which is the lining of the abdominal cavity. First, he sat on a chair and covered himself with a sheet. He then grabbed a bit of the sheet and explained, "This is the liver, the spleen," etc., and by the time all of the indentations were completed, he was on the floor hopelessly entangled. No one dared laugh even after he was mercifully rescued.

Dr. Uhlenhuth's motive was to turn every member of the class into an anatomist. No teacher I have encountered insisted on higher standards. Undoubtedly, we ended up knowing more anatomy than any other medical school class in the United States, more than necessary; yet, we were all served well. So many times in later life, I've been able to call upon the basic wealth of anatomical knowledge he taught me when attempting to solve a clinical riddle.

With two of us working on the upper body and two on the lower section, we dissected the human body. Progress was slow and it was necessary to follow Cunningham's *Dissecting Manual* closely and compare notes with one another. Nerves, arteries, veins, and connective tissue often looked the same until we had developed a certain degree of facility and sophistication in dissection. Periodically, Dr. Uhlenhuth and his various instructors would come to the table to observe the results of our mutilating efforts and ask questions. Once, Dr. Uhlenhuth approached a table and said, "Giff me the phrenic nerve." This student, a little indifferent to say the least, took it out of his white coat pocket and handed it to him! He had just removed it from its proper place. This did not set too well. That particular student failed to survive beyond the first semester, probably because he had no fundamental interest in becoming a physician especially if it required this degree of hard work.

Not only was the course very intense, but a cloud of apprehension pervaded the entire class. Simply, our fear was that if you did not make the cut and successfully pass the first semester course in anatomy, a career other than in medicine was your lot. Everyone started out equally with a fair chance. The issue was one of hard study and plenty of it; cramming just before an examination or at the end of the semester would not do. Without exaggeration, the average student attended lectures and dissection from 8:00 AM until 5:00 PM, took a short supper hour, and hit the books until 1:00 or 2:00 AM. Only Saturday afternoon and Sunday were free from classes, although not from study.

Most everyone soon became accustomed to many hours of daily dissection. The odor of the dissection room never competed with that of gardenias or roses, but was tolerable. Your clothes, hair, and skin soon were permeated with its very special scent. On buses or streetcars, a fellow passenger soon changed his seat. On going home, your presence was known as soon as the door opened whether you were seen or not. Actually, we adjusted to the grisly situation so well that some students placed their conventional brown paper lunch bags in the open chest cavity of the cadaver, just for safekeeping. Lunch was taken at the table side. Once, during a brief visit to Westminster before a major examination, Mother served rabbit. Apparently, I was more interested in the names of the bones and their various prominence and grooves than I was in the meal itself.

Before practical or written examination, there would be a lot of "gas" floating over the class. Usually group celebrations followed. On one occasion, after our final examination, a few of us went to a very shady place on Baltimore Street known as the Oasis. Most of the girls had little coverage, which was nothing

Hugh R. Spencer, M.D., Chairman, Pathology

Maurice C. Pincoffs, M.D., M.A.C.P., Professor and Chairman, Medicine

Louis A.M. Krause, M.D., Professor, Clinical Medicine

Arthur M. Shipley, M.D., Professor and Chairman, Surgery

new to us since we were seasoned experts in human anatomy. It is a little different, however, when one of them sits on your lap.

Freshmen medical students everywhere, in the good old days when you really had to learn anatomy, engaged in horse play, sometimes a little raucous. Amputated fingers cropping up around the fraternity house or in gift wrapping were not uncommon. Once, a deliriously happy fellow, who had just passed a

University Hospital, 1934

major examination, was caught waving a severed arm from a bus window. The police took the matter in hand, but, in those days, nothing was done about it. The rebuke from the professor was much worse than the arm of the law.

There were many laughable experiences which served to lighten the tension. There is time for only a few. Professor Uhlenhuth was drawn to our cadaver because it as a huge man with very small testicles. His interests in endocrinology attracted him to our table. At the beginning of class, he instructed us to inform him when the dissection had progressed to that anatomical area because he wanted the specimens for his collection. At about Thanksgiving, when the first dissection was almost completed, he came into the Gray Anatomy Dissection Hall and tapped on the lamp shades, which was his way of gaining class attention. "Where are my testicles? I want my testicles," he demanded. This broke up the class.

Wilbur Brooks, one of our respected and older classmates (then in his mid-thirties), sat on the front row because of rather severe deafness. Whenever he knew the answer, he could always hear the question. When puzzled, he could never hear the question, which would prompt Professor Uhlenhuth to approach another student. Yet, at a fraternity function, when he was well across the room, Wilbur could hear, "do you want a beer?" This is called proper selective deafness. Wilbur became a very successful radiologist.

We had a great class and we both worked and played together. There was a genuine interest in the other fellow and a lot of assistance rendered through joint study. One of my classmates, who was a dear friend, was Aaron Feder, who became a leading physician in New York at the Cornell Medical Center. Stanley Bradley, who led our class academically, also succeeded in New York and became a professor of medicine and chairman at the Columbia Medical School and Presbyterian Hospital. John Bowers, another classmate, became the dean of two medical schools, Utah and Wisconsin, and later president of the Josiah Macy Foundation and Alpha Omega Alpha, the honorary medical society.

There were four girls in our class—Mary Haylich, Florence (Flo) Gottdeiner, Geraldine (Gerry) Powell, and Celeste ("Susie") Lauve (whom I eventually married!). Celeste had returned to America after residing in Europe for almost a decade. At the time, she spoke French as fluently as English and needed to pick up some of the U.S. slang which had eluded her in France and Switzerland. Someone pinned the nickname "Susie" on her and it stuck.

Later, in our junior year, I took Susie to dinner. I believe it was in the main dining room of the Emerson Hotel which her father had liked. The waiter asked if we wished to have a drink. Susie responded, "I don't drink." I suggested that she have something, whereupon she said, "All right, nothing strong, I'll have a martini." At that point, I wondered just what was happening to me. The waiter sized things up with these two rather innocent babes and suggested an "orange blossom" for her. I'm not sure whether she knows today what a martini really is.

Our second semester was not much fun either but at least some of the heat was off. The course in chemistry just did not make too much sense perhaps, in part, because it was not taught with respect to its relationship to diagnosis and patient care. Much of it comprised memorizing structural formulae without really knowing why. Again, it might have been my poor mathematical aptitude which made it difficult. On one occasion, Professor H. Boyd Wylie had just covered the blackboard with a series of formulae and equations when he noticed an inattentive student in the back row. He asked that student, "Mr. _____, what does this all mean to you?" The response was, "It reminds me of a huge glass jar of jelly beans in the grocery store window with the sign—guess how many." There was pin-drop silence and then a loud reaction. That student had one of the best minds in the class but, unfortunately, it was undisciplined. Later, he took his own life which was a poignant reminder to us that the likelihood of suicide, like addiction, is high in physicians. That is perhaps understandable when one considers the intense need to acquire knowledge, the drive to excel, and the relentless worry about decision making and its consequences.

During that summer, I worked at the Hanover (Pennsylvania) General Hospital in the laboratory unit and had the opportunity to learn many things including the preparation of pathologic tissues by frozen section. This involved freezing formalized fixed tissues, such as appendices, tonsils, and uterine scrapings, cutting them into thin sections with a microtome, and putting the section on glass slides. Performing blood cell counts, smears, and routine bacterial culture work was good practical experience. During the week, I resided in a hospital room and went to Westminster on weekends. Dr. Frederick (Fred) Wright, Hanover's chief surgeon, allowed me to help on operations and it was then that I decided to become a surgeon. His operative technique was as precise as a Swiss watch. This, coupled with his tall and handsome figure and his engaging manner, made him an excellent role model. Dr. John (Jack) Grey also helped start me out on the right track. He was a good diagnostician who allowed me to observe his manner with patients and let me listen or feel for various things. Once he took me into a home and said, "Will you please take the blood specimen for me?" This was my first crack at this and it came out alright. On another occasion, Dr. Grey let me do the spinal puncture on a patient with meningitis. This procedure is a bit more tedious but spinal fluid did come out the right way. No visual aids or computer techniques will ever equal this kind of teaching!

At the end of summer, William (Bill) Mather, a boyhood friend, who was a bit older, and I went to Old Camp Red Cloud on Silver Lake near Binghamton, New York. We stayed there a day or two and I took the occasion the first evening to cross the lake in a canoe to the girls' camp, Red Wing. Strangely, classmate "Susie" was working there as a counselor and tutor that summer and she was a bit surprised when our canoe pulled up alongside hers that evening on the lake. This type of rendezvous was part of a ritual between young men and women then. The next night we dated and went to dinner and a movie somewhere and that was it. My adrenalin overreacted somewhat to this less than chance encounter.

Bill and I put a canoe in the North Branch of the Susquehanna River in early September of 1935 and brought it all the way to Sunbury, Pennsylvania. This was a great vacation. Before starting, I asked Father for a small stake to which he responded by giving me half of all that he had in the bank, $10.00. This was just after the Great Depression. The stake was enough to pull off the whole trip. We made about thirty miles per day, cooked out most of the time, and slept under the canoe. One major mistake was our failure to figure on mosquitoes, which were as large as hummingbirds. We had no nets or repellents. Cigar smoke was a good repellent. One night, I went to sleep frozen stiff on my back with a fresh cheroot glowing. Apparently, I dozed off and the next morning Bill took a picture of me with that cigar popping out of my mouth in the same position.

There was a near serious mishap at Pittston, Pennsylvania, where the river was not so wide and the current was swift. Along the river, there were fish traps made from large rocks shaped in the form of a V. In the center, there was usually a channel where the rapid water was "shot" with great force. At Pittston, just before a bridge, we thought that we were approaching another V-shaped fish trap since the water was deeper and swifter. Just before we reached the apex of the V, we discovered that this was not a fish trap but a dam and there was no option but to go over it. I was in the stern at the time and we both jumped over just when the canoe was headed down. It was about a twelve-foot drop. Fortunately, the canoe did not turn over or capsize perhaps because we held on to the gunnels. All that we lost was one camera and a few pots and pans. It could have been serious, but we were good swimmers and stopped to dry out along the bank.

Negotiating the swift and white water is always the fun part of canoeing. Had there been more time, we had planned to take the canoe to Baltimore which meant portages at Conowingo and Safe Harbor Dams. Medical school was soon to start and Bill had his commitments. We were met at Harrisburg, Pennsylvania, by Stanford Hoff, who took us, canoe and all, to Westminster. He was a good friend who later became a prominent lawyer and member of the Maryland Legislature.

My sophomore year was somewhat more comfortable, knowing that I had survived the first year. Bacteriology was interesting because we had to use our hands in performing cultures, pipetting fluids from tube to tube, and deducing the contents of unknown concoctions. The science of virology had not yet come of age so that our problems were reasonably simple. Professor Frank Hachtel, a medical school "Mr. Chips," knew what medical students had to know. Unfortunately, he always scribbled the daily laboratory exercises on the blackboard in a barely legible script. The previous year, Sam Revell and Joe Gore were copying his directions when Joe asked, "Sam can you read that?" The response was, "God almighty cannot read that." A soft voice behind said, "Well, I can." No harm done.

Professor Hugh Spencer was another "Mr. Chips" whose main role as the chairman of the pathology department was to teach medical students how to be a good physician. He lectured beautifully, took pains to work with each student at the microscope, and was the epitome of what basic science professors should be in a medical school. His teaching sessions in clinical pathologic conferences with clinicians, such as Drs. Maurice Pincoffs, Nelson Carey, Louis Krause, and others, were the highlight of the curriculum later in the junior and senior years. Dr. Spencer smoked heavily, which led to severe bronchitis and emphysema. He was always a great favorite, and in later years, I frequently stopped to see him for brief discussions, including the time when he was hospitalized at the Maryland General Hospital. While he was in an oxygen tent, I asked: "Doctor Spencer, is there anything I can do for you?" "Yes, Woodward, get me a little air." He was a kind and splendid gentleman.

During this year, we took surgical anatomy which was a good review of the anatomical structures which we had forgotten from our freshman session. This brought me closer to Albert (Al) Kump, John Scott, and John Bowers, since we all worked on the same cadaver. Our teachers were accomplished surgeons who taught for the sake of teaching. They included Drs. Thomas Aycock, Monte Edwards, Luther Little, Buss Karns, and Charles Reifsnider, among others. Once, when we were quizzed by Dr. Little while ill prepared, he remarked, "You four put together would not make one poor freshman." Somehow, though, we managed.

The second semester brought us into contact for the first time with living patients in the course on physical diagnosis. We talked to patients, listened to their complaints, and actually examined them. We worked in small groups and the instructor usually took his responsibility very seriously.

Dr. Conrad Wolff and Dr. Milton Kress stand out for me; they took great pains to teach. I remember so well Dr. Kress taking the time to correct my awkward technique of percussing the chest. He had me place the hand firmly on the chest and tap lightly for touch. That can't be learned from the textbook. At the Baltimore City Hospitals, we worked with all types of seriously ill patients, including those with advanced pulmonary tuberculosis, rheumatic heart disease, and syphilis of the brain, spinal cord, or aorta. Now, most of these diseases are museum pieces because of the marked improvement in human health. Modern medical students may never see acute rheumatic fever, complicated syphilis, poliomyelitis, diphtheria, typhoid fever, or typhus fever to mention a few. This is all to the good and is indicative of some of the remarkable progress made in medical science during a relatively short period. Antimicrobial therapy really began in the late 1930s, first with the sulfa drugs in 1936, and then with penicillin in 1940.

After my sophomore year, my summer was spent at the Maryland Tuberculosis Sanatorium in Sabillasville in Western Maryland in the Blue Ridge Summit near Emmitsburg. There were many hospitalized patients there with advanced tuberculosis who were referred by physicians from all over the state. Most were very ill and the death rate remained high since there was no available form of antibiotic treatment then. Dr. Victor Cullen was the director and under him were a dedicated staff of able physicians including Dr. S.S. Stewart and Dr. Paul Cohen. My fellow student trainees were Bo (Bernard) Thomas, a classmate, and Donald (Don) Woodruff, a Johns Hopkins student. Assigned to specific patients, we were expected to conduct a patient history and physical examination and take relevant laboratory tests, as well as prescribe certain medications and even do postmortem examinations. It was a rather eerie feeling, when all was otherwise quiet on the hill, to hear the rasping cough and gurgling sound of a patient coughing up pure blood. All that could be done was to administer morphine, immobilize the patient by putting a sandbag on the involved side of his chest, and pray. Occasionally, it was possible to perform an emergency pneumothorax by injecting air under pressure into the involved side and collapse the lung, but it seldom worked.

Patients who developed tuberculosis of the vocal cords were usually treated by Dr. Thomas Aycock who would anesthetize the pharynx as best he could and cauterize the ulcers. This was a rather crude and painful process. For us young fellows who had become attached to our assigned patients, it was depressing to watch.

The highlight of these summer experiences was the opportunity to work with and examine these tuberculosis patients and to learn, particularly from Dr. Cullen and Dr. Cohen. Dr. Cullen was a full-time, salaried physician for the State of Maryland. His salary was miniscule, yet most of his Sundays were spent examining patients, without fee, for other physicians. He had an uncanny knack for detecting abnormal physical findings and usually his conclusions matched those shown later by an x-ray. He would have his "summer boys" examine patients, without any prior knowledge of them, record their findings, and report to him. Then he would clarify the finer points and humbly demonstrate his skill. There is no finer technique of teaching than this and we all owe him a great deal.

Those were the days when artificial collapse (pneumothorax) of the lung was about the only form of treatment. This involved inserting a needle into the pleural space between the lung and chest wall. Then air was injected under pressure sufficient to fully collapse the lung which allowed it to rest. Occasionally, an adhesion would hold the lung to the chest wall, which then required the complicated procedure of inserting an illuminated instrument, cutting the adhesion with a cautery, and allowing collapse of the lung. Air refills were necessary about every week since some of the air would absorb. It was necessary to keep the involved lung collapsed for a year to eighteen months to allow rest and ultimate healing. On my first day in the treatment room, Doctor Cohen performed the procedure which I had expected to observe. With the next case, however, he said: "Doctor Woodward, would you please administer the pneumothorax to this patient!" One grows up fast.

Celeste and I began looking in the same direction late in the junior year of medical school. Actually, I missed a golden chance early in the year at a class dinner dance held at a local country club. Her date had a little extra "soothing syrup" on board. I gathered enough courage to have a dance or so which was followed by a walk on the golf course and specifically to the ninth green. There was a starlit sky with a moon. I asked her to look up, close her eyes, and point to the big dipper. Never was there such a golden chance of which I failed to take advantage; this attests to the bashful characteristics of a country boy.

During the junior summer, I had started a little more serious courting. That Model A Ford saw a lot of travel from Baltimore to the Blue Ridge Mountains, a long ride. On arriving at the mountain setting, often early in the morning, various treats awaited me by my friends, Bernard Thomas and Sam Novey. Usually, there was a pie bed or a large basin put in the middle of the bed between the mattress and springs. In getting into bed over the obstacles, my time of arrival was noisily advertised.

Without a doubt, those two summers' with Dr. Cullen and his staff helped me and gave me considerable confidence in knowing the physical examination techniques of chest disease. This was to serve me well through the coming years, since careful examination of the human body and often of the heart and lungs can detect things not found on x-rays, electrocardiograms, or CAT scans. One will never hear a crackle (a râle as it is called) on an x-ray of the lungs. The stethoscope and human ear can!

My junior year consisted of hearing a great many lectures—almost 1200—in Davidge Hall, some excellent, others monotonous. One professor actually read the chapter on measles from the textbook. Today's students might sue the dean for such performance. There were reading assignments and opportunities for patient contact in the various clinics. There were two solid weeks of examinations at the end of each semester in all types of subjects. They all had to be passed. Questions were usually written on the blackboards and I honestly believe that Dr. Pincoffs, the distinguished Chairman of Medicine, composed questions as he wrote. One year, one of his first questions was "Describe hepatitis," which landed like a dull thud over the room. Viral hepatitis was unknown at that time.

My senior medical school year was a pleasant experience. After all, we had about "arrived," the curricular responsibilities were not great, and we had an opportunity to study those special subjects which were not possible earlier. The pressures were less intense. The standout events of the year were lectures and patient-oriented teaching clinics by Drs. Maurice Pincoffs, Louis Krause, Nelson Carey, and Harry Stein in medicine. Other outstanding teachers were Drs. Arthur Shipley, Frank Lynn, Thomas Aycock, Charles Reifsnider, George Yeager, and Harry Hull in surgery, and Drs. J. Mason Hundley, Louis Douglass, and W.H. Toulson in gynecology, obstetrics, and urology, respectively. Preventive medicine was a part of internal medicine and who among us can forget Dr. Huntington Williams coming to a whole class lecture with a fifty-pound cake of ice and a vial of smallpox vaccine in the center. This vividly demonstrated the need to keep the vaccine cold or else it became inactive. The class in preventive medicine made field trips to dairy farms, sewage disposal, and water processing plants. During the year, we saw chickenpox, erysipelas, rheumatic fever, and others at Sydenham Hospital. Later, the antibiotics and the favorable effects of preventive vaccines made such specialized isolation hospitals obsolete.

Home Obstetrics

One of the eventful assignments in medical school was the senior student program of outside obstetrics involving delivery of pregnant women at home. After having witnessed the birth process in hospital, we actually served as assistants and also had prenatal clinic experience with pregnant women. After this preliminary hands-on experience, senior students were expected to deliver 10 babies at home all on their own. My assignment came during a two-week period in May in the senior year.

The obstetrical department supplied us with a large black suitcase which included essential equipment. Following a local telephone call, the chief obstetrical resident directed the budding senior student to proceed, day or night, to a specific residence which was usually within walking distance or a short ride from University Hospital. The social environment in Baltimore in May of 1938 was relatively calm and one could perform the task perfectly safely in an atmosphere of persons who not only favored but looked forward to help. Usually, we were assigned to deliver multiparous women who had already delivered one or more babies since complications in this group are less likely.

On arriving in the bedroom, often illuminated with kerosine lamps or candles, hot water was immediately called for and the patient thoroughly examined. With practice, this determination could be made accurately by even a senior student. If the new baby's head was easily palpable, effaced in the pelvis, and the cervix widely dilated, things were going to happen rather rapidly.

Usually, I tied two sheets to the bedposts and instructed the mother to pull hard on the sheets timed with her severe painful contractions. The duration of the labor pains were timed because the longer they lasted, coming with increasing frequency, the closer she was to the main event.

Frequently, when labor pains were not strong or the contractions seemed to have ceased, we would give a hot soap suds enema to stimulate contractions. On one occasion, I had a rather portly patient lean over the side of the bed for proper placement of the enema nozzle. She remarked "Doctor, you're going wrong." I quickly changed direction. On another occasion a woman stopped pulling the sheets and suddenly exclaimed rather hysterically, "I can't have this baby, I can't have this baby." In other words, she quit. I suppose my next action would not receive full psychiatric approval, but I put all of my gear in the black bag and started toward the door. She looked up and asked where was I going and I remarked, "If you are not going to have this baby, you don't need me," whereupon she remarked, "Yes, I can, yes I can," and we proceeded uneventfully from there.

A final case led to a reprimand. It was on a Saturday afternoon when I encountered a woman, at term, in hard labor, with a breech presentation. In such patients, according to instructions, we were expected to call for help. Yet, the breech presentation was very obvious and a foot had been partially delivered. I completed the process without event, but on reading the report, the chief resident "dusted me off" very properly.

On one occasion, under candlelight illumination, just at the critical moment of delivery, a huge gray rat ran across the bed. That very evening, a boyhood friend was with me who had aspirations of studying medicine. This experience changed his ardor considerably and he became an investment counselor. On another occasion, just as the new baby was born, a small child, previously unnoticed by me, came out from under the covers to see what was happening. Occasionally, when we arrived things had already happened: a BOA (born on arrival) or a DOA (dead on arrival). In one such instance, a newborn baby had been placed in a bucket of water. This was a reportable event to the police department.

We were then expected to make postpartum calls several times at home to check the progress of the mother and child. Of course, the child was referred for pediatric care. This was all very good instruction and represented learning the practice of medicine at the grassroots, community level.

Our graduation exercises took place at College Park where a ceremony was held and where we were awarded the coveted degree of Doctor of Medicine. After the ceremony, one of the classmates tipped off a news photographer that Susie (now called Celeste again!) and I were soon to be married. The college president, H. Curly Byrd, was also set up for the picture which we humbly declined.

The June after graduation from medical school is a time similar to "twilight sleep" of pregnancy. The woman in labor was usually given medication which put her in "Utopia" so that she awakened not knowing what had happened. Groups of our class did various things. Some of us went to a cabin in the mountains to raise a little rumpus. Timothy (Tim) Callahan ended up with a broken ankle after sliding into third base which was really a rock!

The State Board medical qualifying examinations were taken on June 24, 1938, and I doubt whether any of us cracked a book. Celeste chickened out and did not take the examination that day because that evening we were to be married. (She successfully completed the examination the following year.) This was a typical hot, humid, June Baltimore day. I took the examination, promptly put on my best suit, and appeared at the right time. We were married at Celeste's father's home since I, as a non-Catholic, was responsible for the break in protocol and a home wedding. My mother and father were there, as were my two brothers, Uncle Theo, Aunt Renie, Aunt Grace, and my cousins, Martha and Lydia Fogle. Tim Babylon was my best man. At the crucial moment, I became aware of a strange noise which turned out to be Tim's knees knocking. The bridegroom and best man should never be concerned because all eyes are on the bride and my bride was a knockout.

The honeymoon was short, just a long weekend, since internship was soon to begin. We went by car to Washington and took the Old Bay Line down the Potomac to Norfolk and Virginia Beach. The Cavalier Hotel was our choice, which was a very nice one though it was a little disconcerting that our room was not ready and permeated with cigar smoke. We had three full days in all, for which Celeste was well prepared—eight pairs of shoes and six pocketbooks. Our happy life together had started in spite of the fact that it was to be marked by inadvertent separations.

Chapter 5

HARD WORK WITHOUT PAY

*P*erhaps one of a young physician's most rewarding experiences is to train in a first-class teaching hospital with the opportunity to observe the medical and diagnostic practices of senior physicians and to participate in the process. Really, the intern and resident, known as house officers, are the backbone of a busy teaching hospital because they are on call, night and day, usually seven days a week. There was no pay (although we did receive full room, board, and laundry) and no real need for any because our reward was practical experience gained under the best guidance and tutelage possible.

There was an occasional night and about every third weekend off starting on Saturday afternoon and ending Sunday night. I do not condone this rigid schedule, but it did induce a sense of responsibility. Somewhere between that intense schedule and today's looser program lies the answer.

It is also important that interns and residents receive adequate compensation for their work. After all, a house officer *is* a physician and is entitled to a proper return for his or her services.

On this point, it is my view that a physician who has spent most of his life preparing for the medical profession is entitled to a comfortable living. The time spent and financial outlay is enormous. I don't believe that one should expect a luxurious way of life either, although I am aware that such occasionally occurs. But generally these represent special circumstances.

Hospital house jobs in our day involved a rotational schedule for assignments extended over a two-year internship. This involved experiences in internal medicine, surgery, pediatrics, gynecology/obstetrics, laboratory service, and surgical specialties such as neurosurgery, urology, and orthopedics. There always were two busy months in an active emergency room. You were assigned with another intern and each worked twenty-four hours, alternately. The nursing staff was excellent and there was a senior physician surgeon or specialist upstairs who was subject to your call and expected to respond.

We saw all kinds of patients who arrived on foot, by ambulance, via the police or by private automobile, from Baltimore and elsewhere. You could count on an average of about one hundred fifty patients daily, some routine and some quite ill. It was

Housestaff 1938–39 (left to right): Standing ———, ———, Houghton, Doeller, Bell, Long, Diggs, Dickey, Bunn, Cornbrooks, Albrittain, Gerwig, Coughlan Stiles, Day, Woodward. Kneeling: Bailey, Ridgon, George, Bieren, Settle, Callahan, Bowie, ———, Haase, McKinney, Cotter. Seated: Waller, Owen, Seegar, Bradley, Talbott, Thomas, Bunting, Wells, ———, Bowers.

here that we soon learned how to be a physician; the growing up process was rapid—or else. After these harassing and tedious two months were completed, we looked back upon that experience as one of the most satisfying possible. All of this was excellent training experience, particularly for the war years soon to follow.

Several experiences in the emergency room stand out, those which were satisfying as well as the mistakes. One night, I was suturing the scalp of an intoxicated man who was using foul language in the presence of the student nurses. He received a verbal reprimand and threat which temporarily quieted him. Then, at the height of my minor surgical procedure he reached in the small basket beside him, took a flashlight, and hit me squarely on top of the head. Soon, Dr. Harry Bowie, my surgical resident, was sewing my scalp.

One night, after a busy day, I crawled into the cot in the back room hoping to sleep through to daylight. Soon, I heard footsteps in the hall. "Doctor Woodward, come, emergency." There were four tables in the large open treatment room. On the second one lay a well-dressed man who was ashen in color with the first signs of shock. The brief history was that an argument began in a bar between two men; he stepped in the way to stop it and caught a bullet in the left side of his chest. To make matters worse, he was an editor of the *Baltimore Sun*. Anyone knew that the first matter was to treat the shock, which was done promptly by the administration of fluids, a blood transfusion, and the lowering of his head by tilting the table. The patient was conscious and had a private surgeon who was called immediately. Just as that situation was stabilizing, an ambulance delivered two adults on stretchers who had multiple leg and arm fractures and open wounds including compound fractures with obvious exposure of bone. They required immediate splinting, stoppage of bleeding, suturing, bandaging, and preventive shock therapy. They were placed on tables 2 and 4. Just then the police brought in a flamboyantly dressed man who was the thug, promptly identified by the editor as his assailant. The officer had put metal claws on his arms, which was a very effective silencer. Momentarily, a man who had discharged a 32-caliber pistol in his ear was placed on table 1. At that point, I called my surgical resident who, after being awakened, listened to my situation. After a full report, Harry said: "Ted, you can handle it, can't you?" As it turned out, I did. The man on table 1 was much beyond any help. There was no cardiopulmonary resuscitation in those days, but it would have been of no help anyway. The fractures of the two patients were splinted, sutured, and bandaged. By this time, Dr. Walter Graham had arrived to minister to the editor. An x-ray had shown the bullet to be on the right side near his liver. He was taken for sugical exploration; the wounds in his chest wall, intestine, and liver were mended and the bullet removed. It had ricocheted along a rib, through the diaphragm to the liver. All three patients came out well.

I recall a mistake never to be made again. A man complained of mild chest pain thought by him to be "indigestion," a common disorder. On examination he had a few crackles (rales) in the lower part of his lungs. I failed to give them proper significance, prescribed something, and asked him to return. Later that day, he had a full-blown heart attack which brought him back to the emergency room. He recovered fully in spite of my ineptness, thank God! That warning was enough.

A boy of about twelve suffered an open fracture of his left shoulder and, while in the hospital, developed a wound infection slow to heal. Also, he had osteomyelitis, an infection of the bone. He was discharged with an open and deep wound infection since some boys often do better at home. The plan was for him to return to the emergency room for dressings. The wound seepage had a horrible odor. On returning for his first examination, after removal of the gauze dressing, the wound was clean and there was no odor. Covering the wound and entire shoulder were maggots which had done a better cleaning job than antibiotics or anything else. He, like all boys, had played on the ground, and picked up the eggs which performed a great job. Maggots were first used to clean wound infections during World War I by Dr. William S. Baer, a Baltimore physician.

One of our favorite Saturday night exercises was the strange need to remove a billiard ball from a patient's mouth. The usual course of events involved playing pool in a hall, generous use of spirits, and a challenge that "you can't put a billiard ball in your mouth." The challenge was usually taken. Invariably, it was the 8 ball! The jaw, or masseter muscles, usually clamped down, making it impossible to remove it because of the clenched and spastic mouth muscles. We had a special instrument to slowly exert even pressure for the various muscles and "deliver the baby."

One Friday night, I first sewed up the left side of the face of a man severed by a razor; but later, he came back with a similar wound on the other side—ear to mouth. Finally, after the third time, now about 2:00 A.M., with a throat cut, I decided to call the police. These episodes were usually the result of Friday or Saturday arguments stimulated by alcoholic spirits.

There are opportunities in an emergency room to practice humanistic medicine if one will simply take the time. On a busy day, late one afternoon, a dear old lady in a coma was brought in from several blocks away. She was waiting for her husband to meet her in front of the old Miller Brothers restaurant on Fayette Street. The lady, in her late seventies, was unresponsive, her blood pressure touched 300, and she had all the signs of a massive brain hemorrhage. I, very young looking at the time, was informed that the son and daughter-in-law were outside. The husband had not yet arrived. Closed doors can be very frightening to loved ones. It was not hard to tell that the problem was serious and my country upbringing dictated but one thing—"talk to the family." A few moments were taken to tell these fine people, unknown to me at that time, that "the lady is very ill, she has probably had a large brain hemorrhage, our senior neurosurgeon is on his way, and the condition is very critical." These were just a few informative words. The neurosurgeon came and I performed a spinal puncture which yielded pure blood. She had suffered a massive brain hemorrhage probably caused by her high blood pressure. She died quietly. Her son became a prominent judge in Maryland. He, the patient's husband, and I became close friends, all because, I believe, time was taken to say a few honest words. There are lessons to be learned here and I am confident that the computer or specialized medicine will not teach them.

Each intern had two busy months in the hospital laboratory. John Wagner and I started the Blood Bank since up to that time, there was no blood reserve. We would take an extra one-half pint from large policemen or firemen who had plenty to spare. In this way, we developed a reserve.

During this time, Celeste was working as an intern at Baltimore City Hospitals. The University of Maryland did not accept women in intern and resident positions at the time.

Surgical rotation was long and tough. If you were selected for Dr. Arthur Shipley's service, it meant being in the operating room at 7:00 A.M. until late afternoon, then working up new patients at night, and starting all over again in the morning, five and a half days a week. There were at least thirty-three active cases to handle. Nights off were unheard of. Mrs. Aikenhead, the chief operating room nurse, would manage a chocolate milk shake for Dr. Shipley and the surgical resident, but not the surgical intern.

During this very tough tour in June 1939, Bill, our first child, was born, one year after our marriage. I was up most of the night when Bill came.

To return to our house officer training . . . Internal medicine is as detailed as surgical training, maybe more so. We worked on both the "free" medical wards and on private medical services. All ward services were informative and instructive. In the 1930s, patients came from all over Maryland and from adjacent states for medical and surgical care. About this time, I concluded that the practice of general medicine was my goal rather than surgery, as I'd decided earlier. The clinical study of patients and the application of diagnostic aids and treatment seemed to afford the best challenge. Let someone else sew the patient together.

Nights off were few but, in the evenings, we could gather in a room for a game of bridge, listen to good records, or talk. There was no television. We worked and thought as a small compact community.

At 2:00 A.M., the medical resident would rout the intern out of bed with the admonition, "Get down to the emergency room and work up that case of pneumonia," or meningitis or whatever. For the acutely ill case with pneumonia, there was a set routine; antibiotics had not been discovered but immune serum treatment had been reported by Drs. Thomas Francis and Colin MacLeod of the Rockefeller Hospital in Manhattan. First, we would examine the patient carefully, collect blood and sputum for blood count, smear and culture. The patient was then sent for a chest x-ray and the ward nurse was alerted to start oxygen. The intern then scampered to the laboratory, performed the blood count, sputum smears, specific typing of the causative bacterium, and the blood culture. The typing procedure involved performing twelve or more smears and the whole process, if we were on the ball, took about twenty minutes. By that time, the patient was in bed, under an oxygen tent. You arrived knowing the specific bacterial cause, reached into the refrigerator, took out type III pneumococcal antiserum, or whatever was the indicated type, and spent the whole night personally giving the curative serum. Now all of this is passé because penicillin and other antibiotics have made this tedious procedure obsolete; things are much easier now. Yet, this is how it was then and the experience was not bad training for learning the rules of the game.

Reluctantly, I recount an unhappy incident. On a late Sunday afternoon after a rare and brief weekend, the chief medical resident, Dr. Kennedy Waller, called to say: "You had better get your ass over here because Doctor Pincoffs is going to round on a sick pneumonia patient who just came in." Actually, one always signed out to a fellow intern who had full responsibility for patients on the entire service. I scampered in at 6:30 A.M., and looked at the patient who was a middle-aged man in an oxygen tent, very ill with a type III pneumonia, which is the worst kind. I went over the chart and found everything in order, except the result of the blood count. The patient had been placed on one of the new sulfa drugs, which had just been discovered, and they were known to occasionally adversely affect the blood. No blood count was performed by the physician in charge before the drug had been started. I promptly took blood for counting and discovered few, if any, white blood cells, which are essential for fighting infection. I surmised that there was possibly a clot in the tube which made the count inaccurate and promptly collected another blood specimen. Just at that time, Kennedy Waller came to the lab and said, "What is the count and get upstairs because the 'old man' is coming on the ward for rounds." Actually the first count had been accurate because the white blood cell population was dangerously low. Before the small group, about fifteen in all, I presented the clinical information, including the results of the physical findings, sputum, chest x-ray, blood count, and sulfa treatment. Dr. Pincoffs, tall, erect and austere, asked "What was the blood count before the sulfa was started?" Response, "Sir, it was not done!" There I stood, naked and disarmed; he looked daggers at me. No one, the intern to whom I had signed out or the chief resident, uttered a word that Woodward was off yesterday. A week later, he selected from the two junior house officers an intern to serve on his private service for two months, a choice teaching service. I was not the one. Much later, we became close friends and I had the honor to succeed him as chairman. Yet, to his dying day, he must have believed I goofed. It was never discussed again and I am quietly proud. Actually, the patient had been his part-time carpenter for his home near Catonsville. The sulfa treatment really had little to do with his ultimate death since the patient more than likely had a serious blood disorder which had made him susceptible to pneumonia in the first place. There are many facets to growing to manhood.

I learned a lot during my two years of rotating internship at the University of Maryland Hospital in Baltimore. Even today, I suspect that an internship of this type would produce better physicians and specialists—surgeons included. Sadly, we do not seem to have time for such any more.

Lasting and valuable friendships were established during this critical time. Eph Lisansky, my assistant resident in medicine, put a bridle on me and helped me shape up. John Bowers, Stan Bradley, Tim Callahan, Bernard Thomas, Sam Novey, and Harry Bowie have been mentioned. John (Jack) Bunting settled in Houston and became a leader there. Joseph (Joe) George went west to establish himself in general surgery. Sam Revell in Baltimore (and later Bedford, Virginia), Bill Long in surgery in Salisbury, Everett Diggs, Ernest (Ernie) Cornbrooks in gynecology in Baltimore, and Winfield Thompson in surgery in South Carolina were among my friends. John Albritton, Chief obstetrical resident, had a distinguished career in the U.S. Navy. These were some of my associates whose ability I salute and whose friendship I treasured.

After my internship, my choice was either to enter general practice, possibly in Carroll County, Maryland or to take another year of training since war with Germany seemed inevitable. My earlier commission in the Coast Artillery shaped my leanings. One growing child and another one on the way practically dictated that I acquire a post with some salary. Up to that time, we had no home and poached on either my parents in Westminster or my father-in-law in Roland Park. Not ideal adjustments, but that was the way it was.

For two weeks during the summer of 1940, Celeste and I went to Fort Belvoir, Virginia, since I held a commission in the Coast Artillery which was later transferred to the U.S. Army Medical Corps. There I functioned as a post physician and most of my evenings were free. Celeste and I had a nice little suite in the Officers' Club with meals plus the added bonus of a steward who liked babies. By this time, Celeste was pregnant with Lewis, who was due in October. During that two weeks, I was paid a lieutenant's salary which helped things a bit.

From Baltimore, we moved to Detroit after I accepted the post of assistant resident in gastroenterology at the Henry Ford Hospital under Dr. John Mateer. The pace was much different, a little slower then I was accustomed to, but I learned a lot. It was my privilege to work with Drs. Mateer, Howard Baltz, and Don Marion, and others who were mature, sophisticated specialists in gastroenterology. Mornings were spent in the outpatient clinics, and afternoons looking after the in-hospital patients who were referred from outlying areas or from the clinics.

In Detroit I learned how to talk to patients, particularly those who suffered from anxiety, tension, or worry, rather than from organic illness. Often gastrointestinal manifestations show themselves in that way. Automotive executives, top baseball players, and successful businessmen were often prone to ulcer-like symptoms, but had no demonstrable ulcer. Dr. Mateer taught me how to talk to such anxious patients, to hear every detail, to encourage, to instill confidence but not to overprescribe. This is what I learned in Detroit, along with how to perform such necessary procedures as a sigmoidoscopic examination, gastroscopic examination (by looking into the stomach with a tube and a light), and draining gallbladders.

We had a great time in Detroit and made such new and good friends as Raymond (Ray) Monto, who remained on the Ford Hospital Staff in medicine and in hematology, and Dalton and Mary Welty. Dalton became a splendid internist in Hagerstown, Maryland. In August, during the heat of summer, I was called for Reserve Army Service for three weeks active duty in upstate New York near Plattsburgh.

While crossing Canada in an old Studebaker on the way to my duty station, I felt a little grubby and pulled into a gas station to refill and use the facilities. I noticed that my stool was clay colored which immediately prompted me to look at my eyes which were yellow. I had no concept then that I was suffering from hepatitis from the injection of yellow fever vaccine which had been given me weeks earlier. In any event, I went ahead, reported to camp, and went through maneuvers for two weeks.

Soon after the camp opened, everyone came down with severe dysentery. There were no facilities, no tents up as yet, and no antibiotics, only sulfa drugs and intravenous fluids. Some men actually went into shock. The camp was a shambles, its personnel on the verge of mass panic. The cause of the epidemic was traced to a mess sergeant who had personally made sandwiches while he had a small boil on his hand contaminating the whole batch of egg salad. Fortunately, there were no deaths and everyone eventually recovered from staphylococcal food poisoning.

After my Reserve duty, I returned to Detroit, where I resumed my happy experiences at the hospital and learned a great deal more about the specialty of gastroenterology. Soon after, our second son, Lewis, was born.

With two children, our small apartment was inadequate and I negotiated a surprise for Celeste. Our salary was $120.00 per month which included everything. There were no fringes, insurance, or hospital benefits, but I managed to rent an unfurnished second-floor apartment just across the street from the Henry Ford Hospital which gave us ample space.

War clouds were brewing for America and in January 1941, I made overtures to enter the military service as a medical officer. I was assigned to Camp George G. Meade in Anne Arundel County, Maryland, and this ended my formal medical training.

Chapter 6

THE MILITARY WAY—
THE ONLY WAY
First Overseas Assignment and "Tooling Up"

*W*ith little advance warning, the formal military orders "requested" my presence at Camp Meade by late January 1941. By now, Celeste and I had two young sons, Billy, age 2½, and Lewis, born on October 3, 1940. We moved from Detroit to a first-floor apartment in West Baltimore, not far from Meade.

The Senior Medical Officer at the base was Major Prather who asked me whether I was interested in surgery or medicine. When I replied internal medicine I found myself at the new cantonment hospital, a branch hospital barracks-type building, where I was put in charge of two wards of about thirty beds each filled with new GIs, most of whose illnesses were a social disorder called gonorrhea. In a way, this was internal medicine!

Rather soon, I learned about this strange and ancient disorder. Happily, sulfa drugs had just been introduced and we were able to apply rather effective specific therapy.

A severe outbreak of epidemic meningococcal meningitis developed in the new young army recruits. This frequently happens when young men, with little prior immunity, are crowded to-

59

gether in barracks. The epidemic was sizeable and swept many military units at Camp Meade. I was placed in charge of a ward and for the first time had the opportunity to observe and participate in dramatic curative medicine of a disease which, until a few years earlier, had usually been fatal.

In the isolation unit, officers were placed in individual rooms and enlisted men in open wards. A regimental colonel was admitted with meningococcal meningitis which was rapidly detected and promptly treated. He responded well and rapidly to treatment which was the usual result. Just at that point, his executive officer, an officious so and so, entered the ward, ignored all posted notices of quarantine and isolation procedures, walked to the colonel's room and demanded attention, "Lieutenant, what is wrong with my colonel?" "He has meningitis, sir." "Well, what are you doing for that?" "We are giving him sulfonamide, sir." "My God, man, that's what's they use for gonorrhea." "Yes sir, we are curing everything the colonel has." By that time, I had gained the colonel's full confidence and learned previously that he had a sense of humor. He laughed, the executive officer was put in his place, and the lieutenant's head was not severed, although it was close.

The new medical CO was Col. Henry Thomas who entered the service from practice as one of Baltimore's Hopkins' outstanding clinicians. He sparked the service through the organization of teaching clinics and seminars. One day, he brought Dr. J.M.T. Finney, Sr. to Meade to speak to the staff. Doctor Finney had been one of Doctor Thomas's revered teachers at Hopkins. It was a great treat to hear this very respected gentleman and dynamic pioneer surgeon speak. He was one of the original pillars upon which the Hopkins Hospital was built. During World War I, he had established an outstanding career as a surgical consultant under General Pershing in France.

The hospital service was very busy which required two, not one, OD's (Officer of the Day) particularly for night calls. One night, after having responded at about 2:30 A.M., I crawled in bed hoping that the next call, to be alternated with my associate, would grant me several hours sleep. Soon, the footsteps of the charge of quarters were heard hurrying down the hall. There was a knock on the next door: "Captain Kirshner, Captain Kirshner, there is a lady over at the station hospital having a baby!" The response was: "Call Woodward, I never heard of that disease." I took the call knowing that Kirshner, as a New York pathologist, might be out of practice. There was no difficulty with the delivery since the mother does most of the work anyway. However, the delivery room was ill-equipped and there was no cord to tie the umbilical cord. A shoestring soaked in alcohol did the job.

Medical life at Ft. Meade became more routine but the war was gathering momentum in Europe and North Africa. Rumblings from the Far East were being heard. I traipsed off to the Personnel Assignment Division in the Surgeon General's Office in Washington and requested foreign service. Col. George Lull was in charge. His staff officers indicated that families were no longer being sent to the Philippines, the post I had requested. He did indicate that a Col. Leon A. Fox was involved in developing a medical program in the Caribbean Islands and was sending families to these stations. I was given his address and on walking out of the office, he walked in. The secretary introduced me and immediately he said that he would arrange a transfer to the Medical Department of the U.S. Engineers, under his supervision.

In no time, I was ordered away from Ft. Meade to take a four-week didactic and laboratory course in tropical medicine at the Army Medical School, now the Walter Reed Army Institute of Research. This was a splendid course. We heard such giants in medical science as Col. George R. Callender, Dr. Max Theiler, Col. Joseph F. Siler, Dr. K. F. Meyer, Dr. John Paul, Dr. John Enders, and Dr. Rene DuBois speak. Col. Siler actually taught us how to dissect mosquitoes effectively and demonstrate malaria parasites. This was a whole new world for me which medical school had not opened (nor was it expected to do so).

Immediately following the course, I was ordered to Bermuda by Col. Fox. I arrived in Bermuda to find a sizeable outbreak of dengue fever which was literally sweeping this small island. The disease is severe, although not fatal, and is transmitted from person to person by a mosquito identical to the one which transmits yellow fever. This was a major headache for medical authorities because of the possibility that yellow fever would occur instead of dengue. Yellow Jack, as it was called, could cause fatal outbreaks of colossal proportions.

At the time, Dr. Max Theiler, at Rockefeller Institute in New York, had developed a new vaccine for yellow fever. Unfortunately, patients with jaundice were cropping up in young, newly recruited military personnel who had recently received the new yellow fever vaccine. Some of the reactions were fatal. Epidemiologic sleuthing by Drs. Karl F. Meyer and Thomas Francis of Michigan pinned the cases, which followed vaccination, to several batches (lots) of the new vaccine. It was determined that human blood serum had been obtained to mix with Theiler's attenuated virus to serve as a vehicle. These batches had been contaminated with hepatitis virus in the serum, something not known at the time. This was an unavoidable mistake of nature and was the forerunner of the virus hepatitis problem.

Military authorities have always been aware of the historical significance and threat of yellow fever. The Bermuda outbreak was dengue which swept the Island. It infected many people and burned itself out by the natural means of infecting most everyone which made them immune. I was able to study and describe many cases including my own, and pinpoint the causative mosquito called *Aedes aegypti*. Also, I learned why they call it breakbone fever. The deep muscle pains are very severe.

A very crisp incident will stress the dynamic personality of Leon Fox. Our British allies were making things difficult as far as bringing in medical supplies, upon which they wished to apply a tax. In Bermuda, our engineers built an airfield by dredging and making a small island out of two smaller ones. Colonel Fox called upon the Colonial Governor who acted typically British and would not budge. He walked to the window, looked out, and remained rigid. On approaching him, Colonel Fox asked what he saw. "Fox, I see that the British Union Jack is flying over the island," a rather firm put-down. Without hesitation, Col. Fox said: "Governor look out in that direction" (which revealed nothing but a vast expanse of water). "Why Colonel, all that I see is ocean." "Well, I wish your eyesight were a little better, because out there, you would see one hundred destroyers bobbing around in the water which President Franklin Roosevelt decided to send you and arrange the details later." At this point, the Governor turned around and said: "You win, arrange the details." Now that is an example of inspired communication.

I spent only a short time in Bermuda and then returned to the States where I soon received orders for assignment with the U.S. Engineers in Jamaica. Not long after arriving and getting settled in the renovated large mansion made into a makeshift hospital, Lt. James New, the ranking officer in internal medicine, asked me to see a patient with him. He indicated his belief that the Jamaican laborer had malaria, but had failed to respond to huge doses of quinine, by far the best and most effective medicine for this serious illness. It turned out that the man had murine typhus fever, the first case to have been so diagnosed in Jamaica. This did provide a bit of personal pride and ultimately caused a bit of a stir in Washington at the Army Medical School. It led to the appointment of a small typhus mission consisting of Col. Harry Plotz, director, Lt. Col. Neil Philip, entomologist, and Capt. Byron Bennett, laboratory expert.

Later that afternoon on December 7, 1941, after I had finished with the patient, Major George Heffernon, the commanding officer of the small medical unit, came in and said: "Have you heard the news? The Japanese have bombed Pearl Harbor!" The sun was going down as I looked to the west; it was then crystal clear that Celeste and my boys would remain in Baltimore and that matters were considerably different.

Just a few weeks later, New Year's Eve to be exact, another incident happened. I was OD, which meant Officer of the Day at night as well, and subject to all matters, surgical, medical, and whatever else. A railroad brakeman had a near fatal accident while riding a box car. He was on a ladder and failed to notice the car approaching a warehouse with little space. He turned his head, front to back, and in the scraping process practically amputated his ears. He was brought in with each ear clinging with a thin piece of tissue. Rather than remove the ears, I decided to apply some of the skills learned at the busy emergency room in Baltimore. Our nursing help was most skillful and patient. For about six hours that night, we took pains to do the right thing, cleaned the area thoroughly, applied local anesthetic properly, and carefully approximated skin, cartilage, subcutaneous tissue. The basic principle taught by Dr. Shipley and others was to avoid too many stitches (sutures) because they can damage the blood supply, which is very poor in cartilage in the first place. Such wounds have to be carefully bandaged and re-bandaged. The threat of infection and breakdown of the wound is always a major concern. Sulfa was available and undoubtedly helped. Three to four weeks of painstaking examination and re-bandaging were required and healing took place by primary union (no infection)—not bad for a non-surgeon!

Shortly thereafter my name was announced over the loud speaker to report to the Office of Chief Engineer. In the room was my patient, his wife, and the boss. "Lieutenant," the wife asked, "why does one of my husband's ears stick out more than the other?" One has to just put up with these things. Actually, they appreciated my efforts and presented me with a gift.

Our unit soon moved from Kingston to Fort Simmonds in the heart of Jamaica's jungle where an air field was being constructed to train B-17 bomber pilots and to serve as ancillary protection for the Panama Canal.

There were new cantonment-like hospital facilities which served the useful purpose of caring for laborers, engineering personnel, and military. We encountered all kinds of acute infectious diseases, malaria, dengue, typhoid fever, dysentery, meningitis, and fungus diseases, so that the tropical medicine training I had received was put to good use.

Scorpion bites caused severe muscle pains, headache, and painful, red, swollen wounds. It was a good idea to check your shoes each morning. Once a veritable epidemic of bites occurred in Jamaican laborers. A little detective work revealed that a nurse had given a healthy dose of rum to a laborer with a scorpion bite which was said to be a good antidote. The outbreak stopped abruptly with change of treatment to an antihistaminic.

Many of our nonhospital activities involved traveling all over Jamaica to examine newly recruited young men to determine whether they were fit for the hard labor of working on the airfield. This provided many interesting experiences and I found the natives to be polite with a mellow, soft lyrical manner of speaking.

There were occasional breaks from duty. We would go north, through beautiful mountain terrain, to Montego Bay on the north shore. On the way, we would go through a shaded cool valley called Fern Gully which was just smothered with orchids growing wild. At Montego Bay, there was a lovely small hotel directly on the ocean, named Casa Blanca. For a pound a day ($4.00), we had room and all meals. We could at least look across the water toward Baltimore and feel a little closer to home.

A lucky break came to me through the misfortune of a foreman who was hit solidly in the eye with a stream of water under pressure. The retina was separated and he was dispatched to Chicago for special treatment. I was selected as the medical escort. First, I took a plane to Miami, then a train to Chicago. Celeste brought young Bill to the city and we remained in Chicago for several days, staying at the huge Stevens Hotel at the lake. We tried the best, plush dining room for the first night. Naturally, I was ccstatic. Bill was popped up in a chair, now about two and one-half years old. A napkin was tucked in his collar; he took a goblet of milk, most of which promptly leaked everywhere. "Dot dam dat milk!" he blurted. Up to that moment, the two dear ladies at the next table had admired this threesome. Before that had passed, another utterance came: "Blue Jesus." This one I had

Walter Reed Army Institute of Research (WRAIR)
Group, 1942: Woodward, Bucantz, Hamilton, Bennett, Philip, Bell, and Reagan.

*Typhus mission, Fort Simmonds, Jamaica, 1942: Woodward, Philip, Plotz,
Bennett.*

never heard. The ladies were horrified. I remarked: "Celeste you
have certainly trained our oldest son very well!" Apparently Bill
had been a willing listener to our maid whom Celeste had in Baltimore.

Soon after I returned to Jamaica, the typhus experts from
Washington came to Jamaica to study the typhus problem. By
that time, a small laboratory had been built for them and I had
trapped a number of mongooses which had been suggested by me
to be the reservoir of this type of typhus, since there were few domestic rats around. The mongoose and bushmaster snakes had
done a good job cleaning up the rats.

In preparing for the typhus experts, I looked around Jamaica
for guinea pigs and there were none. I hopped a ride to Puerto
Rico where there was a good chance to acquire some of these
friendly little laboratory animals. On landing at Borenquin Field
in the nose of a B-26 bomber, I noticed a unique sign over the bar
in the Air Force Officers' Club. "No Air Force Lieutenant
Colonel under the age of 17 will be served at this bar unless accompanied by his Mother." At this time, the war was going badly

in Europe, North Africa, and the Pacific and all forces were rapidly expanding, particularly the Air Force which needed young active pilots.

A ride was taken to San Juan. Not knowing what else to do, I went directly to the office of the chief of Laboratories for Puerto Rico. The Director was Dr. Costa Mandry, who was the top scholar in Medicine at the University of Maryland in 1921. He gave me one-half of his total supply, one hundred guinea pigs, and I promptly returned to Jamaica.

Col. Harry Plotz, Neil Philip, and Byron Bennett taught me all about ticks, fleas, laboratory techniques with animals, and the rudiments of testing for antibodies in blood. This was valuable and needed experience. In a short time, evidence of about thirty cases of typhus in Jamaican laborers turned up which was new and surprising. Also, there was a bit of a ticklish situation because British and Jamaican authorities accused the United States of having transported typhus from Texas and other southern states where rat flea typhus is prevalent. This was a weak accusation since the disease had always been present in Jamaica but never detected.

In retrospect, it is more than likely that this clinical diagnosis and successful laboratory confirmation of the first rickettsial disease in Jamaica served as a stimulus to pursue infectious diseases as a hobby, not a specialty but as a career in internal or general medicine in whatever direction it might take.

While in Jamaica, Neil Philip, the entomologist with the typhus team from Washington, wished to visit a well-known bat cave which had an entrance almost as large as a small two-story house. Even during daylight, bats were flying about. Phil went in to a considerable distance until the floor and ceiling were about six feet apart. In the dim light, bats were everywhere. Flashing a light caused a general storm cloud of these eerie creatures which made loud screeching sounds.

This was enough for me and I retreated, shooing away those on my hat, shoulder, and arms. By this time, Phil was squatting and with his flashlight was picking up young ticks from the dark ghana. Bats had a hard time attaching to his shiny bald head which seemed not to bother him. He came out about 15 minutes later with a broad smile and plenty of new species of ticks. Since he had not brought any alcohol to preserve the new specimens, we stopped at the nearest pub, and acquired a bottle of light rum for the purpose of preservation. Some of the runover was imbibed. Later Phil named one the the ticks after *"Woodwardia Celesteae."*

In May 1942, we bought a small, three-bedroom brick row house in Northwood, Baltimore, for the sum of $5,195. This new setting brought us a whole new circle of associates who became lifelong friends: the Winslows, Orths, Rands, Murrays, and Grahams.

Chapter 7

En Route to Italy, England, France, and Germany via North Africa

The Surgeon General's Office assigned me to a field laboratory unit which was staged at Camp Kilmer, New Jersey. Once you entered the Army Base, everything became confidential, although we all had the general idea that our destination was Africa. I reported to the lab unit and to the commanding officer (CO). Apparently, I had been plugged into a spot vacated by someone designated as a serologist. This was about the most unlikely assignment I could imagine since my training and qualifications were in other directions. Yet, the U.S. Army is not easily reorganized and the CO was not likely to budge.

Soon after, we were taken in trucks to the Brooklyn Navy Yard and at night boarded a ship. It was named the Slyterdycht and turned out to be a reconverted Dutch cattle ship. It fully lived up to its history. Bunks in small squares, called staterooms, were four deep. I chose one at the top since, in those days, my figure was trim and it was easy to squeeze between the bunk and bulkhead. Everything was accomplished in military order. Calisthenics were held on deck at sunup before mess. There were the three usual meals out of mess kits. Numerous instructional exercises were held on deck during the day hours. Always, we were expected to follow strict blackout at night—no lights at all, no striking of matches for a cigarette. One reason we took this seriously was because we were stationed on the right rear of a large convoy whose ships were a prime target for torpedo practice. The German submarines had been quite active with considerable sunken tonnage to their credit. Our destroyers continually circled the convoy, listening and looking, and we were glad to see them.

One night on deck, a GI struck a match to light a cigarette. He was promptly decked with a blow to the jaw which fractured the lower mandible. The next day, the ship's military commander promoted the man who had delivered the blow to the next highest rank.

After about a week, we spotted land which turned out to be the Canary Islands. Our force landed at Morocco, just northeast of Casablanca. There was some, not much, exchange of fire and we disembarked without mishap. Our field unit was assigned to a bivouac area just east of Casablanca along the coastline where we pitched tents. It was December and the weather was cold but not freezing.

Somehow, I had developed a cough and fever which led to my transfer to the Eighth Evacuation Hospital in Casablanca. Looking up, I saw the face of Dr. Byrd Leavell, one of the finest physicians anyone could have. This was the University of Virginia Evacuation Hospital Unit and how lucky I was to meet Byrd in this way. The disorder was virus or "atypical" pneumonia, not serious, and I soon recovered. After the war, Byrd returned to Charlottesville, where he developed and headed the hematology program at the University of Virginia Hospital. Until his death in 1979, he was the most respected internist in that fine medical center.

My CO of the lab unit had no specific assignment for the laboratory nor did it appear that any action would take place for some time. At the time of my conversation with Col. Banton at Walter Reed he had said, "Look me up when things quiet down after landing." I did just that and went to Gen. Mark Clark's headquarters in search of his chief of preventive medicine. Col. Banton took me to the Pasteur Institute in Casablanca which was a recognized center for work on typhus fever, plague, and rabies. Dr. Georges Blanc, the director, was trapped in Vichy, France.

The acting director was Marcel Baltazard, who neither spoke nor understood a word of English. Here my high school and college French came in handy, miserable as it was. Somehow, I conveyed the message that a new technique, using an antibody testing method, could distinguish between the various rickettsial diseases. These disorders include epidemic typhus, caused by lice; murine typhus, caused by fleas; and Rocky Mountain spotted fever, which is transmitted by ticks. Dr. Baltazard, a distinguished rickettsial expert, listened and knew the significance of this. He simply marked out a little laboratory space, and said: "This is yours, come work with us and show us the method called 'deviation du complement' (complement fixation)." This is what Col. Banton had wanted and naturally it suited me since the lab unit bivouacked in the field was not to become active for a number of months.

Naturally, this did not set well with my CO of the field unit. He provided no transportation for me between the camp and the Institute and took a dim view of the whole thing, to say the least. I simply handled the transportation problem by buying a bicycle.

Years ago, the Boy Scouts had taught me their motto to "Be Prepared." Accordingly, before leaving Walter Reed, I had collected all of the essential laboratory reagents and antigens including known positive and negative human serum specimens to enable me to get started. At the Institute, I started to demonstrate the new serologic procedure of complement fixation for typhus fever. I personally bled the sheep from the jugular vein because sheep red blood cells are used in the test. Complement was derived from guinea pig serum and it had to be inactivated by holding a Bunsen burner under a water bath at 56°C for one-half hour. There were no fancy regulated water baths available. Every element which goes into this complicated reaction had to be standardized and it was here that I really learned serologic techniques. I was allowed a Muslim laboratory helper to provide a normal saline solution which should consist of **exactly** 9.5 grams of sodium chloride and not "**about**" 9.5 grams per liter. This mistake messed up everything until the discovery was made.

Finally, after several weeks, the reaction worked and I was able to demonstrate this new and exciting reaction to the scientists at the Pasteur Institute. This gave me an "in" status with an assigned laboratory and run of the place, including their very fine guinea pig and monkey colony. Dr. Baltazard (Balta) and I became close friends and our friendship lasted a lifetime. Dr. Henri Nourry taught me much about rabies (hydrophobia) and when Dr. Georges Blanc returned to Morocco, he shared his scientific knowledge with me.

Typhus Fever in North Africa

The central purpose for me in North Africa seemed that of determining as rapidly as possible the current status of epidemic louse-born typhus in Morocco and North Africa, evaluating the threat and degree of immunity in our military forces, and learning about the clinical and pathologic aspects of this ancient scourge.

Marcel Baltazard, acting director of the Pasteur Institute, himself an authority on the laboratory aspects of typhus, took me to an infectious diseases facility just outside Casablanca. Here all natives with infectious diseases were herded into a small compound consisting of small open wards. Its name was Lazaret Ain

Woodward with Georges Blanc, Director Pasteur Institute, 1944

Chuk, and the best name for it was a pest house. Brought there from throughout the area were cases of tuberculosis, typhoid fever, typhus, smallpox, and plague, all diseases with dreaded and sinister histories.

At this time, I was immature medically and full of the spirit of adventure. One morning, I requested the French physician in charge to provide a fatal case of typhus fever so that I could perform an autopsy. He took me to a small, damp room with little more than concrete slabs upon which there were three bodies, a child, a young woman, and an older woman. He said, "They came in last night with typhus and promptly died." Without thinking, I selected the young woman for examination. There were few instruments and no rubber gloves. Having proceeded to the chest cavity, I cut the lung, and found it to be consolidated and deep red in color. Having just realized the situation, I looked up and said, "This is not typhus, this is plague!" Up to that point, I had failed to reason that a grandmother, a mother, and a child do not come in and die so rapidly of typhus. This is typically true of plague, however. Slides of the lung sections showed large clumps of plague bacilli. That night, I discovered a few fleas in my clothes since this arthropod always leaves the dead for a warm body. Dr. Baltazard was very comforting to me when saying, "Woody, don't worry, plague is a disease of the Old World." I spent a very uncomfortable three days—the incubation period after a flea bite or direct exposure to a patient.

Soon it was possible for me to arrange for a ten-bed ward for the study of typhus patients. The surgeon's office was most helpful in providing sheets, pillows, syringes, needles, antiseptic solutions, medications, and solutions for intravenous therapy. At this time, there was no effective specific treatment for typhus. All typhus patients at Lazaret Ain Chok were screened and admitted to this service. The then-current medical literature reported that the heart was weak in typhus patients (central heart failure) and that digitalis was indicated for treatment and administration of fluids intravenously was contraindicated. My background knowledge of Rocky Mountain spotted fever (RMSF) indicated a contrary view since epidemic typhus and RMSF are similar in many respects. As a noncardiologist, I needed help.

The Sixth General Hospital group was stationed in Casablanca in old school buildings. One day I walked into the surgeon's office whose commander turned out to be Col. Thomas Goethals, the son of the man who had successfully engineered completion of the Panama Canal. After inquiry, he kindly indicated that there were cardiologists in the unit and arranged an introduction to Maj. Edward F. Bland. I had stumbled upon the Massachusetts General Hospital Unit which at that time meant nothing to me. Ed Bland was most gracious in his reception of me. With Dr. Daniel Ellis and their electrocardiographic technician, we went to the Lazaret to examine some cases of early typhus fever. I asked Drs. Bland and Ellis whether they thought the patient manifested signs of congestive heart failure. Their responses were negative which coincided with mine. So, we set out to prove it. Dan Ellis joined us in this little clinical study. Using the simple techniques of measuring blood pressure, pulse rates, venous pressure by the brachial vein method, a few electrolyte studies, and intravenous administration of fluids, we concluded that in practically all instances during the early stages of typhus the heart was not affected, but rather there was alteration of the peripheral vascular circulation. Our work was later published and has stood up to the test of time. Simultaneously, without our knowledge, a similar and more thorough study was conducted in RMSF patients by Dr. George Harrell at the Bowman-Gray School of Medicine. His conclusions were similar to ours.

This work and the opportunity to meet such gifted physicians at the Massachusetts General Unit helped establish friendships which lasted through the years. Dan Ellis, my closest friend, became one of Boston's leading gastroenterologists. Ed Bland, a pupil of Dr. Paul D. White, made his own special mark in cardiology. It was a privilege to meet and learn from Drs. Alfred Kranes, Charles Short, Summers Sturgis, James Halstead, and others assigned to this splendid medical unit.

The clinical work was interesting but the main purpose of work was to determine the protective efficacy of the typhus vaccine which our military forces had received. Soon we determined, after kinks in the serologic tests were corrected, that our soldiers showed a few antibodies as measured in the test tube by the complement fixation test. I visited various military units and obtained vaccination histories and specimens of blood. Few of the men showed antibodies to typhus. I then initiated a different technique, first on myself and then on a few other men. Right or wrong, I surmised that the vaccine as given by regulation doses did not contain enough of the antigen, or rickettsiae as they are called. All three doses were combined in one dose, a single injection of 3 ml instead of 1 ml once weekly for three doses. To our surprise, the antibody titers were as high or higher with a single dose and in a shorter period. The reactions in the arm at the site of injection were tolerable. This study was confirmed in guinea pigs and in a limited number of monkeys. Furthermore, it was shown in these animals that when antibodies had appeared in their blood, they were immune when given the living, fully virulent germ. These were interesting if not important findings.

Soon I was privileged to meet the Secretary of Health for Morocco, Dr. Flye St. Marie; Balta arranged the introduction. It was possible for me to converse with him in French and he kindly took me on inspection trips throughout Morocco. Typhus was rampant in the native population. Whenever there is increased incidence of typhus or another epidemic illness, a quarantine area is designated by the Caid (a local governor) and all patients must be confined to this Lazaret during their illness or until they die. Here, in such primitive settings, I saw patients in all stages of typhus, lying on the cold ground with their eyes directed toward Mecca, particularly in cases of death. There was peace and quiet, no hysteria or panic, and death was calm. This system of rural quarantine must have dated back to Biblical times.

Dr. St. Marie was stimulated by the antibody findings of the American vaccine. This was particularly important since the U.S. vaccine was killed or inactivated without any chance to cause the disease. This was in direct contrast to a living vaccine then being made and produced at the Pasteur Institute. This vaccine, made from infected flea feces, produced active murine typhus in a number of recipients and had the potential of causing wider outbreaks of the disease. Hence, our French allies were delighted with the prospect of using an effective, killed vaccine product. I performed studies of the living flea feces vaccine and the U.S. vaccine in prison volunteers recruited by the Commissioner of Health and the superintendents in several prisons. The results were similar to those found in animals. It was shown that the higher concentrated vaccine dose produced good antibodies. It

Volunteers for typhus vaccine trial, Morocco, 1944

should be said that no one knew at that time, for sure, whether the presence of those antibodies was an indication of protection in humans against the natural disease.

About this time, I was ordered to Cairo, Egypt, where the U.S.A. Typhus Commission, after its organization by Executive Order of President Roosevelt, was settled for work. A strange stroke of fate had placed Gen. Leon A. Fox as director of the Field Typhus Unit in Cairo and I was pleased to see my old boss again. The data which I took to Cairo was of great interest particularly for Col. Harry Plotz, Dr. John Snyder, Capt. Byron Bennett, Capt. Robert Ecke, and Capt. Chris Zarafonetis, who were to become my close friends. Here, on my suggestion, it was decided to follow through with the vaccine-antibody studies and determine whether those vaccinated were really immune to typhus. Further, I agreed to send specimens of serum to all interested, which included Col. Plotz.

At this time I was confident that the French authorities would wish to complete the study in view of the potential hazard of the living-type vaccine. Work was completed in monkeys which established high protection if antibodies were present in their sera at the time of administering living virulent rickettsiae.

The same results occurred with the studies in humans; those with antibodies dropped a little and, after varying periods, a mild, flu-like illness developed in a few. There were no complications whatever in this human vaccine trial and the work established the remarkable effectiveness of adequate vaccination for typhus.

A breach of normal standards of ethical behavior marred some of the gratification of these exciting experiences in North Africa. After completion of the initial vaccine studies, I was ordered to the headquarters of the Typhus Fever Commission in Cairo for discussions related to the vaccine findings. The data showed that immunization of volunteers with the inactivated American-type typhus c vaccine stimulated the production of serum antibodies with high titers even after one injection of vaccine. Results with the Blanc living, flea feces-type of vaccine were spotty and disappointing. At this point, while presenting the results, I commented to a senior officer that it might be possible to make this a complete experiment since French authorities in Morocco were anxious to determine which vaccine, inactivated or the Blanc-type living murine vaccine, was superior as well as safe. A completed experimental study meant giving the vaccinated persons a living suspension of typhus rickettsia to determine whether the antibody immunity to the actual disease was real. This carried a certain potential risk.

Later that day, this same person said, privately, "Woody, if you conduct that experiment and send the serum specimens to me, I will give you a hundred dollars." This flustered me considerably. My immediate response was simply that these blood sera were not mine but rather the property of the U.S. military forces and French authorities. Obviously, it seemed to me that we were all working toward a common goal. I indicated that it was my intention to transmit the sera when the work was completed. Yet, this unorthodox request triggered me to be cautious.

The final stages of the experiment were completed but not until similar tests were performed in guinea pigs and monkeys which showed that the type of challenge contemplated with living and virulent typhus rickettsia was not only safe but that favorable results could be anticipated. After the clinical and laboratory studies were completed in Morocco and showed protective efficacy of the American-type typhus vaccine, I divided the remaining blood serum specimens into three equal parts. One was sent to the Typhus Commission in Cairo, one to the National Institutes of Health in Bethesda, and one retained by me.

Several months later, on returning to my base in Morocco, I was called to the Chief Surgeon's Office. Chief Surgeon Guy Burnett was very indignant over a letter which was dispatched to me through channels from Gen. Leon Fox, who was now the field director of the U.S.A. Typhus Fever Commission. After the first paragraph, the letter read, "Of course, Woodward, you know that _____ took your experimental data, rephrased it, reduced you to the grade of a technician and submitted it to the Surgeon General's Office under his signature. This may be all right with you, but please understand that I expect no such servile attitude from anyone serving with me on the Typhus Commission." None of this was known to me.

Col. Burnett was livid and asked what all of this meant since he knew of the general aspect of my work at the Pasteur Institute and with the French health authorities. I explained everything to him. He responded, "If I were you, I would sue him." I responded negatively. "Then I'll write a letter to the Surgeon General." Again, I declined the offer. "What's the matter, Woodward, don't you have any guts?" To this, I responded, "Yes, but my view is that I and many others know who performed the work and, in the long run, people like that who lower their ethical standards are usually found out." Indeed, that actually occurred because the very person involved never achieved the eminence or respect which he obviously sought.

This was a disappointing eye-opener since it uncovered an aspect of the medical science profession heretofore unknown to me. There is enough room for credit for everyone in our remarkable profession, which makes it unnecessary to indulge in a frantic foot race to beat someone else to publication of scientific data.

During the course of the clinical and laboratory studies, many U.S. military medical officers landed in Morocco prior to their duty throughout North Africa. After a few months, I was settled and had a fairly decent clinical and laboratory program underway. Officers newly arrived were often placed in Replacement or Disposition Pools, usually in a tent setting, until their assignments came through. I arranged to meet them, and to relieve their boredom, took them to the Pasteur Institute, and to my Lazaret Ain Chok where they could see medicine and ancient scourges in the raw. American physicians had heard of typhus, smallpox, and plague, but had never seen them. These visits proved to be interesting and many friendships were formed in this war. Col. Perrin Long, Col. William Stone, Dr. Fred Soper, Dr. William Davis, Mr. David Rockefeller, Dr. Dorland Davis, and Dr. Thomas Reekie, were among those who visited. Actually, it was Col. Long and Col. Stone, among the early visitors, who became familiar with the vaccine work and its significance. Col. Long was aware of the administrative difficulty I was experiencing from the head of the field lab unit to which I was assigned. He became head of preventive medicine and chief medical consultant at headquarters in Algiers. One day the surgeon in Casablanca received a wire: "Capt. Woodward will work on typhus fever and typhus vaccine and be given no other assignment. Signed Eisenhower." This was quite a formidable mandate and with that piece of paper, my transportation and most other problems were solved.

There were a number of interesting sidelights. When the laboratory was established specifically to diagnose typhus by the serologic test tube method, specimens came in large numbers from our allied French forces. The medical officers were anxious to establish a specific diagnosis of an infectious disease. Much later, I learned why they were so persistent. Once a specific diagnosis was confirmed, the convalescent soldier often was eligible for a military ribbon called the "Medallion Infectueuse" to wear on his uniform. Often, when the results were negative, I got pleas to "just make it a little positive."

Frequently, it was necessary for me to visit various medical units as well as the Preventative Medicine Headquarters in Algiers, known as NATOUSA (North African Theatre of Operations). Most of the military transport was via C-47s (DC3) which were the workhorse airplanes of the Air Transport Command. The C-47 had bucket seats, and usually there were no doors since the cabins were nonpressurized and the wings flopped like swinging shutters. On reaching flying altitude after take-off, most passengers usually "hit the deck" covered with a blanket to sleep out the trip. Once, en route on a "milk run" from Algiers to

Casablanca, I sacked out. The run was about 1,000 miles and the highest mountain en route was about 1,200 feet elevation. Usually the trip took about three hours. After about three and a half hours, I looked out the window just to check on things. Rather than viewing land below, we were now over water with the North African coastline some distance to our rear. After a few minutes' contemplation, I made a presumptive diagnosis. Accordingly, I went forward through the door to the pilot's cabin and found the pilot and co-pilot asleep and the automatic pilot on. I tapped the pilot who promptly awakened and I remarked that Casablanca was about one-half hour to the rear. "Oh," he said, "we were just practicing navigation!" Those air fellows had a busy life which often included nocturnal activities. Had we kept going, we were headed for North Carolina with about enough gas for just a fraction of the way!

Louse Verdict in Medical History in Naples, Italy

Naples, Italy, was ripe for an epidemic of louse-borne typhus. This ancient epidemic scourge has a record of causing misery, panic, and death in large numbers in all human populations. It has taken a greater death toll during man-made wars than have the effects of generals, soldiers, and bullets. Italy had not known typhus fever for three or more decades which meant that the younger population was immunologically unprotected and fully susceptible to the disease which is transmitted to humans by lice. The louse bites a human several times a day and if it is infected, its feces causes the illness. Rickettsiae abound in the louse droppings.

Naples was badly overcrowded. The German army, on abandoning the city after the Allied Forces' landing at Salerno in 1944, had bombed the reservoir and stripped Naples of transportation, available coal, fuel, and foodstuffs. Bombing of the city by the Nazis and the Allied Forces, before the occupation of Naples, had caused widespread devastation, flattened houses and apartments, so that as many as three to four families had to crowd into one room. During the day, people foraged for scarce food and clothing. At night came German air raids which forced everyone into air raid shelters deep in the stone caves and catacombs of old Naples. Here Neapolitans, in panic, crowded, rubbed against each other, and, in that way, shared each other's lice. At daylight, the process of spreading lice effectively distributed the disease through the partially destroyed city. Into this setting came the Allied Military Forces with American, French, and English army units.

In November 1943, prior to the Allied occupation of Naples, the B.B.C. first reported a typhus fever outbreak in Naples. This news in itself is a harbinger of bad events for any military commander or civilian health authority. The Typhus Commission, then headquartered in Cairo, was asked to make a preliminary survey of the problem as soon as the military situation permitted. Dr. John (Jack) Snyder and Dr. Andrew (Andy) Yoemans made a quick study. Their findings clearly indicated that the entire city was seeded everywhere with typhus patients. The forecast indicated a calamity of major proportions. Louse infestation in humans builds up in winter, when people bathe less and wear the same clothes, particularly when soap and water are unavailable. Southern Italy can be freezing cold. Typhus epidemics usually are at their worst beginning in January and February, with the epidemic peaking in March. This is the usual pattern of all of history's major epidemics and Naples was not to be the exception.

The U.S.A. Typhus Commission was given control of the epidemic by Executive Order. This caused some ill feeling with the regular army command which, under most circumstances, does not wish to delegate authority to another agency. Nevertheless, this was the order of the day from the Secretary of War, Henry Stimson. My old chief, Brig. Gen. Leon A. Fox was placed in charge of the field operations of the Commission which included responsibility for control activities in Naples. He reported to Brig. Gen. Stanhope Bayne-Jones, director of the U.S.A. Typhus Commission under the Surgeon General of the Army, Washington, D.C. Gen. Fox immediately organized a six-point control program and proceeded to "hit southern Italy like a ball of fire," as he expressed it in a long cablegram to the Secretary of War. The six-point program for control of an epidemic disease of this nature is applicable for almost any similar epidemic situation in a crowded city. The program as organized and the persons responsible for each individual unit were:

U.S.A. Typhus Fever Commission Directors: Dyer, Simmons, Carter (seated), Fox, Bayne-Jones

1. Case finding of typhus patients (Maj. John Snyder).
2. Ambulance and hospitalization of cases (Maj. John Snyder).
3. Contact delousing/refugee delousing/air raid shelter delousing (Dr. Charles "Buzz" M. Wheeler).
4. Mass delousing throughout the city (Dr. Fred Soper).
5. Vaccination with typhus vaccine (Capt. Robert Ecke).
6. Flying squadron for control of all secondary outbreaks in southern Italy below the Rapido River (Capt. T.E. Woodward).

It must be recounted that Col. William S. Stone, head of preventive medicine for the North African theater of operations, was mainly responsible for having DDT available to the military theater of operations. This was an enlightened example of foresight.

When our forces entered Naples, the populace was confused, malnourished, and generally panic stricken. Funerals were frequent and the cortege of hearses often contained two or three coffins. Black garb was the order of the hour.

The comprehensive control program began in January 1944, and before long the city and its people were clouded over

Typhus epidemic, Naples, 1943–1944

with DDT. There was no difficulty in attracting people to be given DDT, "being dusted off," as it was called. Adults, and particularly mothers, came in droves with their children for DDT dusting. The principal problem was one of maintaining order.

All persons and established agencies would call our headquarters to report a case of "fever." The case finding team responded, examined, and, if typhus was apparent, the patient was transported to the "fever hospital" by ambulance. In this way, infected patients were removed from their environment to an isolation hospital for supportive care which, at that time, was meager since there were no effective antibiotics. Immediately the contact delousing teams would go to that area and spray DDT on the clothing, mattresses, and inhabitants of that house and each house adjacent to the one where the typhus case had occurred. In this way, a lot of infected lice were killed, which would then make this setting a much less serious infective threat. As soon as a louse comes in contact with a single DDT particle, it becomes helpless and dies in several hours. DDT sprayed into

Col. William S. Stone, M.C., Head,
Preventive Medicine for North African
Theater of Operations

a person's clothes has a lasting killing effect for lice, extending up to three weeks. This was a most potent weapon for control. While this was happening, mass delousing stations had been established in an available room or store located in a "hot spot" typhus area of the city. Neapolitans came to these mass delousing stations in droves because of the fear and horror of typhus.

Various population groups, such as physicians, nurses, firemen, policemen, priests, and nuns, were offered vaccine, an offer which was not fully accepted since "needle sticks" are not pleasant.

While this was happening in Naples proper, I was busily occupied scurrying about all of southern Italy in an attempt to stamp out secondary epidemic fires before they got out of control. In all, my team blotted out fifty-six separate small-town outbreaks of typhus fever during January, February, March, and April, 1944. Our Flying Squadron Operation was a composite of the system practiced in Naples proper: See the case, identify it as typhus, remove the patients to hospital, and kill lice with DDT in the involved home and adjacent houses with a small, garden-type dust sprayer. All of this could be accomplished if order and discipline were maintained. For this purpose, I soon learned the value of having a few Italian police join our team. My mission responsibilities took me all the way across Italy to Bari and north above Mt. Cassino in a sector under control of French forces. Indeed, I was with a French mortar unit which witnessed the air bombardment of the Monastery on Mt. Cassino.

DDT proved to be amazingly effective in controlling louse infestation. Instead of an epidemic peak of typhus fever in March, which was the usual pattern, the epidemic was broken by late February and early March. This was the first time that a typhus epidemic had been arrested in its tracks.

Typhus patients came from all directions. Refugees poured into Naples primarily from northern Italy since they were forced to go south by German authorities. The military effort came to a virtual standstill because of the rigors of winter, flooding of the Volturno and the Rapido Rivers, and the fact that Mt. Cassino and the surrounding high ground gave the German army a distinct advantage. One day we had word of cases of typhus north of Naples. Before going out of the city, I always checked the military maps for security reasons. The site to be examined looked a little close to military activity but the exact setting was not clear. With my six-by-six army truck, DDT, garden duster guns, two Italian dusters, and an associate, I went north and noticed some rather heavy equipment: tanks, howitzer, heavy trucks, and such. We were in a British sector. At a pontoon bridge, I stopped and asked directions of a British Tommy. "Sergeant, how do I get to Pontecorvo?" He said, "Captain, cross that pontoon bridge, go right two hundred yards, left two hundred yards, and you will precede our patrols into town." We took heed, went in the backward direction, and thereafter I was accused of taking a German occupied town with DDT guns!

Later, while I was still in Naples, I was billeted in the Parco Hotel which overlooked the Bay of Naples. Numerous well-known movie stars who came to Italy to entertain servicemen under USO auspices were billeted in this hotel. Some of these celebrities were Humphrey Bogart, Frederick March, Marlene Dietrich, Adolph Menjou, and John Garfield. They mixed with anyone good-naturedly and ate the food. I do not recall eating spaghetti or ravioli once while in Italy, but we were served cauliflower twenty different ways.

One day, when leaving Naples early, I witnessed a jeep hit and kill a horse along a main road. On returning that evening, all that was left were the bones—the carcass was stripped clean. On another day, at dawn, en route to Bari, Mt. Vesuvius began its historic eruption which added another hazard and threat to the city. The ash reached heights of thirty thousand feet and landed across the Mediterranean on the soil of Africa. Neapolitans again witnessed the anger of Vesuvius and much damage was done. The cone spat fire and ash and smoked for many weeks; the whole contour of Mt. Vesuvius changed drastically.

Transportation was a serious problem for me as head of the Flying Squadron Unit. Naturally, to travel to outlying areas I needed transportation. The colonel in charge seemed intent on focusing his available resources to Naples proper which left me dangling; no vehicles were assigned to my unit which was frustrating to say the least.

Early in the military game, I learned of the silent power of whiskey. I always kept several bottles available for bartering purposes. Near our small typhus central headquarters unit was a large motor pool filled daily with all kinds of government vehicles. One quart of whiskey was usually sufficient to exchange for two six-by-six trucks a month. Later, in the southwest Pacific, it was uncanny how a bottle of liquor would bring the engineers in with a bulldozer to clear a mite-ridden typhus area when reams of official requests failed. In any event, through this devious maneuver, my small team got the job done and we put out about fifty-six small typhus outbreaks which would have been large explosions had they gone unchecked.

By the beginning of spring, the epidemic had been brought under full control through a huge combined effort. Contact delousing performed in the vicinity of individual cases and air raid shelter delousing really did the job. By May and June, 1943, the typhus epidemic in Naples was over and the U.S.A. Typhus Commission was relieved of its responsibilities.

Aden and Yemen

Not long after the Naples epidemic, the British government requested assistance from the U.S.A. Typhus Commission because of an epidemic threat to the Port of Aden. This busy port and city at the junction of the Red Sea and Indian Ocean was vital in the supply route to the Burma area of operations where Field Marshall Mountbatten was in command.

Capt. Robert Ecke and I were selected by Gen. Fox to make the survey and recommend control measures. We knew that Aden was close to the equator and wondered how any louse could be responsible for typhus in such a hot tropical setting. This soon became obvious and, at that point, the only other suspect illness was relapsing fever, a spirochetal disease sometimes transmitted to humans by ticks.

Both Bob Ecke and I were flown to Aden in a British army plane, a Dakota which bumped about a bit. It was hot and I felt hotter than the weather and for the first time became airsick. We stopped at Kameran Island, a small spot in the Red Sea for refueling, refreshing drinks, and a bit of rest taken at Government House. I felt badly with fever, nausea, and a headache which persisted and was present when we landed early afternoon at Aden. The outside temperature was 115°F. We were met in high style by Governor Sir John Hathorne Hall's chauffeur and driven in a stately Rolls Royce to Government House. Sir John met us cordially and we were shown to our equally stately quarters, consisting of a large bedroom, dressing room, and bath, all in grand colonial style.

Bob looked me over and we found seventeen umbilicated vesicles which went along with smallpox, since I had worked with patients for several weeks while in Cairo. Things abated quickly, however, since I did have the protective effect of vaccination and experienced only a mild infection.

The scientific problem in Aden related to the transport of an epidemic disease from Yemen, across a wide and hot desert of eighty to ninety miles to Aden and its port. Typhus could readily cripple any port city as it had Naples, Italy, for a short time. It was necessary for us to travel to Yemen, identify the illness, and counter with control measures, if feasible. We were introduced to the health authorities of Aden and before setting out were provided with a touring car and a truck with an armed squad. Our driver also served as our guide and interpreter. The reason for the armed guard had not been made clear to us. In our left front seat was a young man, fully armed, who was in charge of our military reinforcements.

We had a long, hot ride across that hot sand (there were no roads to speak of) and much of the travel was in a wadi, the dried bed of a stream or river which was now bone dry. Our driver seemed preoccupied and was not pressing on as rapidly as he should. We were anxious to reach our destination before dark, to get bedded down, and to begin work. Darkness came and we still had many miles to go. In the distance, we saw fires arranged in a large semi-circle which came nearer as we slowly moved. Then we stopped, seeing nothing but fires and silhouettes of men surrounding us. Without a word, our front seat guard opened the door, bent to his knee and aimed his rifle. So did the squad in the truck behind us. Thank heaven, the men did not shoot. We were surrounded and soon pressed by many agitated Muslim men, also armed. Even now, we did not understand the problem other than possible highway robbery like the Old West. I remarked to them that we were here to study and help with the new disease. This seemed to do the trick; they could see that we were pale-faced and had medical supplies. This was an adventure.

On we went until near midnight when we reached a village in South Yemen at the base of a mountain. There was nothing to see and we were taken to a vacant building, probably a school house, to spend the remainder of the night. On arising at dawn, we could see a large Muslim city with an enormous number of clay and brick dwellings along the mountainside. It was here that our problem resided.

Just after leaving our makeshift motel, I saw a young boy of about twelve and asked, through an interpreter, for him to take us to a house where someone had just died. He remarked, "You ask for the dead when the graveyards are full?" A rather profound comment for anyone. We went from clay hut to clay hut and examined boys and young men. We encountered patients in all the various stages of louse-borne epidemic typhus. Some were very ill in the acute stages; others who had recovered were now left with gangrenous areas in various parts of the body. A little bedside test which involved mixing a drop of blood on a glass slide with a Proteus OX type 19 strain of bacteria quickly showed a positive reaction. This confirmed the likely diagnosis of louse typhus and not spirochetal relapsing fever.

Bob and I then went from house to house, section by section, and deloused everyone. The anti-louse powder we used was not DDT but a British product known as AL63 which had naphthalene as a base. It killed lice when blown into the clothes with a mechanical hand duster and smarted a bit about the moist parts of the body. This worked to our advantage because of the prevailing concept that "for anything to help, it has to hurt."

Not once during the first several days were we allowed to see or examine the Muslim women. In the Mellah or Jewish ghetto of the village, we were immediately asked to administer help to women as well as men because it was clear that help was being provided. Several days later, though, the invitation came to administer powder to a mother and grandmother in the Muslim section.

Often in Muslim countries, large villages are named for the day of the week when markets are held. All trading is by barter, not exchange of money, and large groups travel from one village to another. In this village, one of the largest, we soon perceived the problem when we looked out to observe several thousand

persons who had come for market day. Here a little American in-
genuity helped.

The local chief or Caid whom we had met earlier came at a
designated time to witness our activities. We needed his full support and confidence particularly if we were to successfully delouse the approximately two thousand market shoppers. His
word was the law.

He rode up on a beautiful horse with his eight guards
mounted on equally handsome animals. The Caid was amusing
to see but we could not display any reaction. He had a white tur-
ban, a white coat with a belt around it, and that was about all
except for a G-string. His police force was dressed about the
same way except for some brass buckles showing here and there.

Through interpreters, I explained the delousing procedure to
the chief. Then Bob Ecke deloused me and I, in turn, deloused the
Caid before everyone. Quickly, Bob and I deloused the guards
and taught them how to use the mechanical powder guns. The
Caid explained things to the multitude and in about three hours,
we had them all deloused. The guards not only kept order but deloused adeptly at the same time.

It then became clear that marketplace delousing each day of
the week would go a long way in controlling lice and their
spread. This, coupled with house-to-house delousing where fever
patients resided, successfully controlled epidemic typhus in
southern Yemen and was the basis of our report.

The threat to Aden was due to the deprived status of Jews
who, rather than suffer more privation and persecution, were
leaving Yemen and crossing the desert to Aden, hoping to return
to Palestine. In the migratory process, they carried infected lice to
Aden which might readily spread typhus among the poorer inhabitants in this busy port city.

We further recommended the establishment of direct travel
routes with delousing stations strategically placed along the way.
These logical conclusions were put into practice to a sufficient
extent to keep Aden free of typhus.

Before leaving Yemen, the Caid entertained us with an elaborate Arab meal. He presented Bob and me with two of the most
beautiful horses one can imagine. He was disappointed when we
told him that we could not accept these handsome gifts. Imagine

negotiating two horses across an eighty-mile desert and then by airplane to Cairo and ultimately to Baltimore, Maryland, during wartime.

The Caid gave us his next best gift, about a dozen gourds each, filled with honey. This was a great delicacy and I still have one of the gourds.

Chapter 8

FROM EUROPE TO
THE PACIFIC ISLANDS
Continued Search for Rickettsiae

*W*ith the Naples crisis at an end, the Commission members returned to their headquarters in Cairo to continue their epidemiologic and clinical studies of this intriguing disease, while I returned to Morocco to tie up loose ends.

For many years, it had been surmised that those persons who had contracted the rat/flea form of typhus fever, called murine (rodent) typhus, were immune to the more severe epidemic form, louse-borne typhus fever. There was supporting historical evidence for this concept based on careful studies in humans and animals. Simply put, a person who has survived murine typhus is immune to epidemic typhus and vice versa.

My earlier vaccine studies in Casablanca had set the stage to prove this supposition, not from epidemiologic deduction or studies in animals, but in human convalescents. Seven patients who were fully recovered from murine typhus volunteered to have their immunity tested against the virulent and often fatal epidemic type of the disease. After appropriate measurement of antibodies in their blood serum, they received live epidemic ty-

93

phus rickettsiae. As expected, they developed no clinical signs of illness whatsoever. There was no fever, headache, or rash. All were solidly protected, which proved the immune relationships between flea-borne and louse-borne typhus.

Another product of the earlier studies at the Pasteur Institute in Morocco was the demonstration that a specific louse, which adapts itself only to monkeys, not humans, was capable of becoming infected with epidemic typhus rickettsia and of transmitting this agent to other monkeys.

By this time, big events were brewing in Europe and soon I was ordered to England with an assignment to help instruct U.S. and Free French forces in typhus fever prevention and control. Gen. Fox was in charge of this major field operation which was closely aligned with the Military Office of Preventive Medicine headed by Col. John Gordon. This assignment brought me more wonderful contacts and new responsibilities.

I often lectured to large groups of Free French medical personnel—physicians, nurses, and allied health workers. Typhus fever was known to them, but only by textbook hearsay. In contrast, I knew something about this subject since for a year or more I had been carrying live lice with me. They were kept in a capsule, like a small pillbox, which was open at one end and covered over with a fine mesh. The capsule, containing a hundred or more lice, was then fastened to my calf, thigh, or arm during the entire day. The mesh permitted lice to feed and suck blood, which the little rascals did about twice daily. They feed only through human skin.

Usually, in lecturing to our French friends, I began in English, but after seeing their puzzled expressions, I switched to my rudimentary French. To add to the confusion, I would take lice from my capsule and place one on each of the lapels of the men or women sitting in the front row. That drew their undivided attention and concern. Proceeding with my lecture, I could convey the important message that lice and typhus were bad. Through all of this, I kept an eye on the crawling lice, as did those who had more reason to do so. Eventually they were returned to their capsular cage. One night that mesh broke away from its capsule and I had a spirited time chasing and immobilizing the hundred or so lice swarming all over my torso!

London was completely blacked out at night because of the Nazi air raids and most everyone retreated to underground shelters until the sirens rang clear. Particularly frightful were the "buzz bombs" or pilotless-like planes packed with heavy explosives in their noses. I recall the first one to hit London. The bomb made an eerie buzzing sound and showed a bright jet flame in the tail; it was shaped like a miniature plane. After the jet quit and the noise ceased, about thirty seconds passed before one heard a loud explosion. Houses were leveled and the bomb could penetrate about three floors of a concrete, steel-reinforced building. It was uncanny how the Nazis could launch these missiles and uniformly hit London and cause great destruction. Later, the buzz bombs were programmed differently so that when the jet cut off and the noise ceased, there might be a full minute or more before the explosion. They were made to glide down before hitting.

The Royal Air Force, particularly Spitfire pilots, deserve great credit for learning how to intercept them over the channel. Flying alongside, they would expertly tip the buzz bomb's wing to make it crash harmlessly either in the channel or in the countryside.

General Fox and I were walking in the dark along Oxford Circle one night when we were propositioned by a lady of the night who obviously had better eyesight than we did. Actually all we heard was a shocking price before we hurried on. Nothing like this ever occurred in Westminster!

Everything in England focused on the pending invasion. Moods were much better now that the war was beginning to go badly for the Nazi forces. Much time was spent in sharing information with our British allies. At their Virus and Rickettsial Research Center, I was privileged to meet Dr. Chris Andrews, head of research at Hempstead. In Naples, I had worked with his associates, Dr. Maurice van den Ende, a pathologist, and Dr. Stuart Harris, a distinguished clinician. Maurice later became dean of the University of Capetown School of Medicine. Stuart Harris, continuing to pursue his research interests, became an authority on influenza and was knighted for his work.

While in England, I maintained my various typhus strains in animals and acquired a strain of scrub typhus from Joe Smadel. This is a type of rickettsia which is an especially bad actor. Joe was stationed in England and headed the Virus and Rickettsial Section of the Army General Laboratory. I met Adolph Felix, co-discoverer of the Weil-Felix test, first described in 1915. Also, it was my good fortune to meet Dr. Patrick Buxton, one of the foremost authorities on lice. Dr. Raymond Lewthwaite was a special visitor to the London School of Tropical Medicine. When Japanese military forces overran Malaya, he escaped to Australia. He was a most easy man to converse with and doing so greatly enriched my knowledge of scrub typhus fever, a rickettsial disease not unlike typhus or Rocky Mountain spotted fever. Little did I know then that, in 1948, our paths would cross again in Kuala Lumpur, Malaya, and we'd establish a warm and enduring relationship.

The Allied landing on the Normandy Beaches which established the long awaited Second European Front came on June 6, 1944. This historic event was especially remarkable because of its careful planning, the courage shown by its participants, and the joint cooperation of three major powers—England, France, and the United States. There were many casualties on the beaches and following the arduous close combat in the hedgerow type of terrain characteristic of Normandy. Yet, the beachhead was established, Normandy was secured, and the major port of Cherbourg was captured. Allied progress toward Paris and northern France, however, was slow and tough.

My assignment was aimed at helping protect our military forces from typhus. Our troops were immunized with a typhus vaccine which we knew from our experiences in North Africa and Italy offered considerable protection. If illness occurred, it was mild and the U.S. forces had suffered no deaths from typhus to this point. In Africa and Italy, the English military had experienced thirty or more casualties because of their initial failure to immunize with typhus vaccine. The fear of louse typhus in Normandy stemmed from the large number of civilian workers who had been transplanted from German-occupied countries, such as Poland, Rumania, and Czechoslovakia. These men had been transported to help construct fortifications, missile sites, roads, etc. They were known as TODT workers and it was my assignment to determine the degree of louse infestation among them and the presence of typhus. Our troops had been vaccinated and their standards of health were sufficiently high which kept them free of louse infestation. Each soldier who had crossed the channel was supplied with a two-ounce can of DDT (which incidentally had been packaged by McCormick and Company in Baltimore). The fighting soldier wanted as light a pack as possible so that much of the DDT ended up in the channel. Later they came scurrying back for additional supplies since louse or flea infestation is not pleasant and makes for an uncomfortable night.

My mission took me to Normandy on D + 6 (six days after initial landing) and I found many groups of civilian laborers herded here and there. It was very clear that louse infestation was high, but happily, typhus fever had not yet occurred. My quick survey also included the citizens of Cherbourg and its surrounding townships. Col. Emory Cushing, chief entomologist for the Preventive Medicine Section of the U.S.A. European Command, came over. "Cush," whom I had met in Naples, was a mild-mannered and most helpful scientist who taught me many things about entomology.

My orders were sufficiently flexible as a member of the Typhus Commission to allow me to go wherever a problem might be. I was on my own, more or less, as far as military assignment was concerned. Gen. Fox had expected me to get to Paris as soon as possible and determine, from the scientists there, just what the status of typhus might be in the French civilian population as well as in the German forces. After a considerable stall caused by the foot-by-foot, hedgerow-to-hedgerow battles, Gen. George Patton's armored column finally broke through German lines and kept going. A jeep was made available to me and I followed at a respectful distance. In one building, we came across warm food on a table and wine in the glasses left by Nazi troops who had retreated hurriedly. Paris was liberated and Gen. Patton and his forces kept going to the Rhine River.

I entered Paris the same day as the Free French, under Gen. Charles de Gaulle, reclaimed their capital city and cultural center. Streets were jammed, vehicular traffic came to a standstill because of the deliriously happy Parisians who crowded around any jeep, truck, or tank. I managed to reach the inner city and secure quarters in a small hotel room not far from the Champs Elysees and the Place de La Concorde. There was continued sniping in the city for several days afterward by those not friendly to the Allies or the Free French.

The next morning I found my way to the Pasteur Institute and went directly to the director's office of Dr. Trefouel. I asked to see the Chief du Service Typhique and was taken to meet Dr Paul Giroud. He was effusive in his greeting and must have talked, nonstop, for several hours. He was loaded with much valuable information about typhus. Earlier, Dr. Giroud had produced an effective typhus vaccine by growing the rickettsiae in the lungs of mice, rats and rabbits. Dr. Luiz Casteneda, a Mexican scientist, had first established this method but, Dr. Giroud had adapted it to large animals, since they have larger lungs and could produce richer batches of vaccine. The animals were infected by having them inhale aerosol mists of infected solutions. The germ reached the lungs in this way, multiplied, and produced typhus pneumonia. Infected animals placed in cold rooms became very ill and produced thick cultures of rickettsiae. Dr. Giroud had a slick way of separating the rickettsiae from lung tissue by using an oil suspension in proper proportions and centrifugation. He was beginning to experiment in sheep and even talked about using camels, since they have such large lungs. One of the dangers of this method was that animals tended to sneeze after they were forced to inhale drops of the solution. This sprayed the whole laboratory and often caused illness in its personnel. Dr. Giroud and I became friends and continued a correspondence for many years afterward.

I had carried a strain of scrub typhus rickettsiae to him, wondering whether his animal lung method would be successful in making a vaccine for this disease since efforts by U.S. investigators proved futile. Although he tried, his separation process failed and nothing came of it.

Several days after the liberation of Paris, the Allies held a huge victory parade from the Arc de Triumphe down the Champs Elysee to La Place de la Concorde. Prime Minister Winston Churchill rode in the same vehicle as General Charles de Gaulle, who was then at the zenith of his popularity. The day was cold and it was amusing to see how General de Gaulle kept urging Mr. Churchill to sit down and cover himself with a blanket while the Prime Minister kept popping up to flash the V sign. This, after all, was *de Gaulle*'s day. The principals came to a viewing stand immediately adjacent to where I was positioned. Mr. Churchill was so close I could see his ruddy cheeks and inhale the aroma from his cigar. Many proud French veterans paraded by that day in military dress, their medals of valor prominently displayed.

Military orders soon sent me back to Morocco. I then received orders to return to the United States via the military transport command in August 1944. The trip was through Preswick, Scotland, and the northern route to New York. The passengers on the plane were mostly high-ranking Air Force officers returning to the states. At Iceland, the traffic officer came aboard and uttered the horrifying statement, "everyone off, you are being bumped for high-priority purposes." Unhappily, the planeload of officers disembarked with their gear. I waited until last and, looking out the door, saw nothing but a vast expanse of gray desolate terrain. I remarked to the traffic officer, "Sir, I would really like to see this beautiful country, but I have on board four guinea pigs infected with typhus fever and I know that there is a law against transporting typhus to Iceland." He seemed horrified and remarked, "You stay on this plane and keep those God damn guinea pigs with you!"

The high-priority item which bumped those officers were sacks of mail. Had they known, some heads would have undoubtedly rolled. I rode comfortably on the sacks of mail to New York. There was little trouble getting through Customs with my infected guinea pigs, which were truly infected with Polish and African strains of typhus. I had already prepared a letter on official stationery authorizing their importation. From that point on, I always carried animals, either mice or guinea pigs, whether they were infected or not. It was a good way to avoid being "bumped."

Once I was back home, I commuted to the Army Medical School to settle the guinea pigs and typhus strains I had brought back with me. I also learned more about scrub typhus fever, since I was earmarked for duty in the South Pacific Islands.

Transport by air across the United States and the Pacific Ocean proved a long and tedious journey. Hamilton Air Force Base was the center for Pacific flights and the usual first stop was Honolulu. At Hickham Field in Hawaii, much of the destruction from the Japanese raid of December 7, 1941, was still evident. My next stop was a small postage stamp of land known as Johnston Island, southwest of Hawaii. And from there we were on to Guam, then Kwajalein, New Guinea, and Hollandia.

Experiences in the Philippines

My assignments in the Philippines differed greatly from those in North Africa, Italy, England and France. Under the Typhus Commission, Neil Philip and I had been reassigned from Europe to this theater of military operations. Through the direction of Gen. Stanhope Bayne-Jones, head of the U.S.A. Typhus Commission and deputy head of preventive medicine, Surgeon General's Office, I was placed under the command of Col. Maurice C. Pincoffs. I, of course, was happy to work under my old medical chief.

There were great differences between the European and Pacific Theaters which included shorter distances, smaller areas of operation, fewer facilities and resources, rain, mud, and tropical heat. It was a different war altogether.

Scrub typhus fever was the only rickettsial disease threat since infection by murine typhus or Q fever was rare. Col. Pincoffs assigned me to the 118th General Medical Hospital, the Johns Hopkins Medical Unit, which had already served with distinction in Australia. In Leyte, they had encountered a great number of cases of schistosomiasis, a liver fluke disease which resides in snails and infects man when he swims or bathes in polluted streams. The small worm, called a cercariae, does not survive in salty water, such as the ocean proper, but can survive and infect at a point where fresh water rivers empty into the ocean.

Army personnel often became naturally infected with this worm from the streams, swamps, and rivers in their jungle operations. Air Force personnel usually got into snail trouble when they bathed in streams or in certain ocean areas with low salinity. A few land-based Navy personnel became infected. Signs were posted in noncombat areas warning about infestations and memoranda had been sent to military commanders, but such signs and directives were seldom read or taken seriously. Many service men became infected, some seriously, and some died. Indeed, so many were incapacitated that the invasion of Okinawa was delayed for a short time.

Assignment to the Hopkins Medical Unit brought me in contact with some old friends and some newly made ones. Tented medical wards were full of "schisto" patients, most of them in their early stages of illness. Medical diagnosis had to be made from a history of exposure and the clinical findings, which included fever, rash, intestinal complaints, and, sometimes, lung involvement. Their blood specimens showed a high count of a special white blood cell called an eosinophile. Final diagnosis was confirmed by finding the egg or the worm in their feces.

Treatment, which consisted of the intravenous administration of a toxic drug called Tartar emetic or the intramuscular injection of an antimony compound, Fuadin, was only moderately effective. The men much preferred Fuadin given in the buttocks because the Tartar emetic caused nausea, vomiting, coughing, and signs of asthma. Nevertheless, most individuals responded to either form of treatment and eventually recovered.

One day on my ward, a naval officer dressed in khaki came down the aisle to inquire about one of his men. The officer happened to be my older brother, Lewis; we actually met in that accidental manner. I had known that his ship was somewhere in the Pacific ocean. He invited me on board his ship for a meal and I quickly accepted. Eating out of tin cans (C and K rations) can be monotonous.

That night we enjoyed preprandial drinks, chicken soup, baked ham, mashed potatoes, salad, real lemonade, ice cream, and coffee. In typical naval fashion, the Captain welcomed me and apologized for the meal because "last night we had steak." The Navy knew how to fight a war! A similar episode happened a month or so later when, in Manila, I chanced upon an old boyhood friend attired in Navy whites. Robert Foothrop invited me on board his cruiser that same night. Again, the same story about "steak." Frankly, I liked baked ham much more than steak. The same evening, when aboard ship with my brother, everywhere we looked were ships readying for the invasion of Luzon and Okinawa. We remarked that our old Westminster friend, John Reifsnider, was somewhere out there. The very next day, he came aboard the ship for needed supplies for his unit.

While in Leyte, having access to the hospital laboratory, I was able to work out a technique to determine the blood levels of para-amino benzoic acid, a drug just beginning to be used for treatment of the typhus fevers. While taking large doses of the drug (as much as 20–24 grams a day), I developed my first kidney stone. Occasionally crystals of the drug accumulate in the kidney, since sweating in a tropical environment excessively concentrates the blood and urine.

The military action moved north to Luzon. Gen. Douglas MacArthur landed with his troops at the Lingayen Gulf, his promise to return fulfilled.

My first night in Luzon was spent at the Fairgrounds, just outside Manila as the Japanese forces retreated to the old destroyed city. There was considerable chaos, misery, and confusion before surrender finally occurred making Manila's citizens a prime target for diseases such as typhoid fever, tuberculosis, dysentery, tetanus, and wound infections. Once Manila fell, lepers wandered its streets frantically searching for help. Because the Japanese military had not supported the Island of Culion, where there was a model leper colony, they had returned to Manila for sustenance.

Gen. MacArthur placed Col. Pincoffs in charge of the health of Manila with full power to act. The San Lazaro Hospital and Health Complex on Rizal Avenue was selected for the health unit. The colonel chose senior and key military health professionals to direct its various disease control sections. I was charged with maintaining standards of health in the hospital units assigned to him throughout the city. Maj. William Tigertt was director of the 406th Medical Laboratory located at the San Lazaro complex. Bill kindly assigned me some space in the laboratory for special work on typhus fever which had to be accomplished in my free time.

In one large medical ward, there were more than fifty patients with active tetanus (lockjaw), which they had developed after a bullet or shrapnel injury. Fortunately, most of the men recovered, in spite of no antitoxin treatment.

Tuberculosis victims were also plentiful. Most of them with an advanced case of the disease came to the health center for artificial pneumothorax (injection of air into the lung space); they stood in line, received treatment, and returned home.

One huge room contained approximately three hundred of the most emaciated patients I have ever seen. Many were wasted down to skin and bones, their bodies twisted in all directions; some were confused, delirious, and barely responsive. They displayed all the horrible manifestations of vitamin deficiency and protein malnutrition. Pellagra, scurvy, and beri-beri were rampant. Many of these people were helped by blood transfusions. Blood for the military forces was collected in the United States and rapidly transported by air for use in the war zones. The blood was discarded after seven days. I was able to acquire and administer many units to these unfortunate patients and found the therapy beneficial. Many, particularly the younger ones, also responded to proper nourishment and vitamin supplements. These scenes resembled those being witnessed for the first time in German concentration camps.

I was often called to diagnose strange cases of fevers with rashes which cropped up in military and civilian personnel. In this way, several cases of murine, or the rat-flea types of typhus, were identified. These had never been recognized before in the Philippines, although Dr. Richard Strong had alluded to their presence years previously. This prompted me to make a search for the rickettsial germ in Manila's rat population. The rat catchers delivered live rats, big ones, to me at the San Lazaro Laboratory. I anesthetized them, drew blood for testing, and then returned them to cages. By testing first the blood for the presence of antibodies, and later the brains, it was possible for me to isolate the rickettsial germs. About 20% of the rats in Manila showed evidence of murine typhus infection. I have a scar to this day on my left index finger from the bite of one of those big, gray rats.

We were notified of a case of scrub typhus in a Navy man on the Island of Samar. I hitched a ride on a military transport to Tacloban (Leyte) and then over to Samar, where the Navy had a base. The young man had severe scrub typhus but ultimately recovered. A blood specimen was taken, allowed to clot in the tube, and cooled in an ordinary refrigerator overnight. That tube and clot were then flown back to Manila with me, processed, injected into live white mice, and a rickettsial strain of scrub typhus was eventually isolated. This taught me a simple lesson—that refrigeration is not always necessary for preserving laboratory specimens and that rickettsiae-like bacteria are very hardy and persistent. This was the first recorded isolation of scrub typhus rickettsia in the Philippine Islands. Before the war, this tropical illness was not thought to occur there.

By this time, many of us were billeted in an old Philippine house within walking distance of the San Lazaro Hospital and Laboratory. The 42nd General Medical Hospital Unit, which had been stationed in Brisbane, was transferred to Luzon just outside Manila. Col. George Yeager had succeeded to the command which years before had been under Col. Pincoffs' charge. Here I caught up with some old University of Maryland Medical School and Hospital buddies: Edward (Ed) Cotter, Everett Diggs, Lewis (Lou) Gundry, Harry Bowie, Walter Karfgin, and Stuart Coughlan. A little later Ed Cotter was appointed Chief of Medicine at the Clark Field General Medical Hospital just north of Manila.

I recall sitting down with others in a remote camp site, muddy and wet, listening to the radio about the victory in Europe. Those assembled showed little emotion, since this seemed to be a separate war, far away, that didn't much influence the one they were fighting.

Things did fare badly for the Japanese military and most everyone was filled with optimism. Neil Philip and I surmised from prior reports that scrub typhus might be present in Luzon as far north as Bagio. This was a very picturesque mountainous area and a favorite site for summer R and R. We went by jeep beyond Clark Field to Bagio. There we saw much evidence of Japanese occupation, including their bogus yen as currency. While I collected blood specimens from a few patients, Phil collected mites. From these specimens, we were able to make the first isolation of scrub typhus rickettsia from northern Luzon. Col. Lewis Gundry made the trip with us and often speaks of the harassing ride over narrow mountain roads.

We had been away from Manila just three days. Yet, during those days, three breathtaking events happened, none of which we knew of because we were beyond radio contact. The United States had used the atom bomb, the Soviets entered the Pacific war, and the Japanese asked for peace. This was a momentous three days.

That night, all Manila went berserk. Anyone with a gun shot into the air and there were many casualties, since whatever goes up comes down! I had seen this happen several years earlier when the German Air Force bombed Algiers at night and everyone went out to see the sights. Flak and many falling missiles hit many an unhelmeted head.

In North Africa, I had suffered intestinal difficulty from time to time. This continued intermittently. While in the Philippines, my symptoms worsened and were coupled with fever and considerable weight loss. Finally, the nature of my illness was detected on a microscopic slide which revealed the amoeba of *Entamoeba histolytica*. Col. Pincoffs isolated me in the U.S. Army General Hospital in Manila. For my amoebic dysentery and liver abscess, I was given two full therapeutic courses of emetine hydrochloride of eleven days each and another of six days. This is a rather drastic form of treatment but quite necessary.

I recovered slowly and was able to accomplish a few tasks after discharge from the hospital. Because of my illness, orders were written for me to return to the United States and to be hospitalized at the Walter Reed Hospital for further studies and treatment, if necessary.

Chapter 9

RETURN AND MEDICAL PRACTICE

*N*othing can ever match the elation of returning home after more than four years overseas engaged in one of the most destructive wars known to man. Many young men and women were not to have that privilege. Celeste had done a great job with the children, who had been fatherless for a long time. Always a good trooper, she had not only cared for things beautifully at home but found time to work as a volunteer physician at the St. Agnes Hospital and as a health officer for Baltimore City.

As a result of my health problems, I spent a number of months at the Walter Reed Hospital as a patient which took more patience than I was willing to give. My intestine and liver slowly healed. For a while, I commuted back and forth to Walter Reed as a patient. Then, Dr. Darius McClelland Dixon, my friend and former fellow house officer, offered me the use of his office in the Medical Building several times a week to see patients of my own.

My very first patient, referred by a prominent Baltimore psychiatrist, taught me a good lesson. The patient came with a built-in diagnosis of "recurrent typhus fever." By that time, I was somewhat of an authority on typhus fever and I knew right away that was not the correct diagnosis. All that the patient manifested was intermittent fever, no pain, no jaundice, and absolutely no positive physical findings. She'd had an attack of typhus fever several years previously. You may presume that a careful and complete examination was performed. Still it took me several weeks to work out the cause of the patient's fever—simple garden-variety gallbladder disease with stones. Typhus it was not.

A month or so later, my old buddies Ed Cotter and Sam Revell and I joined in an associateship with shared offices at 11 East Chase Street, a good central location for a Baltimore medical practice. We shared the costs of examining rooms, a reception area, and a small diagnostic laboratory. We also shared one secretary who found it a tough assignment serving three physicians. But we were not very busy at that stage, so things worked out reasonably well. In my first month of practice, February 1946, I grossed just $225. But at least it was a beginning!

In addition to sharing a laboratory, we purchased a fluoroscope and x-ray unit jointly. The laboratory provided basic services for our patients and each of us knew fluoroscopy of the heart and lungs, then a standard skill for internists. I had learned gastrointestinal fluoroscopy while in Detroit and was able to perform upper G-I series and barium enema examinations in some patients and pass along the technique, including sigmoidoscopy, to my associates.

Sam, Ed, and I found time to teach classes and conduct ward rounds at the University Hospital under Maurice Pincoffs's leadership and guidance. Teaching afforded us a useful outlet and allowed many returning veteran physicians to add their talents to those hardy practitioners who carried the load for so long. To establish a medical practice in a metropolitan area takes time, which made it essential for us to find other sources of income whenever possible. Each morning during the week, I attended at the health center of the Western Electric Company, which involved an early, long ride out and a slow return through traffic to town. For the routine chore of performing medical surveys of old and new employees, plus a little medical first aid, we received a weekly salary of $58. We also found it necessary to perform physical examinations, day or night, for insurance agents for a small fee. Added to these activities were the house calls sent our way by established physicians, nurses, or secretaries who wanted to help budding internists. All of these valuable experiences helped me learn about the real world.

Each Thursday afternoon, I went to Walter Reed Medical Center in order to work in the rickettsial laboratory where Joe Smadel had settled. During the war I had previously met Joe, a freshly commissioned captain in the U.S. Army, assigned to the Walter Reed Army Institute of Research (WRAIR). He had come from the Rockefeller Institute where he had begun a career in experimental pathology and virology. I had met up with Joe again in Naples, Italy. He, along with Yale Kneeland, an astute clinician, and Emory Cushing, an accomplished entomologist, came from London to observe the measures which were being applied to control the epidemic of louse-borne typhus fever in Naples. After the war, Joe became scientific director of the WRAIR, where he functioned as a fund of scientific information for various commissions of the Armed Forces Epidemiological Board, including rickettsial diseases, immunization, virus diseases, epidemic hemorrhagic fever, and epidemiologic survey, a polite name for defense against biological warfare.

I continued to work on typhus and Rocky Mountain spotted fever (RMSF), since para-aminobenzoic acid had come into vogue as treatment. Spring and summer found us busy with cases of RMSF in various hospitals about town and particularly at the University Hospital, where many patients from throughout the state were referred. Laboratory work with blood specimens and guinea pigs was performed on open table counters in the bacteriology laboratories, or in the Bressler building. Dr. Frank Hachtel had kindly made laboratory bench space available to me and it was possible to obtain additional facilities on the fifth floor of the Bressler Building since there was other research activity there. In reflecting back, it was lucky that cross-infections of RMSF to others did not occur since the facilities were not only primitive but dangerous. Simultaneously I taught classes in preventive medicine under Dr. Perrin Long at the Johns Hopkins School of Public Health and Hygiene. There were restrictions against handling such pathogenic agents as rickettsiae, which precluded my performing this research at Hopkins.

Most of my handful of patients who required hospitalization were put in the University Hospital, but I was called to see others in consultation at the Mercy, Maryland General, and Union Memorial hospitals and elsewhere in Maryland. Without really realizing it, I was developing into a specialist in internal medicine and infectious diseases.

My Thursday afternoons at Walter Reed, added to the other times spent there at odd hours, cemented my close relationship with Joe Smadel and the talented staff of that fine research institute. These weekly experiences really afforded me much needed postgraduate laboratory experience. Actually, at this time, there were no other rickettsiologists in Baltimore with whom I could associate or receive much-needed advice and stimulation.

Then, in 1948, an opportunity arose which was to have a lasting influence on my medical career.

Scrub Typhus Mission to Kuala Lumpur

Scrub typhus fever had remained an enigma. Many of our military personnel had died of this disease in the southwest Pacific Islands. There was no vaccine and treatment with para-aminobenzoic acid (PABA) was unsatisfactory. Joe relentlessly pursued leads for better therapy. On Joe's request, Dr. Fred Stimpert, of the Parke Davis Company in Detroit, provided the Walter Reed Unit with samples of any antimicrobial agent which showed inhibitory properties for rickettsiae. Chloromycetin, a new antibiotic, was included in a batch of possible candidates. With Betsy Jackson, his senior technician, Joe showed that this new streptomyces-derived antibiotic could inhibit growth of *Rickettsia orientalis* (scrub typhus) and lymphopathia venereum, a virus-like venereal infection in mice and eggs. Joe and Herbert (Herb) Ley successfully treated a few cases of typhus in Mexico and in the process demonstrated that blood levels of Chloromycetin occurred after oral administration.

Through authorities at WRAIR and each nation's respective Department of State, Joe arranged the Scrub Typhus Mission to Kuala Lumpur, Malaya, for testing the efficacy of Chloromycetin in typhus victims. Dr. Raymond Lewthwaite, director of the Institute for Medical Research (IMR), Kuala Lumpur, graciously approved the proposal. Later, this remarkable man, himself an au-

Typhus Group—Kuala Lumpur, 1948. Traub, Woodward, Smadel, Philip, Ley

thority in the field of rickettsial diseases, became a collaborator and close friend of the scrub typhus team.

As part of his team, Joe selected Herb Ley, Cornelius (Neil) Philip, Robert (Bob) Traub, and myself. The contract, funded by the Medical Research and Development Command through the Commission on Immunization, was awarded to the University of Maryland School of Medicine (the first research grant awarded by federal agencies to the school).

We arrived in Singapore on March 14, 1948. Before we could even change our clothes, we were taken to the bedside of a young Muslim. His medical history revealed headache, prostration, and fever and, upon examination, a tell-tale ulcerative lesion (eschar) in his right axilla with adjacent adenopathy. Blood was taken for the routine laboratory evaluation of hemoglobin, leukocyte count, acute-phase blood serum for the Well-Felix reaction, and injection of mice intraperitoneally for rickettsial isolation. A loading oral dose of 2 grams of Chloromycetin was given with a subsequent schedule of one tablet every two hours

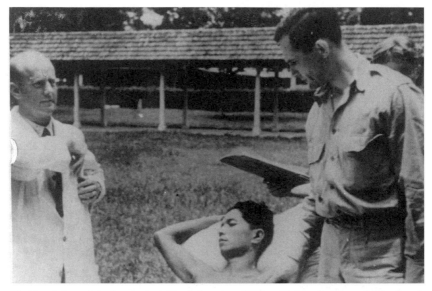

First treated scrub typhus patient, Kuala Lumpur, 1948, with Lewthwaite and Woodward

until the twelfth day of illness. By noon the next day, the patient had noticeably improved. His headache was gone and he was afebrile twenty-four hours after beginning treatment. Subsequently, the diagnosis of scrub typhus was confirmed by isolation of rickettsia from his blood and a rising titer of proteus OX K agglutinins. Recovery was prompt and complete.

Our second patient was Corp. Bebbington of His Majesty's Forces, who was treated in the military hospital. Initially quite ill, he, too, responded dramatically within thirty hours and did not relapse.

A steady flow of suspect typhus patients from the civilian and military hospital and the nearby rubber estates, medical wards, and surrounding villages ensured an adequate clinical trial. Among these patients was a hardy group of Gurkha soldiers whom we treated in the military hospital. There was no simultaneously untreated control series. Patients believed to have scrub typhus were selected and treated consecutively. Of the first forty patients, thirty were confirmed to have scrub typhus. The ten not having scrub typhus included two with murine typhus, two with malaria, one with blackwater fever, two with leptospirosis, two with typhoid, and two with GKW (God knows what). This represented a diagnostic batting average of 75%.

We experienced a striking example of the rapid spread of news. Dr. Lewthwaite received a telephone call from Dr. Stanley Pavillard, a prominent Singapore physician, whose patient, a banker, was desperately ill with advanced scrub typhus. While walking in the Botanical Garden in Singapore, he had evidently contracted illness from an infected mite. News reached Singapore via a British army officer traveling by train from Kuala Lumpur. Familiar with the recovery of Corporal Bebbington, he related the miraculous event to another passenger, who was visiting the ill banker's family. Dr. Lewthwaite coerced Joe, in spite of his protestations, to broaden the area of patient selection and treat the banker, particularly in view of diplomatic amenities. I volunteered to go to Singapore. When we first called for an airplane ticket, we were informed of "no seats available." A call to Government House got me a seat. The afternoon plane from Ipoh which flew to Singapore had only a few passengers. They were prominent Hindus from India and the plane cabin was strewn with flowers. On the front seat was a burial urn which contained a portion of the ashes of Mahatma Ghandi. The ashes were to be dispersed over the sea of Singapore, which is a Hindu burial custom. Approximately 30,000 mournful and excited native Hindus met that plane. Dr. Pavillard cleverly extracted me from the multitude via the baggage compartment and drove me directly to the hospital. In spite of impending vascular collapse, delirium, and a purplish exanthem, the patient recovered. This response established beyond doubt that the antibiotic was remarkably effective at all stages of illness.

Very early in the trials, Sir Howard Florey, en route to London from Australia, stopped off in Kuala Lumpur to observe our project. After personally witnessing the twenty-four-hour recovery of a scrub typhus patient and observing the clinical responses of the few cases treated already and graphically displayed, Sir Howard remarked, "I'll buy it, you don't need statistical evidence."

Joe directed a tight laboratory program. Initial and convalescent blood specimens, daily temperature and pulse responses, and an audit of Chloromycetin tablets were all duly recorded.

Once he observed a technician pouring serum from a tube of clotted blood into a sterile tube. His quick retort, "Chum, hereafter the tube will be centrifuged and the serum pipetted." This admonition, with additional epithets, ended this practice.

It was soon clear that Chloromycetin cured scrub typhus promptly. Based on the subsequent observations, the therapeutic regimen was reduced to one day's treatment and a single 3-gram oral dose. This, too, led to recovery without relapse provided treatment was initiated not earlier than the fifth day of illness. Relapses were later encountered in patients treated prior to the fifth febrile day. These clinical results provided a basis for understanding the difficulties subsequently encountered in our chemoprophylactic field trials.

On Saturday night, April 3, 1948, I was informed of two new febrile patients, who were transported from a plantation where scrub typhus was prevalent. By candlelight, I completed my brief history and examination and obtained specimens from them for laboratory evaluation. Both were toxic yet neither had an eschar. In twenty-four hours, one patient was improved dramatically as was in keeping with our prior experience in scrub typhus victims. The second patient was unchanged; he appeared toxic and apathetic and suffered severe abdominal pain and diarrhea. Enteric (typhoid) fever was suspected. Since blood cultures were not included in our routine, I made an attempt to retrieve typhoid bacilli from the peritoneal exudate of mice inoculated with his blood the night before. Though these smears were not confirmatory, cultures of peritoneal exudate, and other specimens of the patient's blood, yielded typhoid organisms. Therapy was continued. Joe Smadel was annoyed that precious Chloromycetin tablets were being expended on a non-typhus patient, but he relented. Within two days, some clinical improvement, based on bedside findings, was apparent; the patient's temperature dropped to normal in about three days. Treatment was discontinued after five days of normal temperature. Ten days later, the patient greeted me with a full-blown relapse and a toxic psychosis, which is a serious complication of typhoid. Both his relapse and the psychosis responded to additional therapy.

The second typhoid patient treated responded in less than four days and did not relapse. Among the ten treated typhoid pa-

Volunteers exposed to typhus-infected mites, 1948

tients, two relapsed, one became temporarily psychotic, one developed gross intestinal hemorrhage which required transfusion, and one incurred intestinal perforation with peritonitis and shock. This patient's intestine perforated two days later; yet, he, and all the other patients, eventually recovered. Despite this inauspicious beginning, we were convinced of Chloromycetin's therapeutic benefit and soon published the data based on our original ten typhoid patients.

After the obvious dramatic therapeutic response we obtained in scrub typhus patients, Joe directed the program to determine whether the antibiotic could prevent the illness. We advertised in the newspapers for volunteers and got a vigorous response. We selected healthy young men who had been carefully screened medically. American, British, and Malayan volunteers were purposely exposed by having them sit eight hours a day for ten days in a mite-ridden, typhus-infested area. Bob Traub, Cornelius Philip, and Ralph Audy had pinpointed a highly infectious area at the Seaport Rubber Estate (which had already provided us with many of our patients). I had learned that Japanese soldiers who bivouacked in the area during the occupation had experienced high scrub typhus attack rates. These human field trials, which extended for several years, revealed that typhus infection could be suppressed by administering the antibiotic at intervals of every four or five days for about seven weeks. Shorter, intermittent regimens resulted in rickettsemia and clinical illness. When Chloromycetin was given simultaneously with the first day of infection and then daily for twenty-eight days, the incubation period was merely extended and classic illness occurred a week after stopping the drug. The therapeutic findings in our patients and the results of our field trials in volunteers demonstrated that Chloromycetin suppressed the infection but did not kill the rickettsia. These field trials effectively demonstrated the immunologic relationships between host, microbe, and antibiotic and provided firm guidelines of chemoprophylaxis for typhus and other similar illnesses based on active immunization. Drs. Charles (Charley) Wisseman, Bennett Elisberg, Robert (Bob) Traub, and others took part in these later studies. Joe, himself a volunteer, developed a severe attack of typhus.

The initial venture to Kuala Lumpur ended in June 1948, with a total cost to the United States government of less than $50,000. This imaginative medical mission to Malaya was the forerunner of considerable scientific collaboration in subsequent years between scientists of the IMR in Kuala Lumpur, WRAIR, and the University of Maryland. Its pioneer discoveries serve as a remarkably stimulating contribution by a vigorous and talented group of medical scientists.

Chapter 10

PURSUIT OF ACADEMIC MEDICINE

Private Medical Practice Versus Academic Medicine

fter the happy and rewarding events in Malaya, I found myself at a career crossroads requiring serious decision making. Dr. John Mateer, my old chief at the Henry Ford Hospital, called to offer me a full-time post there. This was an attractive opportunity in many ways but it would have taken us away from our home, family, and friends. World War II had accomplished that unhappy circumstance and Maryland was clearly our home.

Dr. Perrin Long, head of the preventive medicine program at Hopkins, who had given me a teaching appointment, offered an equally attractive post in internal medicine and preventive medicine. The reputation of Johns Hopkins was a lure in itself.

One evening, Dr. and Mrs. Pincoffs graciously entertained Celeste and me at Markland, their lovely home along Old Frederick Road. After dinner, Dr. Pincoffs did not press an offer but in his careful way indicated that a full-time faculty position at Maryland might well suit my needs at this time. He knew that I had been unwell and that a steady position in medicine might be an ideal arrangement. On asking about my role, he said, "Ted, we need to develop medical residency training programs and research in the department, since we are lacking in these fields."

Some of my friends, including Dr. Thurston (Turk) Adams, whom I always liked and respected, suggested that I remain in private practice while simultaneously keeping up my research and teaching interests. Although a good suggestion, I knew that one or the other would take second place, and that if private practice was to be my principal source of income, then research and teaching would have to suffer.

Celeste assured me she would support any decision I made. I spoke with two astute and distinguished physicians, Dr. Charles Austrian, one of the best clinicians ever to practice in Baltimore, and Dr. Kenneth Maxcy, a wise epidemiologist and medical scientist. They both gave me the same advice—"Why not return to your alma mater and help work things out there? There is a need for Maryland to build its programs and, in the long-run, there might be more satisfaction in watching things grow than in working in an institution where there is less academic need." This sounded alright to me and I decided to leave private practice and take a full-time, salaried position at the University of Maryland. I was, in fact, the first geographical full-time, salaried physician in any clinical department at Maryland, a wide departure from any previous arrangements there since the school's opening in 1807.

My initial contract in 1948 provided an annual salary of $5,000 with an overpractice privilege of $2,500, making a total of $7,500. An office with furniture and telephone was included, although no secretary. The problem with extra overpractice privilege was that there was so much to do I had no time to see private patients. Teaching, arranging conferences, recruiting staff and house officers, performing meaningful clinical investigation, and acquiring laboratory space occupied me fully. Yet I never refused to visit other hospitals in Baltimore or throughout the state to see patients or give talks. Only in this way was it possible for me to draw attention to our growing academic medical program.

The Department of Medicine simply lacked funds. Indeed, the annual budget at that time was about $40,000 which included three small salaries for Dr. Pincoffs, Dr. Milton Sacks, head of our clinical laboratories since 1941, and myself, as well as stipends for part-time teachers in laboratory medicine, physical diagnosis, cardiology, and departmental secretaries.

After a year or two, I asked Dr. Pincoffs if we could hire a half-time secretary, which he had to refuse because there were no available funds and he did not feel disposed to request such support from either Dean Wylie, or University President H. Curly Byrd.

By this time, our research programs in infectious diseases had achieved a measure of success. By chance, Mr. Charles P. McCormick was ill, suffering severe and lingering joint involvement and a touchy gastrointestinal tract. One evening, upon reaching Sherwood Forest where we had a summer cottage on the Severn River, Celeste informed me that I had been asked to consult on Mr. McCormick, a man whom I knew only by reputation. It was not my intention to examine him since he was the patient of Dr. Wetherbee Fort, one of my former teachers. But as it turned out, Dr. Fort was on vacation and after several telephone calls, I went "up on the hill" to see the patient. Not only were his knees enlarged and tender, but a sigmoidoscopic examination revealed a damaged intestinal membrane and the presence of amoeba in his stools. Charley was the son of a missionary and had spent many of his early years in Puerto Rico.

To make a long story short, treatment for amoebic disease relieved his joint involvement for almost a year. Previously, he had needed a cane and could not personally attend to his very successful tea and spice company for months at a time. His joint problem later returned and it was only then that its cause became fully clear. He developed a typical attack of gout in one of his big toes which rapidly abated after he was given colchicine. In short, he had two medical problems: a sensitive intestine, which often causes a form of arthritis, and gout.

I have never known a more generous man than Charles McCormick, who ultimately became a close friend and benefactor for the school and hospital. For three consecutive years, beginning in 1949, McCormick and Company awarded a $10,000 grant to the medical department each year. It was upon this solid base that we were able to establish a real teaching program with fellows and senior medical residents, and also a research center in Puerto Rico to extend our studies of infectious diseases. Once given our start in research by the generosity of a tea and spice company owner, it then became possible to attract funds from pharmaceutical firms eager to have their antibiotic products tested. Soon to follow was financial support from the Medical Research and Development Command of the Department of Defense, the National Institutes of Health, and other granting agencies. Getting started is one of the problems for any new or growing group. The Parke Davis company alone, beginning in 1952 and up to 1975, contributed approximately $10 million to our programs in antimicrobial study and basic research.

Major Revision of an Old Curriculum

A contribution to the school and hospital of which I am proud was my chairmanship of the Curriculum Committee from 1951 to 1954, when major changes were undertaken. The clinical curriculum of the medical school, which had not been significantly revised for several decades, was badly in need of change. The junior year, for example, consisted mainly of hearing lectures in Chemical or Anatomical Hall for an interminable period. Juniors were subjected to more than one thousand lectures embracing all clinical subjects. Many were excellent when carefully prepared and presented by faculty members, such as Drs. Pincoffs, Krause, Frank Lynn, Harry Hull, and other devoted teachers. But others were quite inadequate, consisting of little more than a professor reading a chapter from the text. The best conferences were organized by the Department of Pathology and centered around a clinical case history followed by presentation of the postmortem findings. Drs. Hugh Spencer, Pincoffs, Krause, T. Nelson Carey, Lewis Gundry, among others, were the stars. Each semester ended with two weeks of written examinations in Davidge Hall which required incessant writing in the blue examination booklets. Major, minor, and subminor disciplines were represented in these writing marathons and a student's fate depended upon them. The junior year involved no experiences with live hospital or clinic patients.

On June 11, 1951, Dean H. Boyd Wylie appointed me chairman of this important committee with the charge to compare our program with other medical schools and to recommend changes. This was a tall order and one which was not to prove popular for a new, young faculty member full of vigor and desire to do the right thing. Members of the committee were Drs. Edmund

Harry Hull, M.D.
Professor Surgery

Louis H. Douglass, M.D.
Professor Obstetrics

Bradley (pediatrics), Louis Douglass (obstetrics), Jacob Finesinger (psychiatry), Harry Hull (surgery), John Krantz (pharmacology), Milton Sacks (medicine), Henry Marriott (medicine), Detrick C. Smith (physiology), Edward Steers (microbiology), and Frank Figge (anatomy). Consultants consisted of senior members and department heads of the preclinical and clinical faculty.

The committee conducted its study during 1951, and held many meetings and workshops. Many medical centers were visited, catalogs studied, advice requested, and sincere attempts made to develop ideas and programs which could best serve the needs of our school and hospital.

The day of reckoning came in June 1952, when the bold new program was presented to the entire assembled faculty in Chemical Hall. Each seat was occupied on that occasion and the mere idea of changing a well-established curriculum made the hot, humid condition of the hall even more uncomfortable.

Slides, graphs, and statistics were presented to compare Maryland's program with other prestigious institutions. Comparisons of programs can be helpful to a point, but the bottom line is the faculty—its interest, capability, and willingness to perform its job.

What was recommended was to greatly curtail the didactic lecture program and put the students on the medical wards in small groups under a preceptor–preceptee type of teaching. This was the old Edinburgh system which involved placing students in their initial clinical years on the medical wards under proper supervision. Osler's system at Hopkins had involved assigning junior students to the outpatient clinics and seniors to the wards, one which we did not follow.

The surgical department and its subspecialties were the ones to suffer most, particularly because of a limit in the number of faculty teachers, essential for such preceptor–preceptee teaching. A transitional compromise was reached which provided for two full lectures each day from 8:00 to 9:00 A.M. and 9:00 to 10:00 A.M. Following the lectures, junior students then broke into groups for practical ward work in pediatrics, surgery, medicine, gynecology-obstetrics, psychiatry, and preventive medicine.

The discussion in Chemical Hall was spirited with favorable and dissenting opinions. But it was not pleasant to stand up and defend such a radical change. Dr. Pincoffs strongly endorsed the new program which helped greatly.

The recommendation carried, and the new program, with its new scheduling, was adopted. Matters then had to be clarified pertaining to participation of the school's affiliates, such as Mercy Hospital. This went smoothly. The advisory board of the faculty accepted the recommendations at its meeting on June 19, 1952, and Dean H. Boyd Wylie appointed a committee of clinical department heads on curriculum to carry out the recommendations. This action was necessary for the dean to obtain new funds from College Park in support of recruiting new faculty, personnel, and other accommodations.

The road ahead was to be bumpy but ultimately succeeded to everyone's satisfaction, particularly the students, whom we serve.

Early Growth and New Departmental Enthusiasm

Although the "new" University of Maryland Hospital opened in 1935, it soon became crowded and inadequate for the number of medical students and house officers who were to be trained. Even before the acquisition of new beds and laboratory facilities, there was a need to recruit a faculty consisting of internists who qualified as effective clinicians, teachers of medicine, and researchers. Preliminary requirements were office and laboratory facilities and adequate support funds. None came easily but with interest, enthusiasm, and some salesmanship, such things happened and the Department of Medicine led the way among the clinical units.

Success can only occur with teamwork and a unified effort by all involved in the process. Dr. Sam Revell, a marvelous clinician, joined the faculty to head up the medical outpatient clinic and later the Curriculum Committee. Dr. Charles Van Buskirk was recruited from the Henry Ford Hospital and developed a first-class division in neurology. Dr. Thomas Conner came to us after five years as a fellow in endocrinology-metabolism at Hopkins under Dr. John Eager Howard. Soon to follow was Dr. John Wiswell from Baltimore City Hospitals and Hopkins. Together Tom and John developed a most creditable endocrinology teaching and research program. They were joined by Drs. Joseph Workman and Robert Bauer who organized and developed a program in nuclear medicine, the first such activity in the school and hospital. Dr. Leonard Scherlis, having finished his cardiology fellowship under Dr. Charles Friedberg at Mt. Sinai Hospital in New York took over the division of cardiology from Dr. William S. Love. He nurtured the growth of this division, particularly in-house officer training and expansion of diagnostic facilities in a rapidly moving field. The program in infectious diseases which I had initiated was taken over by Dr. Robert T. Parker, who was later succeeded by Dr. Fred R. McCrumb, Jr. This division was already active in research, teaching, and consulting throughout the city and state. Dr. W. Carl Ebeling began a modest program in gastroenterology after his return from the Massachusetts General Hospital where he trained under Dr. Chester Jones. Later, he entered private medical practice and was succeeded by Dr. Howard Raskin, who had made a name for himself at the University of Chicago under the tutelage of Dr. Walter Palmer and

Dr. Joseph Kirsner. Pulmonary medicine had the wise help of Dr. William S. Spicer and Dr. Patrick Storey. They were later joined by Dr. David Simpson, who had worked under Dr. Amberson of the Bellevue Hospital in New York. Among the younger group were Dr. Kyle Swisher and Dr. Frank Borges who were destined to play important roles in Maryland medicine.

Dr. Sheldon E. Greisman was appointed to the faculty in 1954. I met him in Korea in 1952, and it was a happy day for Maryland when he decided to begin his remarkable academic career with us. No one has exceeded his talents and dedication to teaching and research. He excelled in each and in no small way helped the school and hospital to find its place on the medical map. Dr. George Entwisle, who had trained under Dr. Chester Keefer of Boston's Memorial Hospital, joined the Department of Medicine as teacher, head of the medical clinic, and later head of the Department of Preventive Medicine and Rehabilitation.

Already on board were such established teachers and clinicians as Drs. T. Nelson Carey, Harry Stein, Louis Krause, Samuel Morrison, Frank Geraghty, Wetherbee Fort, George McLean, Edward F. Cotter, Kennedy Waller, William Helfrich, and other dependable and able practitioners. They could always be relied upon for teaching the practical aspects of medicine to students and house officers. Dr. Cotter reorganized a most effective teaching program for sophomore medical students in introductory clinical skills and directed those sessions for a number of years.

Teaching and medical practice were well-served by Dr. Milton S. Sacks, Dr. Carroll L. Spurling, and Dr. Rouben M. Jiji. Later, Dr. Sacks and his associates manned a large hospital laboratory, taught a first-class course in laboratory medicine for students, and promoted a medical presence within the city and state.

Particular comment must be made about Eph Lisansky who had an enviable World War II record and who, after the war, undertook special training in psychiatry under Dr. Jacob Finesinger. He served for many years as an important bridge between internal medicine and psychiatry. Later, as a well-earned reward for his work, he achieved local and national recognition for these important contributions.

Too much cannot be said about Dr. Harry M. Robinson, Jr. (Robby) who took a good teaching Division of Dermatology, made it better, and developed a very creditable research program.

Sam Revell, Jr.
Professor and Head Division Hypertension

Edward F. Cotter
Associate Professor

T. Nelson Carey
Professor Medicine

Lewis P. Gundry
Professor Medicine

Many able men and women assisted him in this most laudable endeavor.

From 1950 to 1956, these were some of the important developments which made it possible to carefully, but effectively, integrate teaching, medical practice, and research at our medical school and hospital.

Ephraim T. Lisansky

A New Department Head

On a Saturday in June 1954, at 7:00 A.M., a faculty associate, Dr. Merrill J. Snyder, called to congratulate me on having been appointed as chair of medicine at the University of Maryland Hospital and School of Medicine. Merrill had read the notice in the *Baltimore Morning Sun*, which carried this news as well as the announcement that my chief, Dr. Maurice C. Pincoffs, was appointed to chair a new Department of Preventive Medicine and Rehabilitation. Since I had not been interviewed or asked to assume this important role in the medical school and hospital, this was shocking news to say the least. The University of Maryland structure, including the professional schools in Baltimore, is responsible to its Board of Regents. At its meeting the preceding day, this action had been taken and since the sessions are open to the public and press, this startling news was released.

By this time in 1954, I had about six years of teaching and clinical research under my belt. It was common knowledge that the Board of Regents desired a full-time faculty in its major clinical departments at the medical school. Dr. Paul Knotts of Denton, Maryland, a respected senior physician in Maryland, was the only medical member of the Regents. He had great confidence in Dr. Pincoffs, as did the senior authorities, including the president, H. Curly Byrd. By this time, Dr. Pincoffs had more or less fully relied upon me to spearhead teaching and research in the department. It seemed obvious that I was Dr. Pincoffs' choice as chair, since he had wished to step down and devote his interests to the preventive and social medicine fields.

The news release caused considerable discussion, confusion, and some unrest among our academic circle and it was no sinecure for me. Advice came to me from all directions, particularly from one senior person who advised that I not accept the post and insist that the normal channels of committee action and faculty selection be taken. Actually, my initial inclination was to follow this advice since it was not my wish to chair a department in an academic medical center in the first place. Others advised that to decline the appointment would embarrass the president of the university, the regents and above all, Dr. Pincoffs, a man whom I admired and respected so much. Dr. John Krantz and Dr. Frank Figge told me to take the job. So I became the chair of medicine; incidentally, most of the appointments in the medical school back through the decades have been made in a similar manner, like arranged marriages. As related elsewhere, Dr. Shipley was responsible, more than anyone else, for the role which Dr. Gordon Wilson played in recruiting Dr. Pincoffs to the chair of medicine in 1922. This system of appointments has gone through a lot of changes, usually for the better, although such arrangements are not so bad in some circumstances.

My first action was to assemble the entire medical staff faculty. This included the few local full-time faculty and the many devoted, nonsalaried, part-time practitioners of internal medicine, who had served so well for so many years. We met in Gordon Wilson Hall which occupied parts of the seventh and eighth floors of the hospital. The auditorium was full.

My first comment was to pay homage to the part-time faculty members and say to them that they were important members of the growing department and that their teaching services were sorely needed. Also, they were assured that hospital beds would be available for their patients and that failure to accommodate them would be an expression of failure on my part. The message was well received and in the decade to come, many part-time faculty members played vital roles in the department's progress.

During that first meeting, the teaching program then in progress was explained and many present played important roles in its success. Suggestions about house staff training, better diagnostic facilities, more beds, parking, and ancillary problems came from all directions. Not all the problems were solvable, but a start was made.

The following comments were made to the medical faculty assembled in Gordon Wilson Hall:

> The reputation of a medical institution is the sum total of the reputation of the human beings who compose it. The able faculty member, full-time or part-time, contributes individually to the prestige of the institution and in turn shapes the total prestige.
>
> The part-time faculty member, through his contacts with students, becomes a better physician himself. In return for this opportunity to be a student with students and house officers, the part-time member contributes to the institution. As faculty members, because of their contacts in the community, they can interpret the institution, its problems and objectives, to the people, medical and non-medical, in city and state. In the educational program based on the precepts of small group instruction and careful supervision, the part-time faculty member can make possible a better quality of medical education.

To these ends, many nonsalaried, faculty physicians made major contributions to the department and hospital in the fifties. Dr. C. Edward Leach headed the cardiac clinic. Drs. Perry Futterman and Charles E. Shaw headed the diabetic clinic. Charley and his associates evolved the low-insulin dose concept for treatment of diabetic ketoacidosis. Dr. Vernon Langeluttig headed the chest clinic and the student health program was directed by Dr. James R. Karns who succeeded Dr. T. Nelson Carey. Drs. Samuel Morrison and Anthony Lewandowski attended in the GI and renal clinics, respectively. Dermatology, under Dr. Harry Robinson, was ably supported by Drs. Eugene Bereston, Israel Zeligman, Joan Raskin, and many other worthy dermatologists who comprised an excellent teaching division. Until their deaths, Nelson Carey and Louis A.M. Krause maintained their enthusiasm for teaching. Drs. Lewis Gundry and Conrad Acton were regular participants. All of these able physicians served as attending physicians on the medical wards and teaching clinics. During the war years, Dr. Kurt Levy directed the medical outpatient clinic and gave devoted service. Drs. Irving Friedman, William Helfrich, and W. Kennedy Waller contributed regularly. After completion of their training in medicine, Drs. Ramon Roig, Joseph Shear, and Samuel O'Mansky never wavered in their contribution to the teaching clinics. For a number of years, Ed Cotter taught clinical neurology before a division was finally organized.

Without the contributions of these able and devoted physicians, the department would have been much less successful in its growth and development during the decades from 1950 to 1970.

Further Development

The 1950s and 1960s were exciting and rewarding times for the medical school and the Department of Medicine. Changes, growth, and redevelopment occurred in all clinical departments and the medical faculty was proud to have played a substantial part in the school's rebirth.

In medicine, the established divisions of cardiology, dermatology, endocrinology-metabolism, gastroenterology, hematology, infectious diseases, neurology, and pulmonary diseases were improved and expanded. New units were developed in rheumatology, nephrology, and nuclear medicine. Each gradually acquired a head of the division, a second full-time faculty member, a secretary, and a technician, paid for by the growing budget of the medical school and hospital derived from Maryland legislative funds.

The Division of Infectious Diseases led the way in obtaining outside research funds to provide extra income for the depart-

Merrill J. Snyder, Professor, Experimental Medicine and Microbiology.

ment. Merrill J. Snyder, M.D. joined the infectious diseases group in 1949, coming from the Viral and Rickettsial Diseases Section at Walter Reed. His strong capabilities in immunology and enthusiasm for teaching medical students, house officers, and fellows were instrumental in helping organize and promote our infectious diseases program until his retirement in 1984.

Research and training grants in general medicine, cardiology, neurology, endocrinology-metabolism, nuclear medicine, and pulmonary diseases brought in new funds and enhanced the research and teaching activities in many ways. The school and hospital could not have attained and sustained its growth without the help of these outside ancillary financial resources.

Sam Revell and Frank Borges developed a program in renal medicine and were among the first in Baltimore to utilize twin-coil dialysis techniques and renal transplant procedures. Facilities were sparse to say the least. Sam obtained financial seed money from private sources to purchase the necessary technical equipment. Dr. Henry (Barney) Marriott began the teaching program in rheumatology. Dr. Maureen Henderson came from England as a fellow in rheumatology and stayed on in this area. Later, she succeeded Dr. George Entwisle as chairman of preventive medicine. Dr. Adalbert (Dal) Schubart joined our program as medical resident from the St. Louis School of Medicine and Hospital. He was an excellent house officer and chief medical resident. Following this experience, he trained at the Massachusetts General Hospital in rheumatology under Dr. Walter Bauer. He then returned to Baltimore and assumed leadership of the Division of Rheumatology. Illness in Dal Schubart's family forced his return to Germany, where he was appointed to a senior faculty post at the University of Mainz. From the National Institutes of Health came Dr. Werner Barth, who, for several years, gave equally able leadership to this specialty division of medicine. Dr. Robert T. Parker, an able physician, after fellowship training in infectious diseases, later became head of that division.

The house officer residency training program in medicine needed careful attention. The medical residency program was limited, undermanned, and lacking in research activities, though training at the bedside was of a high order.

My first venture in early 1950 was to assign a medical resident to a ward of patients and make him responsible for consulting in various specialty fields in another section. For example, a third-year resident cared for assigned service, yet he rendered consultative service to another ward unit, such as infectious diseases, cardiology, endocrinology, etc. All residents served in this manner. Attending specialists then had a direct and responsible role with patients. In this way, specialty medicine was encouraged while maintaining full interest in general internal medicine. It worked, provided everyone performed their jobs. The system served as a forerunner of a fellowship training program in specialty divisions. Our main accomplishment was the establishment of a quality internship and residency program in internal medicine.

In 1958, Dr. Richard B. Hornick, a graduate of The Johns Hopkins School of Medicine, joined the department after military service at Ft. Detrick. Dick brought a keen clinical and research sense, served as chief medical resident, and ultimately took over direction of the division of infectious diseases from Fred R. McCrumb, Jr. Dick was appointed to the chair of medicine at the University of Rochester and since 1987 has been vice president for medical education at the Orlando Regional Medical Center in Florida. Dr. McCrumb, whose contributions to our knowledge of leptospirosis and measles vaccine will always be remembered, was appointed director of the school's program in tropical medicine and international health training with its research center in Lahore, West Pakistan.

Because of an obvious need, the department organized a training program in general practice in 1954, now known as family medicine. There were no such residencies in Maryland then, and prime graduates were seeking this training elsewhere, the nearest being in Wilmington, Delaware. In general, these residents received internal medicine experience with hospital inpatients, outpatients in the ambulatory clinics, and special work in pediatrics, anesthesia, ear, nose, and throat, minor surgery, and obstetrics and gynecology. All the training was under the sponsorship and guidance of the Department of Medicine. During their third year of training, general practice residents rotated to those outlying hospitals where they planned to establish their practice, such as in Hanover, York, Salisbury, Hagerstown, Frederick, or in various Baltimore hospitals. Each year, we had two to four trainees who, when their training was com-

pleted, were fully qualified for certification by the American
Board of Internal Medicine. For a number of years, the Maryland Academy of General Practice and certain pharmaceutical
firms provided fellowship funds to spark the program. It
worked.

In most academic centers changes occur, particularly in the
shifting of personnel or interests. Sam Revell took charge of the
medical outpatient clinic and was later succeeded by Frank
Borges. Frank, a splendid physician, had helped develop the renal
program and the important field of rehabilitation for cardiac patients. This was the first such program in Maryland. He, then, on
request, directed the successful medical program in rehabilitation
at the Montebello Hospital. Because of lack of financial support
from the State of Maryland for Montebello, Frank took over direction of the Medical Outpatient Clinic. This was in his capable
hands until his tragic death in 1973. Dr. Herbert Kushner succeeded Frank as director of this clinic and proved to be a talented
teacher of medical students and residents.

In 1963, Charles Van Buskirk decided to leave academic
medicine which was a disappointment since he had developed
such an effective specialty division in neurology. His successor,
Dr. Erland Nelson, became the first chairman of the new
Department of Neurology. All of the resources in neurology, faculty and residency positions, and office and laboratory space

Medical Department picnic, 1963.

were transferred from medicine to the new department. This was the first administrative move which weakened the medical department.

Drs. Bill Spicer, Pat Storey, and David Kerr developed a research program on environmental pollution and its relationship to lung disease, particularly emphysema and asthma. Bill received two solid years of excellent training as a fellow (provided by the American College of Physicians) at the University of Pennsylvania Hospital in Philadelphia, under Dr. Julius Comroe. Outside funds were acquired and other resources obtained for an environmental chamber which permitted detailed lung studies in animals and humans under controlled conditions. A residency and fellowship training program in pulmonary diseases followed.

By 1960, the endocrine division had grown in all aspects— research, training, and practice. The National Institutes of Health awarded the division a grant (with Dr. Thomas B. Connor as principal investigator) which made it possible to develop a clinical study center. Seed funds acquired from private sources were used to construct a unit on the 3A wing over the x-ray department. It contained 12 beds, its own kitchen for metabolically balanced studies, nursing, and individual bed units with personal toilets and refrigeration. Supporting laboratories made it one of the finest small clinical research facilities anywhere.

In 1950, the annual departmental budget was about $40,000. In less than two decades, the department's legislative budget alone had reached $5 million. This represented a considerable commitment by the university and by the State of Maryland. Our annual research budget grew from nothing in 1950 to an average of $3.5 million. For more than a decade, the Department of Medicine's research budget from off-campus sources was 25% or more of the entire Baltimore professional school campus. Beginning about 1975, with growth of other departments, these figures changed, particularly in basic sciences.

Without the available faculty and bed resources provided by the Veterans Administration, the school, and particularly the Department of Medicine, could not have fulfilled its important teaching and research role during this mid-century phase of growth. Student enrollment increased because of a presumed shortage of physicians in America. Actually, the problem was more one of distribution than number of physicians, a fact which many authorities failed to comprehend. Without the Baltimore Veterans Administration resources, there could have been no rational expansion of our program in internal medicine at Maryland. This is a reasonable statement, in spite of the availability of affiliated hospital services, such as the Mercy and Maryland General Hospitals. In these hospitals, the patient-oriented and teaching programs were later to achieve high educational standards with assistance from the Department of Medicine.

During this crucial period of reorganization and growth, emphasis was placed on the importance of small group teaching in preceptor–preceptee teaching. The attending staff, bolstered greatly by younger faculty members and fellows, carried out their teaching duties enthusiastically. Groups of four junior students together with a senior medical student, an intern, assistant medical resident, and an attending faculty member (who contributed at least twelve weeks of teaching annually) composed the teams. The attending physician willingly mothered a group of two to four sophomore medical students for their introductory medical course (physical diagnosis) for a semester which changed to a full academic year in mid-1950. In addition to these significant curricular assignments, attending staff joined the part-time faculty in either the general medical clinics or specialty clinics, such as cardiology, endocrine-metabolism, pulmonary, hematology, and others. Those interested in research found time to pursue these interests and those oriented primarily in clinical diagnosis and practice pursued these skills to the betterment of the department's educational, research, and patient practice programs.

For many years, teaching was regarded as a privilege. Rewards were measured in growth and maturity of medical students and the satisfaction of a job well done. In spite of meager or average salaries, particularly for those hospital-oriented faculty members, these were the main returns. Those who contributed grew in stature and confidence and their labors contributed mightily to the school and hospital. All were the result of honest and wholesome teamwork which embraced the clear overlapping with other clinical departments, particularly pediatrics, surgery, and preventive medicine.

The halcyon years were from the early 1950s until late in the 1960s. Research was not the department's prime goal but it was regarded as essential to its evolution as a topnotch outfit for any medical school. The research budget derived from off-campus funds grew, parallel with faculty, house officer, and fellowship development. Growth brought better technical equipment which, when coupled with the application of proper clinical bedside skills, made for a sophisticated program. The legislative budget of the department, derived from university sources, and simultaneous growth in research and similar advantages derived from the Baltimore Veterans Administration Hospital, combined to place the department in an enviable status. Recruitment of house staff, fellows and junior faculty members were vastly facilitated because news of a satisfied staff travels well. All of this was the result of teamwork, not the least of which was the quality and devoted service of the nursing staff, technicians, and classified personnel. The administrative staffs of the medical school and hospital were responsive to the essential needs of a growing medical center, as were the university authorities and the State of Maryland.

FAMILY MATTERS

S oon after my year at Henry Ford Hospital, fate, in the form of World War II, separated me from Celeste and my growing family. Happily, there would be some short returns to the United States during 1940 and 1941 which, in addition to permitting us a joyous reunion, added to the size of our family.

Bill and Lewis, just a little over a year apart, were highly energetic and inseparable most of the time. They were good young athletes and knew how to play in most of the conventional sports. Bill was more organized in his daily routine but could easily be egged into all kinds of boyish pranks. Lewis was more outgoing, ready for almost anything, and best described as a boy who "liked to explode things."

Celeste kept me alive in their minds by reading my letters to them and showing them my pictures. She held things together in handsome style. Once, on a short revisit from Europe, she and the boys met me at Penn Station in Baltimore. Lewis spotted me first, ran up for a hug and said, "Pop, I'm three years old and plenty tough." Never is it possible to regain those four years from my three loved ones but we made up for it afterward.

Calvert School in Baltimore was great and enabled the children to gain a broad education and confidence in themselves. The Calvert School system expects parents to participate in the development process and it is here that Celeste shone. Later, I contributed some to the book work, but arithmetic and spelling were not my strengths. When Celeste entered Lewis in school, the advisor recommended starting him two years behind Bill. After he was tested, he quickly showed his ability to keep up and more and entered only one year behind. This was splendid for him since he met such fine boys, later his close friends, including Duck Martin, Ken Marty, and Dorsey Brown. Teaching the boys to ride a bike, throw and hit baseballs, play football, swim, and a few other things were ventures assigned to me and I accepted them with much pleasure.

After the war, we found a remarkable outlet by spending July and August at Sherwood Forest. This is a summer colony on the Severn River just around the point from the Naval Academy. It provided an organized summer camp program with competitive sports and class instruction in nature and community responsibilities. Bill, Lewis, Craig, and Sis, who came a little later, really enjoyed this.

One evening, while seated on the porch overlooking the Severn River (Round Bay), Lewis dared Bill to swim across and back. Immediately we went down to the Sherwood Forest dock; off they went and each swam over to the red buoy just off Rugby Hall point and back to the dock. Later, Lewis entered a competition for teenage boys, stroked all the way in excess of two miles and took eight minutes off the river record.

After completing their studies at Calvert School, Bill, Lewis, and Craig attended Gilman School. At Gilman, Craig had just as great a time as at Calvert. He was everywhere and into everything. For several years, he broke the demerit record for several of the lower classes. Mr. Callard, the Faculty Headmaster, and his delegated assistant, sent short notes announcing each new demerit. One such read, "Your son, Craig, has earned sufficient demerits as to require his attendance at school on Saturday morning." Offenses including "pushing his classmate off a window ledge to the ground" or "throwing a lacrosse ball in the new auditorium." On this occasion, Craig went dutifully to Gilman on Saturday to find Mr. Callard in the auditorium with ladder, mortar, and a new tile to replace the one broken in the ceiling. Craig was made to hold the ladder and pass required materials to the Headmaster. This settled the demerit problem; there were no more.

Lewis, our second son, was jolly and friendly; everyone liked him and he, them. Little things came easily and naturally to him. When tragedy struck Lewis in June 1955, so many friends rallied to our side. On returning from Manila, Craig and Sis, who were younger, were at the airport with family. Craig asked, "Pop, how did it happen?" Even today, we are unsure as is so often the case in summer swimming accidents. The nicest tribute came from one of Lewis's classmates. Jewish boys were just being admitted to Gilman at that time and things were not always easy for them. Nathan Carliner wrote us such a touching note to tell us that Lewis put his arm warmly around him on the opening day of class to tell him how glad he was that Nathan had come to Gilman and that he would be his friend.

Fathers always dream and so often do I. Lewis would probably have chosen medicine and on the way he would have been our Olympic swimmer. He had a beautifully formed, coordinated body and a remarkable will to achieve. God bless him.

Bill gave full measure and was a good winner. He hated to see John Unitas and the Baltimore Colts lose more than anything else. He and his sister were the neatest of the children. Intolerance and unfair play or bullishness of bigger boys for the smaller ones often made him angry. He was strong enough to back it up and did so on a few occasions, usually aligned on the correct side. His best sport at Gilman School was wrestling at the lower weights and for three years he was Maryland State Champion in his class. Bill worked hard for his education and later attended Princeton and the Johns Hopkins Medical School.

Craig and his brother, Lewis, were cut from the same cloth, alert, bright, attractive like their mother, and solid competitors. Craig knew how to make noises at any time and slept lightly; he seldom understood why it was necessary to retire.

Craig made many friends beginning early at Calvert School, then at Gilman, and during his summers at Sherwood Forest. He competed intensely, wrestling and football being his best sports. Twice he was the Maryland State Wrestling Champion. He matched brains with a strong and coordinated torso. He liked body contact and made a hard-nosed linesman in football. His last year was marred by a fractured leg which kept him out of the last few games of the senior year. Today, Craig and I are the best of friends. His life has been conducted in a friendly, outgoing manner, serious when he has to be but not about himself. If our family had a "blithe spirit," Craig would be my choice.

A touching incident occurred years later with Craig as a practicing physician in Atlanta. He helped care for a dear friend who was widowed and in difficult circumstances with widespread cancer. Craig went to her home, put her dog in the car, and drove directly to the hospital. With the dog under his coat, he went to her floor and put her dear pet on the bed. This brightened the day and accomplished much more than medicine ever could. An agitated floor nurse reported to the supervisor that "Dr. Woodward brought a dog to the hospital." The supervisor responded, "Do you want to tell a dying patient that she cannot see her dog?" Craig never lost his touch of sensitivity.

Sis was not an afterthought. Celeste and I both came from large families. There were so many boys in them that we doubted the spell could be broken. Pregnant during the war, Celeste decided to be confined at the Woman's Hospital, which was in downtown Baltimore, with our friend Darius Dixon as her obstetrician. That evening, there were so many new babies being delivered that the hospital ran out of anesthesiologists. I assumed that role and was busily engaged keeping Celeste under anesthesia when she delivered. The nurse, who had a glancing view, said, "It's another boy," and, for a moment, I was satisfied to have a quartet of boys. Happily, her designation was inaccurate and Darius spent the next few minutes explaining to her how one tells boys from girls. We had a good laugh and all was well.

We named the baby Celeste, but she has always been Sis, even to this day. From the start, she did everything just about right and, for once, we learned the difference between raising boys and girls. We tried to pawn off the boys; no one would take them nor would we have responded to an attractive bid! Sis studied hard, more than she needed to perhaps, but she wanted to get things right. She was neat at home and in her daily activities. When the occasion demanded, she could wrestle on the living room rug and keep up with her brother Craig.

Many times, even later in college, I urged her to study a little less intensively, turn out the light a little earlier, and have a better time. Yet, she had the remarkable capacity to work and play hard. Bill and Sis were very much alike. Her competitiveness matched that of the boys and had she been of their sex, Gilman would have had another star athlete.

Sis attended Roland Park Country School and at her graduation in 1964, Ms. Anne Healy, headmistress, had this to say:

> It is now time to give our full attention to the graduating class and to all they represent in the school. Among them is one who is gifted in leadership as few young women are; in her treatment of each girl in the upper main as an individual and her quiet, almost unknown helpfulness to a number of girls; in her rare qualities of modesty and discretion; in her ability to see all sides of a problem and her respect for the points of view of both faculty and students; in her sympathies and wise counsel she is a superior leader, and by these words, I wish today to pay tribute to Celeste Woodward, who has the esteem and the affection of all the faculty and students.

Sis, Aunt Grace, and Celeste, 1968

Celeste, my wife, has headed the list of pretty girls known to me and somehow has held onto her striking good looks throughout our more mature years. For our senior dance, she made a pink satin evening gown which bared one shoulder. When we walked to the floor, no eyes were on me and Dr. Monte Edwards, our surgical anatomy professor, pushed me aside on the dance floor a number of times. To me, she was queen of the evening. Unfortunately, Celeste, a splendid dancer herself, married a less than average one who knew only one step and tried to make it count for everything.

During my war absences, Celeste handled things beautifully at home and simultaneously worked as a physician for the Baltimore City Health Department and the St. Agnes Hospital. With it all, she wrote me long, newsy, and loving letters at least twice weekly.

She loved the beach and for several summers, we visited either Ocean City or Rehoboth Beach. Those were happy times

Woodward Family: Craig, Bill, Celeste, Ted, and Sis, 1979

50th Wedding Anniversary, June 1988

because she made detailed preparations to ensure everyone had a good time. Summers at Sherwood Forest were so successful for us because of her ability to manage well and never spare herself. In spite of the load of four children and a demanding husband, she found time to entertain friends and almost the entire medical house staff several times a year for at least twenty-five years.

During all my years of maturation and medical growth, Celeste held the fort and gave us the happiest of homes. It was always open to my parents and, later, to my Aunt Grace and my cousin Helen Woodward from Wilmington. My relatives were hers. Mother and Aunt Grace loved to visit Sherwood Forest, sleep on the screened porch, and enjoy the fresh air and singing of the birds.

Celeste made a considerable sacrifice by allowing me to pursue my career and denied herself the same chance because of me.

Her family came first and that is why each of us is so richly blessed. Yet, she kept her medical interests alive. When her schooling was completed, she, on her own initiative and hard work, took refresher courses, worked in the clinics, and became proficient in internal medicine and in dermatology. This was partially in preparation for a sabbatical year we took in 1964–65 to direct the school's program in tropical medicine in Lahore, West Pakistan. While there, Celeste single-handedly established a most active dermatology clinic in one of the medical school hospitals and turned up cases believed to be rare in that area. Each evening she would tell me of a new case of leprosy or cutaneous leishmaniasis that she had spotted and confirmed.

This was a good year for us and we were able to spend more time together, including taking interesting weekend trips to the Kingdom of Swat and Afghanistan. Her reputation grew and she received a request to visit Kabul to examine the children of the Commercial Attaché. Her wise advice was most appreciated.

Celeste continued her medical interests and on our return from Asia put in a tough one-half day (equal to most people's full day) in the emergency room at University Hospital. Here she took time to listen to the complaints of patients including those who were down and out and those who used alcohol and drugs to excess. They were given something by her called sincere interest and empathy which went a long way to provide needed help. Often, patients would come to the emergency room and say, "I want to see that lady doctor."

Even this experience was not enough to satiate her appetite to provide medical help for those in need. She offered her services as a volunteer physician in the Far East. Twice she went to Vietnam under an American Medical Association-sponsored program and twice to Thailand to minister health and good will to Laotian and Cambodian refugees who had fled their respective countries for help in Thailand. Here she worked like a trooper though no longer a young physician like many of the volunteer medical personnel. So many physicians and allied professional people have told me of her selfless and skilled contribution. I look to her with pride, a feeling shared by Bill, Craig, and Sis.

In 1971, Sis became engaged to and married Mark Applefeld, who was our chief medical resident at the University of Maryland Hospital 1974–1975. After having finished their re-

Three brides: Celeste (1938), Sis (1971), and Anneke (1971).

spective training programs in pediatrics (Sis) and cardiology (Mark), they settled in Roland Park and presented us with two lovely grandchildren. Lewis was born in 1977, and Grace in 1980. Lewis will finish the University of Richmond in 1999, and

Mark and Sis Applefeld, 1976

Anneke and Craig Woodward, 1995

Lewis and Grace Applefeld

Mia and Ted Woodward

Grace will graduate from the Roland Park Country School in 1998. She was president of the student body in her senior year. Our enlarged family brought us closer to Willard Applefeld (a medical school classmate in 1938) and his affectionate wife, Bernice. Through them, we became friends with their families.

Bill and Mathew Woodward, 1995

The Woodward home in Roland Park

Craig met Anneke, an honor law school graduate from Columbia, in New York. They were married in Summit, New Jersey in 1971, and ultimately settled in Atlanta, Georgia. Here they gained a host of friends and two lovely children. Mia was born in 1977, and Ted II in 1979. Now grown, Mia will finish her baccalaureate studies at Yale in 1999, and Ted will graduate from Westminster High School in Atlanta in 1998. He is headed for Yale.

Puddin Talk

"A dog is man's best friend" were the immortal words of Lawyer George Graham Vest, uttered in a court room over a century ago. One can argue the point since a loving wife or husband, intelligent and affectionate children, and a few warm and caring friends rank several octaves higher. Yet, these desirable traits are expressed in their own special ways by the family dog.

Our first dog was a squat, alert, and interested Black Scottish Terrier, which when standing up was still very close to the ground. We named the dog "Puddin" and thus began a long line of Woodward female Black Scottish Terriers named "Puddin." The whole family was completely "mesmerized" and the Woodwards now had a second daughter (with full respect to Sis), and a Scottish Terrier dynasty became fully implanted in Roland Park.

So many warm, loving, and affectionate stories of each vintage Puddin could be related. These would include their lives as members of the Woodward family, their independence and almost challenging nature "to almost never come when called," and their constant wanderings in the woods behind the house. Each lived about 12 to 14 years. Puddin #2 went to Europe, Asia, and around the world. Puddin #1 developed polyps and small skin tumors which are apparently fairly common in the Terrier family. Intestinal polyps are serious because of bleeding. Initially, I noted a small nodular growth on her abdomen and decided that a specimen should be taken for microscopic examination to determine the nature of the growth. One Sunday morning I took her with me to my office with the intention of soliciting the first surgeon who walked by in the hall. Dr. Rober Buxton, the chief surgeon, was the first and I decided not to drag him into this bizarre affair. The next to pass was Dr. Robert Johnston, a more junior but very competent general surgeon. "Bob, would you come into my office a minute for a consultation?" He said, "Of course." By this time I had shaved the abdominal hair, had all the necessary instruments ready to perform a tissue biopsy with syringes, needles, local anesthetic, forceps, scalpels, and suturing material. You can imagine that he was a little "taken back" but graciously agreed to be the operating surgeon. I applied the initial anesthetic with comforting words and holding her "bottoms up." Bob quickly removed the small tumor and applied the sutures and a small bandage. All was over in a few minutes. I urged him to charge me his usual surgical and standard fee. In about two weeks his statement arrived on his regular billing form showing a total bill of $1,800, broken down to Professional Services $1.00, Defamation of Professional Character $1,799, "prompt payment is desired." We had a good laugh over this.

Also, I sent this specimen to the Department of Pathology using the standard patient request form for such surgical pathological services. A brief clinical description of the patient's problem is always requested. My clinical statement read, "The presence of a small skin tumor in a young female patient between the 3rd and 4th nipple on the left side." Apparently the specimen included a piece of long black hair with the skin. The pathological report to me read "and in the future would the Professor of Medicine try to give a more accurate and complete clinical history." As it turned out, the specimen was ultimately sent to the Armed Forces Institute of Pathology in Washington whose veterinary pathological experts reported that the type of neoplasm was very rare and had given them considerable interest.

Puddin #4

Currently, we have Puddin #4, a proud and fiesty 5-year-old clone of this Scottish pedigree. She had aristocratic parents which boast grand champion characteristics. Of all of her canine Woodward predecessors, she ranks as the most intelligent, playful, affectionate, and most irascible of the four. All have been raised thoroughly spoiled, but with affection and reserved tolerance for their misbehavior.

Puddin #4 relishes untying men's shoestrings, particularly while we play bridge with friends. It took me awhile to teach her this feat. Actually, it was meant to be a harassing and distracting ploy when the cards were not going our way. However, Ham Whiteford seemed to like this extra canine attention. In spite of this diversional tactic, Ceil and Ham usually beat us. Yet, Puddin and Ham became close friends.

Dogs have been an integral part of our family. All families need a dog.

Chapter 12

SOUTH AFRICA, MADAGASCAR, AND PLAGUE PLUS A POLIOMYELITIS MILESTONE

During the winter of 1950–51, Joe and Elizabeth Smadel, Ken Goodner, Celeste, and I took a short, sunny leave of absence in Florida. Over a drink or two, we turned to the problem of biological warfare and particularly the status of the capability of our country to protect itself against an unexpected exposure to a virulent biologic agent. Plague was high on the potential list of such biologic weapons simply because the human illness incites panic and is rapidly disabling and lethal. Furthermore, interest along these lines had been augmented by the fact that a strange plague vaccine had been encountered in North Korea during the war there.

Gen. Douglas MacArthur's forces had overrun North Korea as far as the Yalu River when he was ordered to stop. During this sweeping invasion, several Communist hospital units had been captured. Among the seized medical equipment were vials of a vaccine labeled "E.V. Plague." Surprisingly, the bacterial material which comprised the vaccine was packaged in sealed vials in a dried state. This in itself indicated that plague was a potential threat to the military adversary. Samples of the vaccine were

151

transported back to the United States and turned over to Dr. Karl F. Meyer, director of the Hooper Foundation in San Francisco. Dr. Meyer, known as K.F., was a distinguished medical scientist. Sometimes considered the American Louis Pasteur, he was the world's authority on plague. The dried vaccine was reconstituted by dissolving it in liquid culture media. Surprisingly, the material was viable and produced living plague bacteria. E.V. plague was known as a nonvirulent strain of plague which began initially as a highly virulent strain. It was first isolated from a case of bubonic plague in Madagascar by G. Girard (the French plague expert). The initials of the patient from whom the vaccine was made were E.V. After numerous transfers or passages in appropriate culture media, the virulent (or hot) strain of plague bacteria became nonvirulent but retained its living status. This led to the production of a living, avirulent strain of plague vaccine expertly developed by Dr. Girard of the Pasteur Institute. The vaccine, when given, caused a local reaction much like the smallpox vaccine. It was used effectively in plague countries including Vietnam to protect against the ancient and devastatingly lethal "black death."

In discussing the potential effects, our minds turned, almost simultaneously, to the key question: How would we protect anyone against illness following an aerosolized exposure to a powdered aerosol dispersed over a wide area, in a dried state? There are various ways to detonate a small-package explosive weapon which contained an infected powder other than dynamite. Such an exposure device would be devastating simply because one small particle inhaled could immediately set pneumonic plague, or the black death, in motion. Moreover, a dried, infected plague powder could be put in the ventilatory system of a large building with devastating results.

In 1951, the only known and reliable treatment for any clinical form of plague was streptomycin. This very effective antibiotic needed to be injected intramuscularly once or twice daily since oral administration was not effective.

It so happened that tularemia, or rabbit fever, was equally responsive to streptomycin treatment. In many respects, plague and tularemia resemble each other. Fever, great prostration, and enlarged lymph glands or "buboes" occur in each as does a serious and often fatal pneumonia. The only difference is that plague with pneumonia is always rapidly fatal without treatment. Plague is simply tularemia multiplied in severity by four times. Naturally, our imagination and somewhat inquisitive minds turned to the important question of whether the newly discovered broad-spectrum antibiotics, chloramphenicol and aureomycin (the tetracyclines), would cure plague. These antibiotics are quite effective when given by mouth. In Baltimore, we had determined, first in mice and guinea pigs experimentally infected with tularemia, that these new antibiotics were just as effective as streptomycin. It was illegal to perform laboratory work on plague in the eastern United States because plague was not an endemic disease. Some work was permitted at Ft. Detrick, Maryland. In the test tube, the newer antibiotics showed some inhibitory action against the plague germ.

Joe, Ken, and I were obviously concerned and concluded that we needed reliable information regarding practical treatment for humans infected with plague. Joe was scientific director at the Walter Reed Institute for Medical Research and, at this time, he was one of our country's distinguished medical scientists. Ken and Joe had worked together at the Rockefeller Institute. I was simply a medical teacher who kept up an interest in certain specific infectious diseases and remained concerned about how better and more practical treatment could be developed. Good fortune was on our side. Dr. James H.S. Gear was a senior scientist at the South African Institute for Medical Research in Johannesburg. He had worked at the Rockefeller Institute during the WWII years. Joe wrote to James who indicated that small but sizeable outbreaks of plague were occurring in African natives (Bantu) throughout South Africa. An invitation to conduct a clinical therapeutic trial in South Africa followed.

On the way, we stopped in Paris and had the great privilege of spending a day with Dr. G. Girard. We learned much about plague from this gentleman and scientist. We (I) decided that a side stop should be made at Casablanca for a brief visit at the Pasteur Institute in Morocco. We received a warm reception from Dr. George Blanc (now retired as director) with whom I had worked during the war. The next stop was at Dakar primarily because Dr. Blanc had given us a personal letter of introduction to

South Africa, 1951—Goodner, Guard, Woodward, Smadel

Dr. Durrieux, the director of Pasteur Institute there. I remember hearing a description of their unique vaccine which combined the virus of smallpox (vaccinia) and yellow fever. The vaccines were delivered simultaneously with a scratch in the upper arm. This was a new and somewhat innovative procedure. We asked about the possibility of bad reactions. We were told that there were no bad reactions. However, after vaccination, the natives returned to their villages and there was no recorded evidence, one way or another, whether a reaction had occurred. That large scratch which Ken Goodner referred to as "the Cross of Lorraine" placed on the arm looked rather reactive in the few that we examined.

We arrived in South Africa to find that a sporadic outbreak of plague among the Bantu, which we had planned to evaluate, had subsided, which negated our chance to perform a treatment and trial there. Yet, James Gear had arranged a meeting of all the medical authorities in South Africa who knew plague. They had lived with and studied this disease which was endemic to South Africa. Assembled were the plague experts of the continent. We learned much. One of the bits of valuable information was data about the response to a new vaccine. These data prompted Joe to cable WRAIR in Washington because the information was adequate to enable cancellation of a sizeable contract. Government funds were saved. This type of conference and workshop was an eye-opener to me. It showed that open discussions and exchange of information by informed persons can help solve difficult problems.

A special bonus that came from this exploratory plague mission related to the poliomyelitis problem. At this time, the only known effective way to prevent poliomyelitis was to administer immunoglobulin (gamma-globulin) to those persons who had been exposed to active cases of this illness during the period of incubation. Dr. William Hammond had made this important contribution while he was at the University of Pittsburgh School of Public Health. The inactivated Salk vaccine concept was just in its developmental stages and the living polio vaccine of Drs. Hiliary Koprowski, K.F. Meyer, and Albert Sabin was just a thought. In any event, during our discussions of plague, James Gear showed us his polio laboratory which was impressive in every way.

James, the great scientist that he is, related a simple Pasteurian-like experiment which he had performed over the previous several years. What he had in mind was to develop a new approach and a new effective method for polio immunization. He carefully observed infants born to South African mothers. He studied the blood specimens of newborn infants and found antibodies to the poliomyelitis virus. The presence of such antibodies was also demonstrated in the mother. These tests had to be conducted in many monkeys since there were no simple test tube methods. The work was tedious and expensive. Not unexpected was the finding that mother and infant had high levels of antibody to poliomyelitis. James had followed these infants for several years and noted that the children did not lose the antibody concentration, a finding which was in direct contrast to the type of pattern in the United States and other westernized countries. Rather, the babies in South Africa, as they grew older, played in the soil, and undoubtedly were exposed to polio virus almost daily. Their toys and diapers, if they had any, were not washed or sterilized. Furthermore, these children were carefully followed continuously for several years. Not only did they **not** develop clinical signs of poliomyelitis, but their antibody concentrations **rose** rather than fell. In a significant number of them, the active, virulent poliomyelitis virus was recovered from their fecal specimens. This was a remarkable observation which showed that they had been actively infected but had not become ill. This prompted Joe to remark, "James, you have the answer; administer active poliomyelitis virus and immediately follow up with administration of immune globulin." Hammond had shown part of this concept with his work in immunoglobulin. The Koprowski and Sabin living poliomyelitis vaccine followed after the inactivated Salk vaccine which revolutionized the story of polio.

Returning to our discussion of plague, a chance for a therapeutic field trial eluded us in South Africa. Dr. Girard had suggested a visit to Madagascar and had generously arranged a visit with Dr. Robie, director of the Pasteur Institute in Tannarive, capital of this large island. The proximity to South Africa afforded only a slight detour. Dr. J. Robie, another accomplished French scientist, received us most hospitably and had previously arranged meetings with appropriate public health authorities. Plague is endemic to Madagascar with its mountains and valleys. Much of this country is rural and rats abound which are important for the plague cycle—rats–fleas–man. Rats and fleas die of plague infection. Humans are not necessary to perpetuate the cycle but when infected with bubonic plague, and particularly the septicemic or pulmonic form, they die in large numbers. Indeed, cases of plague occurred within a short distance of the Pasteur Institute in Tannarive. We were taken to active cases of plague, observed them, and were able to treat a few positively confirmed cases, including the pulmonic and bacteremia types. Chloramphenicol was used initially. If treatment was given sufficiently early in the course of illness, the response was excellent, similar to that following streptomycin. Results were encouraging but there were not a sufficient number of cases to prove the point. Medical science standards require adequate confirmation which is statistically acceptable; conjecture or a promising lead are not enough. In any event, we were encouraged.

While in Madagascar, word came to us of an active case of plague in a southern province. As the clinician of this group, I went to observe and possibly gain more information about treatment. After a very long trip over narrow winding mountain roads, I arrived to observe a young Malagashe woman during the last stages of pneumonic plague. She was almost gone and at the time was feebly expectorating bloody mucous which is typical of the fatal disease. Her son, like all Malagash people, was very caring and solicitous. He had spent the previous several nights attending his mother and even cupped his hands and collected the bloody sputum in order to ease her in every possible way. Unfortunately, she died. I, rather unwisely, performed a limited postmortem examination to examine heart and lungs. Smears of the lung tissue revealed the plague bacillus which confirmed the diagnosis. This experience was reminiscent of the earlier plague vignette in Morocco during the war.

It seemed obvious that the young son who had been so intimately exposed would surely develop the illness. Over the next several days, he was observed carefully in a protected room because he should surely come down with the disease. If he developed plague, early treatment would certainly cure him. Fortunately for him, the illness did not occur which led us to the realization that why, how, and when plague occurs is unclear.

This unscheduled side trip provided a chance for other interesting experiences. My physician associate, a French medical officer, showed me a hurried sacrifice and butchering of a cow. The meat would end up in the black market, since meat was a rationed item. The animal was obviously not healthy and even the liver was infected with tuberculosis, a common disease of cows. Joe and Ken like their beef rare, but when they heard this story, for the remainder of the Madagascar visit, the diet was hard, well-done scrambled eggs preceded generously with adequate alcoholic spirit.

We felt that our mission had been successful, although it raised new problems. The long trip home via West Africa and the Azores was relatively uneventful. The stopover in the Azores was brief. In New York, we maneuvered through customs in spite of native spears, knives, wooden trophies, etc. We took the train south, dropped Ken off in Philadelphia and went on to Baltimore. Celeste, Bill, and Lewis met us at Penn Station. I did not feel well and asked Celeste to drive home. After an hour or so, Celeste called Joe to inquire about my fever elevation and general ill feeling. Joe responded, "We think he has the plague but don't worry, chloramphenicol will take care of it." It did and later I had antibodies.

There is a happy addendum to the plague trip. Based on the preliminary clues, we selected Fred McCrumb to complete the work. He went on assignment to The Hooper Foundation in San

Francisco to learn about plague from Dr. K.F. Meyer and the splendid group there. Fred then went to Madagascar during the following plague season and worked with the Pasteur Institute group. Chloramphenicol and tetracycline (Aureomycin) worked just as well as streptomycin in the *pneumonic* form of illness. However, to be cured, any of the three drugs needed to be given not later than twenty hours from the onset of illness. Hence, the oral route of therapy can be successful, if needed, and represented a practical public health expedient in case of an epidemic. This came to full fruition in India in 1994 when plague struck and tetracycline saved the day.

Chapter 13

SABBATICAL IN KIPLING COUNTRY

In 1959, the Congress, through the Department of State and National Institutes of Health, established a few select centers to strengthen the discipline of tropical or global medicine in certain of our medical institutions and, through them, to develop scientific centers in some foreign countries. These were called International Centers for Medical Research and Training (ICMRT). Funds were set aside in the amount of $5 million a year for such activities and a similar amount for operating expenses each year for an indefinite period. Ultimately five such centers were authorized: University of California (Kuala Lumpur, Malaya), Tulane University Medical Center (South America), Louisiana State Medical University (South America), The Johns Hopkins Medical Institutions (Calcutta, India), and the University of Maryland School of Medicine (Lahore, West Pakistan).

An initial invitation to our university came from Drs. Joseph E. Smadel and James A. Shannon, deputy director and director of the National Institutes of Health, respectively. Maryland's proposal, jointly composed by the Division of Infectious Diseases of

Joseph E. Smadel and Colin M. MacLeod

the Department of Medicine, and the Department of Microbiology, was successful in obtaining a grant.

Dr. Colin M. MacLeod, a distinguished biologist and respected governmental advisor, assisted us in this greatly. Memorable was our long train ride from Karachi through the hot desert to Lahore. Accommodations were primitive and air conditioning was nonexistent; we had to traverse a rickety roadbed for more than twenty-four hours through the Sind, a vast expanse of desert. To venture a snack from the available train rations or at infrequent stops was an invitation to establish a close association with conventional tropical vermin, such as amoebae, dysentery bacillae, and innumerable others.

We decided to rely on liquid carbohydrate which came from a bottle. This satisfied us, but our two fellow Muslim cabin mates, squeezed together with us in a small, hot "compartment," took dim view of their American compatriots. Indeed, we got a small lecture! That all-night ride will never be forgotten. Like it or not, our two new friends woke at dawn for their morning prayers to Mecca, though there was barely enough room to kneel. One stop the next day was at Multan, where Alexander

Pakistan Medical Research Center, Lahore, 1964

School boy—note fluoride line on teeth

the Great sustained his last serious wound when he led his forces over his enemy's fortress walls. With this wound, the great general began his downfall. The temperature in Multan that day was 115°F.

Upon arriving in Lahore, we were met by the American consul, Andrew Corry. Mr. Corry was a dedicated diplomat who gave us much assistance. He wisely advised us to place our Research and Training Center in Lahore; he likewise recommended that we locate it sufficiently distant from the West Pakistan government and military center (then in Rawalpindi) to avoid interference, but to remain close enough in contact with the central government to avoid being forgotten. This was ultimately accomplished. The Center Building, planned and constructed at nominal cost, was adjacent to the long established School of Public Health, central to Lahore. Our neighbors and new friends gave sound administrative and intellectual counsel. Dr. Merrill J. Snyder, our senior laboratory scientist, deserves much credit for his work in seeing to it that a useful laboratory building was constructed.

Dr. Eugene Gangarosa was the first director of our center in Lahore. He was innovative and established many important institutional relationships which were of great assistance in developing a scientific and training program. Dr. Herbert Barnett, an expert entomologist, served next as director. In 1964, it fell my lot to direct the Lahore ICMRT. By this time, after a full decade of chairmanship of medicine behind me in Baltimore, I had a talented and dedicated faculty in place and it seemed reasonable to take a break and help shore things up in Lahore. The dean and university administration granted me a sabbatical leave, provided I found supportive salary funds for it. This was accomplished and my appointment was approved by the appropriate NIH Committee.

Celeste was equally enthusiastic and geared up for her contribution. She spent countless hours boning up on internal medicine as well as dermatology since many patients in impoverished countries experience dermatologic disorders of all kinds.

Celeste and I decided to take a short detour en route to Asia and stopped first in Greece with our baggage and our No. 2 Scottie dog (Puddin). This was a delightful interlude and our first accommodation was at the King George Hotel in downtown Athens. A maid took care of "Puddin" while we traipsed around this historic country. The Acropolis and the Parthenon remain a world wonder and never fail to excite. Luckily, we saw a play and series of folk dances in the Odeum to Herodus Atticus just below the ruins of the Parthenon. One day was spent at Corinth (Kolinos), where we were instructed about the ruins by an intelligent guide and taxi driver. The Corinthian channel, cut through sheer rock to join the Gulf of Corinth and Salamic Gulf, nearly rivals the Panama Canal as an engineering accomplishment.

Our best interlude was on the Island of Cos (Kos), the birthplace of Hippocrates, the acknowledged Father of Medicine (fifth century, B.C.). An Olympic Airways DC-3 transported us. Poor Puddin had to ride in a box in the baggage compartment (the first such experience for her.)

Cos is a small Greek Island, shaped like a dolphin, just off the coast of Asia Minor. Its small airfield, which does not accommodate large planes, is in the center of the island. Cos was not, and is not, a conventional tourist site because it lacks the air facilities and top hotel services demanded by most tourists. This suited us very well. At the airport, we were met by Mr. George Sultanas, with the greeting, "I am George Sultanas, the only English speaking guide in Cos; I will be your guide for your stay." This was accepted and his general fee for services negotiated satisfactorily.

Our hotel was the Xenia, a small, beautifully placed hotel-inn directly by the sea. We had a delightful view, and docked just outside our window was a small cruiser the likes of which represented much of the bulk of the Greek Navy. At this time, as later, there were sharp differences of opinion between Greece and Turkey. We watched the ship leave the dock for maneuvers frequently during the day and night and observed the drills of the sailors on board. Our hotel was within easy walking distance of the town of Cos (city and island each named Cos) and, with Puddin along, we made many visits there. Once, during a drill on the cruiser, one of the sailors in formation spotted Puddin, whereupon the whole unit broke ranks to come over and observe this strangely shaped dog. The Roosevelt dog, Fala, was undoubtedly on their minds because that black Scottie was the best known dog in the world. We felt guilty for having breached the discipline of the Greek Navy.

The Cos harbor is quaint, surrounded by fishing vessels and several forts. One fort, which is well preserved, was built by the Crusaders during their Asian treks.

Its most historic medical site is the Plane tree under which Hippocrates was said to have taught medical students. It is a large tree with many spreading branches whose leaves are not unlike those of an American maple. Our guide, George, proudly boasted of Hippocrates (he called him Hippoc) and about his teachings under that tree. On being asked, "George, how old is that tree?" he responded, "four to five hundred years." Then we queried him about Hippocrates' time of life in the fifth century, B.C. On being caught, he responded, "Well, Hippoc planted the tree under which he taught and this is a descendant." This made everything correct.

In the village is a splendid museum with a statue of Hippocrates, the only one known. The sculptor is said to have derived his likeness from ancient coins. He is cloaked in a fully covering garment and his visage is sad. The statue was discovered during excavations which began much earlier by German and Italian archeologists. It was found in an alcove adjacent to the Odeum (theater) just outside the village. This is a lovely little tiered theater with a line of cedar trees at its entrance.

Further beyond the Cos is the Aesculapian (hospital) where Hippocrates taught and practiced his art. Its setting is a lovely hillside overlooking the sea and Asia Minor. It is mostly in ruins but the original structure can be visualized as one ascends wide steps. Immediately on this level is a large marble slab where offerings to the Gods (votives) could be made, usually sheep or goats. On this large first level sits the Temple of Apollo with many of the large, well-preserved, original columns. One faces a beautifully sculptured wall with recessed arches and statues. The water from the fresh spring dates back to ancient times and, when drunk, is said to cleanse the body and give long life. To the east are several large chambers, one said to represent Hippocrates' operating suite. He was a physician, surgeon, psychiatrist, and philosopher, all combined. Adjacent to this area is a large, roofless enclosure, at the base of which are numerous, closely placed stone pillars about a foot high. This was the steam room or sauna. On the pillars were slabs with heated water running underneath. Here one bathed, meditated, and prayed to the Gods. A partially preserved statue of Aesculapius, the God of Medicine, is outside the entrance.

The hospital proper, on the next highest level, is approached by well-preserved marble steps. The whole setting is most beautiful and picturesque with a view beyond description. Greeks came here to meditate and recover from an illness, not to die. Small, stone-walled rooms were placed in the front of the Aesculapian where those judged too ill to live waited for family to come and take them home. Hippocrates' hospital was not a place to die.

On the eastern side of Cos are several villages, mostly for fishermen. The largest is Cephalos, which is clean, quaint, and made up of white cottages and friendly people. Here Puddin was a great hit and everyone came out to see her. Taken into a friendly café, we made a rather gross public health error which could not be avoided. We were offered cream and Gruyere cheese which looked so inviting. Yet, this is a known endemic area for brucellosis and cheese is a great culture medium. Nevertheless, we were not about to sever Greek–American relations and went all out. This interlude was justified by the rationalization that most of the causative brucellae would probably succumb to the wine we generously imbibed. False reasoning, but nothing happened.

Just within view of Cephalos was the site of Hippocrates' birthplace, a small cottage on the hill. In East Cos the steep mountains fall off to the sea, while in the island center, there are low mountains. On many hills are olive trees planted in steep slopes. This is a good system because all one does when the fruit is ripe is to shake the trees, go below at ground level, and pick up ripe olives in abundance.

The streets of Cos are narrow and lined with numerous cafés and shops which sell local crafts and wares. Directly across from where we ate delicious shis-kebob were old ruins of ancient Greece that have been excavated within the past thirty years in diggings that still continue. The marble and stone pillars, columns, stone streets, pathways, and the remnants of several temples were in clear view. One could imagine Greek men and women walking the streets, shopping, bartering, orating, visiting the temple to meditate, or entering the Aesculapian to seek help. Actually, modern Cos, which has many attractive dwellings, sits over an ancient Greek city probably much larger.

Residence: Shah Jamal, Lahore.
Celeste Woodward, Abdul, Sardar, and Ali

Cos is recommended as a delightful place for anyone who would like to set a slower pace and enjoy the friendly comraderie of very nice people.

It was necessary to leave Cos by larder to meet a cruise ship too large to negotiate Cos harbor. This contact occurred shortly after midnight which allowed us to have a view at dawn of the sun rising over Asia Minor. The panorama of emblazoned red was memorable. At Rhodes, we easily glimpsed the site of where the Colossos once spanned the harbor. About the only lasting memory was the number of tourists there as we proceeded by taxi to the airport and back to Athens.

Our main memory of two days in Istanbul was how beautifully the city sits on a hill, its minarets projecting into the sky. Most were built about the tenth century and the sky is penetrated by the spires of mosques, particularly St. Sophia and the Blue Mosque. Through the centuries, St. Sophia has changed hands from Catholicism to the Muslim faith. The Galata Tower, built in the fifth century, A.D., dominates the Istanbul skyline when viewed from across the Bosphorous.

Karachi Airport in Pakistan is always hard to negotiate. It is crowded, disorganized with transportation, and comfortable facilities are nonexistent. In general, it is a nightmare. The next day we were properly met in Lahore at a spacious and organized air terminal and promptly taken to our quarters, which were delightful to say the least. Our residence for the next ten months was a one-floor villa in Shah Jamal with more than adequate space and a lovely garden. Furthermore, we had house help by prearrangement, since servants are more or less passed down by departing American residents, provided their service has been satisfactory.

Abdul, the number one boy, was a pleasure throughout our stay and he managed things well. Sardar, under him, was young and less responsible but honest and clean. A gardener, Mali, and *dhobi* (launderer) as well as a *chokedar* (night guard) represented the house force. We were now living in the style of the Older British Raj but did not object to the system because soon we were to be thrust into a battery of interesting but pressing matters.

The research and training center, known as the University of Maryland Pakistan Research Center, was well organized and centrally located. The city was the cultural center of old India, a city of contrasts, ancient, with daily life and customs similar to those of centuries ago. In the countryside the ways and customs date to biblical times. Yet, in Lahore, there are modern developments which would rival any urban settings in America, although the internal arrangements, such as kitchen, bathing facilities, and temperature controls, would hardly please the modern American.

Requested by the NIH to make a survey of skin disease in West Pakistan, Celeste was put to work almost immediately by the Fatima Jinnah College which was solely for women students. Single-handedly, she established and organized a dermatology clinic which steadily grew in numbers. She devoted about equal time to the King Edward Medical College which was co-educational. Daily she came home with stories of having detected cases of leprosy, prevalent in Lahore, kala azar (leishmaniasis, a protozoal disease), scabies, psoriasis, and contact dermatitis caused by too much and unnecessary skin treatment. She treated hosts of other disorders. Immediately she made a name for herself and for the medical center. She was called on for all kinds of consultations to the affluent or the impoverished. Indeed, she was able, as a woman physician, to examine other women thoroughly, something denied to male dermatologists. Her friend, Dr. Ghulam Shabbir, would say, "Kindly tell me what the lesion looks like, I have never seen it." His earlier training in dermatology had been in England. Yet, this variety of skin disorders in Lahore and similar settings seemed limitless. Celeste was happy and kept very busy, and when we left, her departure left a dent in the dermatologic services, particularly the one at Fatima Jinnah which she had so devotedly and efficiently developed.

Her star patient was a most grateful gentleman, Mian Said Saigol, a splendid, intelligent, and most successful industrialist. He had unfortunately been treated excessively with radiation therapy for common warts located in a delicate anatomical area. Skin necrosis and wide inflammation had produced a horrible mess. Initially, there was reluctance on the part of family and house personnel to accept a woman physician. Yet, she carefully and authoritatively took over and in a few days her treatment had produced striking results. She was quickly accepted into the family's inner circle and even the guard at the entrance of his mansion came to attention when she approached. On a memorable occasion, we were entertained at dinner with the entire family, children, grandchildren, and several of his wives, in attendance; all were served at a huge table setting. The chef had trained as a Cordon Bleu Chef in Paris. Needless to say, I was a little nonplussed to have a huge helping of Johnny Walker's Black Label presented to me as soon as we set foot inside. The dinner, out of Arabian Nights, was elaborate and delicious. Following dinner, Celeste was presented with an intricately hand-tooled, wide gold bracelet imbedded with many precious and semi-precious stones, which, we understand, had been part of his fourth wife's wedding gifts.

When he had improved sufficiently, Said graciously took us to the Lahore Race Track where he had a horse entered in every race. With his steady medical improvement, he informed Celeste that she was now his "blood sister." Indeed, he offered air travel and use of one of his magnificent mansions for Billy and Sue who were on the verge of marriage. This was graciously refused; Celeste traveled in high circles at times!

My chores were a bit different. We had young physicians and technical staff members at the research center who needed

Larry Gallagher and Allan Ronald, Lahore, 1965

guidance, discipline, and help. The laboratory research facilities were primitive and needed modernization. There was no library, and patience was necessary in awaiting replenishment from the States. Indeed, I purchased a slide projector and microscope in Tokyo rather than wait for another through normal requisition procedures. On several occasions, I found it necessary to provide personal funds to meet the laboratory payroll, since the Baltimore home base was a little erratic. Yet, we made it.

Before going to Lahore, my clinical interests had prompted me to seek an academic appointment to the two Lahore medical schools, the King Edward and Fatima Jinnah Medical Colleges. I was granted a visiting professorship in each school.

Accompanying us to Lahore were Dr. Allan Ronald, his wife, Myrna, and Dr. Larry Gallagher and his wife, Anne. They were assigned special work on infectious diseases since there were a plethora of cases of all types. With my faculty professorship opening doors for clinical study, I was asked to teach junior and senior medical students at each school. Ward rounds started at 7:00 A.M. Much of the teaching was done in small groups of about ten each, every other day from 7:00 A.M. until noon. Laboratory backup was almost nonexistent which, at times, was not a bad system at all. Most of the physical examinations had stopped at the navel previously, but I changed that, at least, in men. I taught the students sigmoidoscopy, much to the consternation of everyone. Yet, amoebic dysentery and bacillary dysentery are very common in tropical countries and such examination is often essential.

Once, when rounding with senior medial students soon to graduate, they presented a case which sounded clearly like a patient with a brain tumor—headache, poor vision, vomiting, and other typical findings. In these cases, careful examination of the eyes, retinae, and optic nerves is essential. I handed my ophthalmoscope to the senior student to examine the eye. He knew nothing of the procedure and actually shone the sharp, bright light into his own eye. Just then, Larry Gallagher walked by and I asked: "Larry, when did you first buy your ophthalmoscope?" He replied, "the first year," whereupon he examined the patient's eye and saw the classic diagnostic findings.

The students then informed me: "Oh, Dr. Woodward, this is research, we are not expected to perform these procedures, the Professor of Ophthalmology would not like that!!" By this time, January 1985, I had been accepted into the system and decided to do something about this when it became necessary to return briefly to the States for pressing matters. Before leaving Lahore, I wrote the Welsh-Allyn Company which made the best available ophthalmoscope and otoscope (for examining ears) and pleaded for a sale price not much above cost, explaining my reasons. By the time I left, I had 150 American ophthalmoscopes for medical students and faculty members for each of the two medical schools in Lahore. Somehow, custom officials did not pick them up (probably they were labeled as laboratory equipment) and full distribution was made. These instruments are still in evidence in Lahore!

These were great times. Allan Ronald and Larry Gallagher had a field day studying febrile patients of all types—typhoid fever, amoebic dysentery, liver abscess, leptospirosis, and malaria, among others. We were able to develop a special clinical ward for the study of typhoid in a municipal hospital just outside Lahore. Several clinical disorders, new to Pakistan, cropped up in these clinical studies; the presence of West Nile virus fever, leptospirosis, dengue fever, and others, for example. We were able to identify a case of profound anemia due to a deficiency known as glucose-6-phosphate dehydrogenase deficiency for the first time in Pakistan.

Malaria has always ravaged Asian people and this mosquito-borne illness was prevalent. Our research interests were directed to identifying the types of malaria, the mosquito types which caused them, and controlling the spread by attacking these mosquitoes. A new technique involved the placing of small, vinyl, plastic-like strips impregnated with an anti-mosquito chemical agent in village huts. A number of villages north of Lahore were made available for our use by health authorities. It was possible to make studies of a village with the vinyl strip, and at the same time, one without the strips to serve as a control. Samples of blood were taken by finger stick on a regular basis and spleens of villagers were palpated, since enlargement of this organ is a good index of the presence of malaria.

These rural studies allowed us to learn about Pakistani life, which maintained customs of centuries before. Chapati, a flat type of bread like a pancake, is made by a few village women. Each woman brought her dough, rounded into a ball, to the bake, a woman with a huge terra cotta vase sunk in the ground for an oven. Coals at the bottom provided heat. Women sat around a circle, gave their dough to the baker, who flattened it into pancakes, scored each with a special mark and placed it by hand at the top of the oven. When baked, Chapati, which is full of good vitamin B and protein, was returned to the dough owner. For each ninth cake, the baker kept a ball of dough. There was no exchange of coin, just payment in kind. The conversation around this bread factory rivaled that of our small town barber shop, the flour mill, firemen's hall, or hairdresser's.

Hookah smokers (the use of a water pipe and tube for smoking) were an interesting group. In the evening, men sat in a circle, well-cloaked because of the winter chill, and passed the hookah around so that all could smoke. The boys sat in the background and often sneaked in a puff or two. The older men, wheezing heavily, would ask us for help for their "tightness of breath." The suggestion that hookah smoking be stopped brought a blank or very uncertain stare.

One eventful trip to the villages and to Sialcot remains fresh in my mind after twenty years. With me in our staff car was Dr. Nur Ahmad, our deputy director and driver. Near the Indian border, on a hard macadam road, we rounded a corner and came upon a tragic scene. Just seconds before, a Volkswagen driven by a single occupant had rounded an opposite curve and struck a small shepherd boy and several sheep in his small flock that were crossing the road. The Volkswagen, a new one, was badly jammed against a tree and I quickly observed that the driver was not seriously injured. I asked Dr. Nur Ahmad to tend to him while I examined the boy about age 10 lying flat on the road. He had a broken leg and compound arm fracture. A weak pulse was present, but he was not breathing. By this time in 1964, mouth-to-mouth resuscitation had come into practice and I quickly applied it. Soon, and happily, the boy began to breathe on his own and his pulse improved in strength. He soon came around and whimpered in severe pain. We practically commandeered an approaching car, used a back seat for a stretcher, and back-tracked a few miles to a small town which had a small hospital, really a first aid center. We were able to obtain some intravenous fluids, pain killer medicine, and better splints than the ones applied at the scene of the accident. The Volkswagen driver, a successful young business man who had been driving entirely too fast, was not badly injured, a broken arm and nothing more. After we were satisfied that the boy was stable, Dr. Nur Ahmad and I proceeded to Sialcot to conduct our business in a clinic there. We returned via the small town in order to check on things, which provided me one of the most rewarding experiences of my medical life. The boy was much better and was in the process of being transferred to a large hospital in Lahore. In the meantime, more than a thousand Muslims had assembled from the surrounding countryside. As we were leaving, Dr. Nur Ahmad said: "That is the boy's mother," who was standing by the car within a foot of my rear window. She did not speak my language nor I hers. Yet her eyes expressed her feeling more than words or a portrait. I felt happy for her and her son, who did make a full recovery. My mind went back ten years to the time of our Manila experience when the technique and benefits of mouth-to-mouth resuscitation measures were not known.

A pleasant part of our Lahore experience was that of receiving visitors from the United States. Dr. William (Bill) Mosberg, an able Baltimore neurosurgeon, came to Lahore from Karachi where he had consulted for USAID. Dr. James Steele, a prominent veterinary scientist and educator, came with his son for a few days. He was en route to India to advise about contraceptive devices for cattle that caused this large Asian country considerable trouble. Charley and Anne McCormick broke their round-the-world trip at Bombay and came to Lahore for a few days. We had a great time showing them such sights as the Bad Shaii Mosque the Red Fort in Lahore, Kim's Cannon, "Zam Zammah," on the mall just across from the Museum, the old city and Jehangir's Tomb just outside Lahore to the north, as well as the famous Shalimar Gardens.

We accompanied them to Delhi to visit the Taj Mahal in Agra which was a special treat for everyone. Our last stopping point was as a guest of Mr. Naval Tata at Tata House in Bombay. Here we were royally entertained at dinner one memorable evening. There were more than fifty dinner guests and the cocktail party continued for about two hours. This festive event is a

Taj Mahal, Agra, 1960

serious matter in India because alcohol is at a premium and its use is really frowned upon. Delay in dining was due to the fact that Simone Tata's servants felt that there was insufficient food on the large table for so many guests. The chef from the Taj Mahal Hotel, which Mr. Tata owned, kept sending more food but could not understand the dilemma. He had prepared turkey and chicken, aspic sculpted in the form of animals, and other decorative dishes which had eluded the imagination of the servants. Late that evening, Anne and Charley exited India through the Gate of India initially built to honor the visit of Queen Victoria to this vast country. They joined their ship and we returned to Lahore.

In early January 1965, Colin MacLeod, then with the Office of Science and Technology of the White House, cabled an invitation for me to join a small working group as an official delegate in Tokyo to help develop a joint U.S.–Japanese Medical Science Program. I gratefully accepted. Shortly, I was associated with Colin, Dr. James (Jim) Shannon (Director of the National Institutes of Health), Thomas Francis (University of Michigan, Preventive Medicine), John (Jack) Weir (Rockefeller Foundation), and Stanley Bennett (University of North Carolina). We met first at the American Embassy in Tokyo and later with Japanese scientists to inaugurate the U.S.–Japan Cooperative Medical Science program which has contributed mightily to the control of diseases, such as tuberculosis, leprosy, encephalitis, cholera, schistosomiasis, and filariasis. These diseases are prevalent in southeast Asian countries. The program remains viable and productive and is now in its fourth decade. It is a model of international scientific cooperation.

The air trip from Lahore, Karachi, Bangkok, Hong Kong to Tokyo was long and tiring, but an interesting incident broke the monotony of the trip. Two new passengers boarded at Hong Kong and took seats several rows ahead of me. When the flight attendant came down the aisle, I remarked to her that now she had two distinguished passengers. I had recognized Mr. Lowell Thomas and presumed that his wife was with him. Soon after reaching our flying altitude to Tokyo, Mr. Thomas came down the aisle and asked if he might speak with me. He presented a medical problem; obviously, the flight attendant had mentioned that a physician was on board. Mr. Thomas remarked that he and his wife had been "shooting" animals, with a camera, in Africa and were now en route to Tokyo and each had a bad case of what has euphemistically been called "Delhi Belly," "Gippy Tummy," "Montezuma's Revenge," or "Tourista" (in other words, diarrhea). He asked if I had any suggestions to "prepare them for that good Japanese food."

Now it is a little difficult to make a clinical diagnosis at 32,000 feet, with the patient fully clothed and traveling at a high rate of speed. But, as we always advise medical students, the medical history is more important than the physical or anything else. To my mind, his problem was more likely dysentery with an active inflammation of the lower intestine than the more mild toxic types of diarrhea. He had a little fever and a specimen which I was able to examine in the lavatory fitted in with the more acute bacterial type of infection (dysentery). I always carried a supply of antibiotics for such circumstances and mapped out a treatment plan for them.

He could not have been nicer and after our medical discussion inquired about my doings in this part of the world. I spoke some about our tropical medicine program in Lahore and had remembered an earlier venture of his into the high Himalayas when, by accident, he fractured a leg and was carried out on a plank, so I asked him about it. He knew well the northwest Asian frontier and had been instrumental in helping to stimulate some of the archeological diggings at Taxila. This ancient city was an old Buddhist Grecian civilization near Rawalpindi which had been excavated several decades before.

In any event, I chose my time and pulled three old coins from my pocket: one a small, silver Alexander the Great coin. The other two were copper of the Kushan era. As I proudly fondled these three coins, a good conversation piece, proud as anything, Mr Thomas took his key chain out of his pocket. Hanging from it was an authentic gold Alexander the Great drachma. Few of this type of coin exist anywhere. I remarked: "Mr. Thomas, a coin of that quality and antiquity, hanging on a key chain?" He remarked: "Woodward, my friend, the Director of the London Museum is giving me two more for a pair of cuff links." Moral of story—don't try upsmanship on a pro.

Weeks later, I received a nice note from Mr. Thomas with a personally inscribed book. He remarked that the antibiotic regimen had been successful.

Numerous festive occasions added greatly to this interesting period in West Pakistan. Weddings usually were planned for the autumn when the weather is very agreeable. House, trees, and bushes were gaily decorated with colorful electric lights and bright decorations of all kinds. At night, they resembled a huge Christmas garden. Weddings were segregated and, on arriving, men were ushered into a huge tent were conversation went on for hours. The beverage was usually a lime or orange squash, a shock to many Westerners. After a while, band and trumpet music announced the coming of the groom. He, along with his father or brother, were met by the bride's father and brother who went to the men's reception area where the marriage agreement was signed and witnessed. This is not a bad idea since the bride is thence assured her full share of inheritance.

The ladies had a much better time. They were gaily dressed and were shown the various lovely wedding gifts which, I understand, always came in pairs. Celeste was my informant. Indeed, the dressing of the bride was often with help of guests and friends. Then a special dramatic event, unwitnessed by the men, occurred. The bridegroom, who, if this was a fully orthodox wedding ceremony, had never seen his bride (the marriage was usually arranged by family), was led to the ladies' tent, blindfolded, and seated in a chair. The marriage chair is low with the seat several inches off the ground. The bride was also seated, blindfolded, in a similar chair, the two separated by a partition so that they could not see each other. Then, at a crucial moment, blindfolds were removed and each looked into a mirror which would allow the first glance. I mentioned to Celeste that the low chair was a good idea because if he had a sudden attack of syncope, he had not far to fall. The nuptials were then followed by a buffet in each tent, men and women.

A particularly happy assignment for me while still in Pakistan was a visit every week to Rawalpindi and the privilege to lecture to officers and ancillary health personnel of the Armed Forces Medical School. Mornings were spent in ward walks with the opportunity to see and discuss many interesting cases—

typhoid fever, amoebic liver abscess, meningitis, encephalitis, malaria, etc. Cases were clearly and formally presented. These rounds were followed by a lecture, indeed, a series of lectures were given over the eight-month period. These visits brought me in contact with Maj. Gen. Ayub Kahn, Col. Burney, Col. Hussain, and so many others. For about a decade after returning to Baltimore, the surgeon general of the Pakistani army selected a military medical officer to come to Maryland for a three-year period of training in internal medicine and a subspecialty of his choice. Three excellent officers came, and the one who stood out was Zaheer-Ud-Din, who made a hit with everyone in Baltimore. Later, he became surgeon general of the Pakistani army.

Chapter 14

ATTACK ON ASIATIC CHOLERA

hen Joe Smadel left WRAIR as its scientific director in
1956 to assist Jim Shannon as deputy director of the
National Institutes of Health, it was at a time when
the world was generally peaceful. This prompted member nations
of the South East Asia Treaty Organization (SEATO) to think in
terms of peaceful endeavors. A handsome sum of $400,000 was
allocated to stimulate responsible agencies to develop some type
of program which could help alleviate illness and suffering in
Southeast Asian peoples. The U.S. Department of State sought
the advice of the National Institutes of Health, which charge Jim
Shannon placed on the capable shoulders of Joe Smadel. Not one
to shirk a chance to be of help, Joe quickly fixed upon a medical
problem which had tormented Asian peoples for centuries. Joe
assembled his team to survey the possible areas for study and
called upon Colin MacLeod, Ken Goodner, John Dingle, Dick
Mason, and me to join in the search. Asiatic cholera was the
prime target and, for this reason, the only geographic countries
for survey were those where this horrible diarrheal disease was
known to occur.

John Dingle, Ken Goodner, Dick Mason, and Colin MacLeod—Cholera mission group

Our first visit was Tokyo where many great microbiologists had contributed so importantly to the evolution of knowledge of cholera. Ken Goodner and I took a taxi hoping to visit the Japan National Institutes of Health. Our imperfect Japanese tongue ended us at the Kitasoto Institute, the home of the great Japanese pioneer on plague. There we met the famous man's son and were fortunate in being treated to a viewing of the memorial marker to Robert Koch who visited Japan and the Institutes in 1906.

From Japan, the group visited Taipei where the U.S. Navy Research Unit #2, under the direction of Cmdr. Robert Phillips, had spearheaded a new vigorous treatment using intravenous fluid replacement. Bob Phillips received the team graciously and taught us much about the physiologic abnormalities involved in cholera. Simultaneously, this important research unit had trained a team of expert investigators.

In Taipei, we were graciously entertained by the medical school dean and faculty. The dinner, in addition to numerous toasts of "gombe" (means "bottoms up") sandwiched between the many courses, was a rather strenuous proposition. The dinner course involving a roast pig was very easy to handle, cracklings and all. Each roasted shoat placed on the various tables had small lighted electric bulbs in each eye. Also, we learned of a ranking system when eating a roasted pig. The ears go to the lesser dignitaries and the tail to the number one guest. Joe ate the first tail. After each round of bottoms up, between courses, we returned to various tables. One of the later dishes was a fully feathered pigeon, beak and all, placed in the center of each of the circular tables. Deftly, the waiter carved each bird and, in front of each of the American visitors, he placed the head, neck, eyes, and beak. This is a formidable sight and challenge. Each of us very graciously tried to pass off this choice morsel to one of the faculty members' wives seated beside us. "Oh, no, doctor, that is especially for you!" A special treat like that once in a lifetime is enough.

Next we went to Manila, which, in 1959, was being visited by a strange form of cholera infection known as El Tor (the lion). Ken Goodner had long recognized this strain as a virulent form of the old and ancient explosive diarrheal disorder. Subsequently, many deaths occurred from El Tor cholera.

In Manila, there was much enthusiasm to place the cholera center there. Numerous circumstances suggested a cautious decision. Cholera was not regularly present in the Philippines nor was there a clear ideal regarding the lines of authority should a center be placed in Manila.

Bangkok was especially exciting because of a sizable outbreak of cholera that had occurred in 1959, which had caused great concern and some panic in various places. Fortuitously, the undersecretary of health, Dr. Luang Mungman (Dr. Pyn), had the ear of the Crown and the key to Thailand. Dr. Pyn was a close friend of Ken Goodner and a former graduate of the Jefferson School of Medicine where Ken served as its distinguished chairman of microbiology. Not only was every medical door in Bangkok opened to us but we had the added pleasure of an audience with the young king which Pyn had arranged.

In Thailand, then known as Siam, there is strict protocol. Not only did we arrive at the Palace reception hall well ahead of time, but we received diplomatic instruction as to how to conduct ourselves and how to respond in the presence of the King. "One answers questions, not asks them. Do not cross your arms or your legs and don't touch your body in the presence of the King." The audience was to have lasted for fifteen minutes. The

Meeting with King of Thailand

next hour and a half was delightful and memorable. Joe, as our "great leader," was placed to the right of the monarch, who was a most affable man. We were seated in a circle around a small table with a center floral display. The young king kept speaking about practical solutions to medical problems and Joe, the intense person that he was, kept stressing the need for research. The King kept wisely responding, "But how will that help my people?"

Two site visits were planned for India because the Ganges Delta had always been the home and reservoir of Asiatic cholera over the decades. In Delhi we visited with members of the health ministry including Dr. C.J. Pandit, a recognized authority in the field of enteric infections. We gained considerable information and later in the afternoon we were invited to a reception and tea attended by cabinet members of the government. In typical British-Indian tradition, each us was paired to talk with a specific minister and for 20 minutes my partner was the minister for birth control. I learned from him that the increase in population rate in India was a huge 5% annually, that women conceived as soon as possible, that children were on the streets in poverty, etc. He indicated that an attempt was made to control population growth by sterilization of men; about 90,000 were sterilized by a vasectomy in the Bombay area. He stated, "We realize that we were not making a dent in the problem, and furthermore we men don't like that!" Then he said, "You Americans have invented a pill. Let's make two assumptions, one that it works, and also that the United States would sell it to us for a penny each." He then said, "it would cost us a billion dollars just to deliver the pill to the mouth and we doubt whether she would take it in the first place!" I understood the problem.

That very afternoon Prime Minister Nehru came into the room and graciously met each of the American visitors and warmly shook our hands. We then went to the hotel to prepare for a reception and dinner given by Dr. Pandit. Ken Goodner predicted a dry evening and insisted that we have a drink or two before going to the reception. On entering the front door of the lovely residence, each of us was greeted by a waiter with a tray of fully filled glasses. "Do you wish bourbon, gin, or scotch?"— enough for that site visit.

Following our visit to Bangkok, we proceeded to Delhi and Calcutta because in India there were many medical authorities who were knowledgeable in the field of cholera. Much was learned there of a practical and fundamental nature. We saw numerous cases of cholera in Calcutta under very primitive circumstances.

Our last site visit was to Dacca in East Pakistan, now known as Bangladesh. This was the true home of cholera because the disease had been endemic there for years and was recognized as a continuing major cause of death and suffering. The governmental

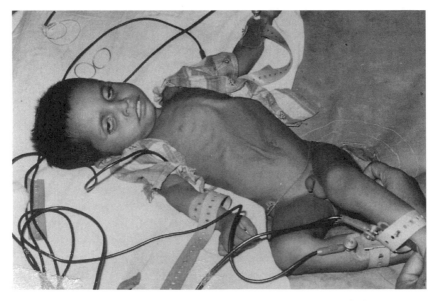

Asiatic cholera. Note extreme dehydration. (Photograph courtesy of Dr. Charles Carpenter)

doors were opened and Joe and his team were persuasive ambassadors. The various laboratory facilities were visited as were the hospital clinics, the villages, and the village bazaars. Several simple reasons led to the decision to place a clinical study center in Dacca. Cholera was widely prevalent there, the governmental and medical authorities were enthusiastic in their invitation to develop a research and treatment center, and the need for help was obviously apparent. This country has one of the highest population densities in the world.

The visiting team with Joe Smadel as its dynamic leader unanimously reached this decision. Jim Shannon, director of the National Institutes of Health, willingly accepted the recommendation and added his considerable administrative and scientific advice. As a sequel to this visit, a new center was developed and with it began a new explosion in the modern era of research on cholera which expanded greatly the development of new knowledge, not only for cholera but for other disorders.

On a personal note, I relate an event which stresses the importance of simple clinical observations. Bob Phillips, the uncontested authority on cholera, once remarked to me during the early days in Dacca, that cholera patients were not thirsty because they had an isotonic type of dehydration. However, the extreme cholera patients observed by Ken and me in Dacca and Calcutta were remarkably thirsty. They were usually too weak to reach for a bottle placed at the bedside. To be sure, the fluid was often vomited which was a major problem. This prompted me to suggest that an anti-emetic might allay the nausea and vomiting and thereby assist in treatment by replacing fluid loss. I also suggested that a fair trial should be given to the broad-spectrum antibiotics which had been discarded. A few years later, investigators showed dramatically that oral rehydration of cholera patients with carefully designed fluid solutions is usually sufficient for cure. This new information remarkably precluded the voluminous use of intravenous fluid replacement. Also, antibiotics have been shown not only to reduce the total fluid replacement requirement in seriously ill cholera patients, but also to cut in half the period when the pathogenic vibrio of cholera is shed in the diarrheal specimens. **Lesson learned**: The clinician with an open eye can occasionally put in a sensible word or two.

Chapter 15

KOREA AND
HEMORRHAGIC FEVER

*W*henever young military personnel are exposed to new unexplored terrain, new diseases are encountered. Malaria, scrub typhus, and other types of serious infections invariably occur and are often fatal or highly debilitating. Epidemic hemorrhagic fever was such an encounter in Korea, particularly when American troops became engaged near the 38th Parallel. Not only were we ill-prepared for the events to follow, but the disease rates and high incidence of fatal cases were alarming, in addition to being of significant strategic importance.

Under such circumstances, our country has always mobilized its scientific personnel, who have freely contributed their collective talent to work collaboratively with the military services to help clarify and control the problem. During World War I, there were notable examples of such collaboration, required to develop an understanding of those measures necessary to control pneumonia, influenza, typhus, and meningitis. These joint efforts were used effectively during World War II in the European, North African, and Pacific Theaters. Korea was another example.

Tom Wayne, Joe Smadel, Colin MacLeod, John Dingle, Ted Woodward, and Adam Rapalski

Numerous well-qualified and patriotic medical scientists such as Drs. William (Bill) Jellison, Barry Wood, Fred Bang, Robert (Bob) Traub, Marshall Hertig, David Earle, and others had made fundamental studies in an attempt to settle the hemorrhagic fever enigma. Joe decided to take on a direct approach and garnered Drs. Colin MacLeod, Adam Rapalski, Ken Goodner, Richard (Dick) Mason, Thomas (Tom) Wayne, and me for a fresh evaluation. On the way out, we stopped at the Hamilton Air Force Base in California. While waiting, we engaged in a game of draw poker with suitable reinforcements. Believe it or not, Joe held a royal straight flush in diamonds which prompted us to freeze the deck. Everyone put his name on the ace of diamonds. Years later, I gave the five cards, suitably encased in lucite, to Joe when he retired from WRAIR.

In Korea, we became immediately involved in a difficult and serious problem. Whenever young American soldiers contracted hemorrhagic fever and developed shock syndrome, about 20% died in spite of any form of treatment. This is a death rate which for any disease is unacceptable. Colin and Joe looked over the roster of medical officers who had trained in important medical centers in the United States and came across the name of Dr. Sheldon E. Greisman whom Col. Dick Mason happened to meet coincidentally. He was a graduate of New York University and a protegee of Dr. David Earle with whom he had worked as a physiologist on capillary circulation. Joe arranged for Dr. Greisman's transfer from the psychiatric service to which he had been assigned. The disease in Korea, with its physiologic abnormalities, was the kind just made for Shelley Greisman because it involved shock and an understanding of the small circulation. His bedside observations and direct observations of the capillary system led to a significant advance which turned out to be one of the few new additions to our knowledge of hemorrhagic fever. This experience gave me the opportunity to meet a remarkable and brilliant young clinician and physiologist.

After separation from the military service, Shelley came to the University of Maryland to join our faculty. Here he made important contributions to education and research in the medical school and hospital, and he became one of the country's leading authorities in the field of bacterial endotoxin.

This same trip enabled me to meet Dr. William (Bill) Spicer who was busy with an infantry unit at the 38th Parallel in Korea. Bill also joined our department at Maryland and performed important work on the relationship of environmental pollution and lung disease. Later, he developed a training program which showed the importance of nurses and other allied personnel to the health care system.

The medical mission to Korea proved to be of great value to the University of Maryland School of Medicine and Hospital. At the U.S. Army M.A.S.H. Hospital near Seoul, I also met Dr. George Entwistle, a very capably trained Boston physician with special talents on problems related to hypertension. While treating critically ill soldiers with Korean hemorrhagic fever and shock, George showed that very small doses of adrenalin and carefully measured infusions of serum albumin sustained kidney function and led to recovery.

George kindly accepted the invitation to come to Baltimore. He joined me in medical practice for several years and headed the general medical outpatient clinic. After Maurice Pincoffs's death, George was made head of the Department of Preventive Medi-

*William S. Spicer, M.D., Professor of
Medicine*

*Sheldon E. Greisman, M.D., Professor of
Medicine and Physiology*

*George Entwistle, M.D., Head,
Department of Preventive Medicine
and Rehabilitation*

cine and Rehabilitation. These three highly qualified persons—Greisman, Spicer, and Entwistle—gave much strength to our medical school and hospital academic and practice programs in Baltimore during the growing period.

Chapter 16

THE ARMED FORCES EPIDEMIOLOGICAL BOARD

*I*f ever there was a bureaucratic love story in Washington, DC, the Armed Forces Epidemiological Board (AFEB) deserves high consideration because of the close collaboration and spirit of cooperation developed and continued between military and civilian medical scientists and government officials. This board was founded on logic and necessity by some of the brightest minds of twentieth century medicine. World War I was a nightmare partially because of the great threats of pneumonia and influenza which devastated the world population, whether civilian or military. No vaccines or specific methods of treatment were available, making these horrors even more alarming.

In 1941, at the debut of another world war, these visible threats stimulated the minds particularly of Drs. Stanhope Bayne-Jones, Stephen Simmons, and Francis Blake. They, along with the wise input of Dr. Colin MacLeod, conceived the plan to form a special board of civilian medical advisors to guide the military services and develop new methods of prevention and cure. The diseases to be evaluated were not only those involving the respiratory tract but other important microbial epidemic diseases, which had traditionally attacked military personnel throughout history, such as malaria, meningococcal and streptococcal infections, plague, yellow and typhus fever, and many more. For example, from 1915 to 1922 there were 30 million cases of typhus fever and 3 million deaths in Russia and the eastern border of Poland alone.

Toward these ends in January 1941, a Board for the Investigation and Control of Influenza and other Epidemic Diseases in the Army was inaugurated. Its organizational structure included the board itself, comprised of seven members, and a group of commissioned officers including leading medical scientists who were expected to study relevant special medical problems at their various medical centers and develop new and necessary knowledge vital for keeping Army military personnel healthy. In 1944 the name of the organization was changed to the Army Epidemiological Board. After World War II, the Board was expanded to include officers of the Navy and Air Force. It was redesignated the Armed Forces Epidemiological Board as an advisory group for the Surgeons General of the Army, Navy, and Air Force. On November 29, 1949, it was established as a Tri-Service Board and so continues.

Commission on Immunization of the AFEB

My first exposure to AFEB activities was via its Commission on Immunization which was first chaired by Joe Smadel, followed by Geoffrey Edsall and Bud Benenson. I was asked to serve as a consultant because of my past experience with rickettsial infections, human vaccine efficacy trials, and work on scrub typhus and typhoid vaccines. The first meeting I attended was in Philadelphia at the Jefferson Medical College where Ken Goodner served as host for a two-day meeting. At the time I could not understand why two full days were needed to discuss anything. As it turned out, there were many scientific and strategic details which needed to be thoroughly evaluated, discussed, and agreed upon before further studies on any specific problem could be approved.

Also, the results of many ongoing projects were heard, sifted, and ultimately put into action. There was close collaboration, complete understanding, and trust between military and civilian scientific investigators which was absolutely essential if any extensive program of this type could be successful. This was, and continues to be, a basic tenent of modus operandi of the board, its commission members, and military representatives.

Plague was an important topic at the time. Not only was plague then an infection of worldwide importance, but it ranked highly as an effective weapon for biologic warfare which was a very hot topic in the early 1950s. Our Russian adversaries were highly sophisticated and very active in this general field. The studies on plague conducted in South Africa and elsewhere were conducted under the sponsorship of the Commission of Immunization and are described in a preceding chapter.

Out of these meetings came a much better understanding of immunologic principles, and the methods to develop new vaccines for such diseases as influenza, poliomyelitis, adenovirus infections, rickettsial diseases, typhoid fever, tularemia, plague, and others. All such work was group supervised and carried through from its planning and implementation of field studies, to final testing in humans to evaluate efficacy.

Commission on Rickettsial Diseases

This commission of the board had a proud heritage and it comprised the leading rickettsiologists in the country. It was privileged to have the consultative advice of world leaders in this field such as Drs. Raymond Lewthwaite and Ralph Audi (United Kingdom) and Marcel Baltazard (France). Joe Smadel and Charlie Wisseman were its directors for many years, with heavy and steady input from Jack Snyder, Bob Traub, John Fox, Charley Shepard, Buz Wheeler, Andy Yeomans, Ed Murray, Paul Fiset, Neil Philip, Willy Burgdorfer, Dick Ormsbee, Bill Vinson, Henry Fuller, and Lew Barker. I was privileged to serve as a member of this Commission.

Epidemic typhus fever was not a threat to our military forces during World War II because of better health standards, an effective vaccine, and DDT which prevented louse infestation. Indeed, there were no deaths from louse-borne typhus except those few suffered by our British allies. In North Africa alone there were 33 cases in British military forces and three deaths which could have been avoided. During this war louse typhus was quite prevalent in civilians in North Africa and in Southern Italy, particularly Naples. When the British adopted use of the American typhus fever vaccine, this problem ceased.

Q-fever was another matter in the Mediterranean area, particularly in Italy and has been mentioned previously. Rocky Mountain spotted fever (RMSF) was never an epidemic threat nor was murine typhus which involved a rat–flea–man cycle. Scrub typhus transmitted by mites was another matter and during WWII it was responsible for disabling and killing a number of American military personnel in the southwest Pacific area.

The Commission on Rickettsial Diseases helped solve many of these riddles. Actually the typhus project mission in Malaya in 1948 was channeled under the umbrella of the Commission on Immunization of the AFEB. The important contributions which resulted from this work were: 1) the first known specific treatments of scrub typhus, murine typhus, and Rocky Mountain spotted fever; 2) the first known specific treatment of typhoid fever; and 3) the first known demonstration that an antibiotic given prophylactically and intermittently to persons exposed to scrub typhus fever in the field could prevent them from developing the illness. The latter was a contribution of significant military importance. The total expenditure for the project was less than $50,000. Thus, potent weapons were now available which practically guaranteed protection against death from any rickettsial infection, particularly scrub typhus. Also, patients promptly responded to specific antibiotic treatment with full recovery. Better understanding of the pathologic and physiologic changes in patients even led to recovery in advanced cases.

Effective vaccines for the rickettsial diseases, particularly epidemic typhus, RMSF, and Q-fever, were developed under Commission auspices.

These studies and those of others have pushed rickettsial diseases "backstage" but their potential threat remains. Even now, scrub typhus fever is a considerable problem in North Thailand and accounts for about 25% of the cases of obscure fever (FUO).

Commission on Epidemiological Survey (CES)

After WWII, the western world experienced a "cold war" and an "iron curtain" as phrased by Winston Churchill. Military authorities and the newly formed AFEB considered it vital for the United States to develop an understanding and full knowledge of biological warfare (BW), particularly with reference to adequate defensive measures. A new CES was organized in 1954 along different lines from the original commission formed under the initial board. The executive order charged the Commission with responsibility to evaluate the potential of bacterial warfare (BW) as a weapons system and to formulate those criteria and safety measures necessary to maintain our posture against any enemy attack. In the late 1940s and early 1950s, BW was considered a major risk.

Dr. Richard (Dick) Shope of the Rockefeller Institute, and one of our nation's distinguished biologists, was wisely chosen to head the new commission with membership including Joe Smadel, Colin MacLeod, John Dingle, W. Barry Wood, Thomas Francis, Geoffrey Edsall, and me. A little later, Ivan Bennett, Dick Hornick, Vernon Knight, and Shelley Greisman joined as members. Col. William Tigertt, MC, was the first executive director who was succeeded by Col. Dan Crozier. These officers exemplified the highest standards of knowledge and capability.

Frequent meetings were held in the "war room" at WRAIR as well as at Ft. Detrick, which was then designated as our nation's BW center. Originally the center was administered under the Chemical Corps and later it had direct attachment to WRAIR.

Throughout the thirty years of its existence, the CES avoided any adversarial posture. Cooperation and trust between military and civilian scientists flourished throughout these three decades, and our country developed an innovative and effective defense system. Much new knowledge was gained regarding how highly pathogenic microbes such as bacteria, rickettsiae, viruses, and toxins cause illness. Each important pathogenic agent, particularly those that produce toxins, was studied, its antigens defined and characterized. New vaccines useful to protect against various illnesses were painstakingly developed, which included those for the rickettsial diseases and Q-fever, anthrax, botulism, plague, tularemia, typhoid fever, the various viral forms of encephalitis, Rift Valley fever, dengue, and yellow fever. Such milestone studies made at Ft. Detrick were conducted in collaboration with academic centers throughout the United States. These joint efforts represent a model of their type rivaling any others performed elsewhere.

The studies of Q-fever described earlier was really a CES activity. Smadel, Goodner, and I, following the leadership of K.F. Meyer, ranked plague as a high-priority agent and in 1951 went to South Africa and Madagascar to learn more about this dreaded disease, and the use of vaccine. This experiment and work are described in a previous chapter. Co. (Pops) Randall, VC, developed a Venezuelan Equine Encephalitis (VEE) vaccine at Ft. Detrick under this broad program. Years later, available stocks of this new vaccine were taken to Texas and other southern states for immunization of horses naturally infected with VEE virus which began in Central America. Without doubt, our major horse population in America was saved through this example of inspired preparedness.

Several interesting happenings are recalled. We learned of experiments conducted by our potential enemy which involved placing thousands of *Aedes aegypti* mosquitos (which transmit yellow fever virus) in small plastic spheres. They were then released from an airplane at an altitude of 30 or more thousand feet. On hitting the ground, the spheres collapsed and the mosquitos flew away. The full scenario simply meant that infected mosquitos could have been placed in such spheres, launched in a missile from a submarine off the east coast of the southern United States, and programmed to drop over Texas, Mississippi, Louisiana, or Alabama. Here, there is a large human population concentration without any immunity, whatsoever, to yellow fever. The *Aedes aegypti* mosquito was prevalent throughout the southern United States and an epidemic of this devastating illness (Yellow Jack) could be readily initiated. Added to this was the realization that no more than 5 million doses of yellow fever vaccine were available in our nation's stockpile.

When the cold war began to soften a bit, President Nixon directed that research on BW would cease at Ft. Detrick and elsewhere. All major nations joined in the belief that BW and chemical warfare (CW) should be outlawed.

Our CES group, in an attempt to bring the subject of BW into the open, invited a small team of knowledgeable Russian scientists to visit WRAIR and Ft. Detrick in Frederick for the purpose of a joint meeting between our authorities and the AFEB. It took a lot of maneuvering and persuasion with authorities in the Pentagon and the Department of State to have such a radical idea approved. Nevertheless, the meeting was held with our Russian guests who were given a tour of WRAIR and the highly technical laboratories at USAMRIID in Frederick. The actual scientific meeting between the two groups was held at a motel in Frederick.

A few years later in 1990, I was privileged to join an ad hoc group appointed by the National Academy of Sciences and the National Security Council to visit Russia for the purpose of holding open meetings there regarding BW. The group was also expected to explore the vexing problem of a large anthrax outbreak which was said to have killed more than 1000 Russian citizens. Dr. Joshua Lederberg, President of the Rockefeller University, Ivan Bennett, Paul Marks, and I were members of the group including a member from the Department of State. We all met for initial briefing in Frankfurt, Germany while en route to Moscow. The four-day meeting was open and cordial. Our group pressed for openness and full agreement including a plan to stop smallpox vaccination which was practiced at that time by the Russian and United States Armies. Smallpox virus is a potentially potent BW agent. Ultimately smallpox vaccination was stopped and now there is talk of destroying all supplies of this virus. This is ill-advised in my view since a potential threat remains and we must continue to be alert not only for any terrorist intervention, but for a natural outbreak which could possibly begin from a primate source starting in Africa.

With this meeting in Moscow, we were told that their prior anthrax outbreak at Sverdlovsk was caused by spread of infected dust from infected cattle and ingestion of contaminated meat by Russian citizens. This was untrue and it now has been openly stated by Russian authorities that there was a laboratory break at a BW center which released anthrax spores that ultimately spread widely throughout this area.

Even the desert Gulf War profited from the innovative preparedness developed under our nation's BW defense program. During this war, the possible use of anthrax and botulism organisms was very real. Iraq possessed this capability. Our U.S. forces were in a favorable position because vaccine supplies were available for our units and our allies. Steps were taken immediately to ensure this posture.

The CES ceased as a commission in 1971 when all of the commissions of the AFEB were terminated. Yet, our country does remain alert and maintains an effective capability through open and relevant research at Ft. Detrick and elsewhere. Studies of highly pathogenic biologic agents must be continued because humans can be attacked from natural sources at any time.

Space does not permit a more detailed description of the breadth and application of the CES program. Let me say simply that I was proud and privileged to be in a position to help ensure a defensive posture when it was of considerable importance for our country and our society. How lucky I was to have served under Dick Shope and the team and later to serve as chairman of the Commission beginning in 1959 with Dick's retirement. This was a unique privilege which enabled me to mature and grow professionally and develop a broader understanding of microbes, their potential for destruction, and how to counteract their threat.

Presidency of the AFEB

In 1975 during a meeting of the board in Texas, I had to leave early because of pressing problems in Baltimore. During this absence, my fellow board members nominated me to serve as president, which was ultimately approved by the respective Surgeons General of the three services. At this time, the president was expected to serve for two years.

After Gus Dammin retired as president, the board suffered growing pains simply because the commission system had been summarily stopped by executive order and a new organization with a new charter became effective in July 1973. Surgeon General Jennings suggested that the new AFEB assume responsibility for rendering advice in four categories: 1) communicable disease control, 2) health maintenance, 3) environmental quality, and 4) physician standards.

The board meeting on April 18, 1973 was a little maudlin and to quote General Jennings, "This meeting signals the end of a glorious era which I want to assure you isn't going to cease just because the Department of Defense has made a new charter for this organization as required by new laws that have been enacted and other factors."

Ed Lennette succeeded Gus Dammin, who had served expertly for twelve years as president. During the next several years, there were numerous difficulties in working with a new type of ad hoc committee system. A sense of discontent prevailed simply because board members perceived their role as diminished with less responsibility and authority. Its role now was purely advisory, which was a marked change from the previous commission research system.

It is a tribute to everyone involved that the new AFEB succeeded and found its important niche as an advisory group whose services became eagerly sought by the military. I succeeded Ed Lennette as president from 1976 to 1978. Herschel Griffin took the gavel from 1978 to 1980 and somehow the gavel was returned to me from 1980 to 1992.

During these memorable times we dealt with many problems: 1) prevention of heart attacks in Air Force personnel, 2) the

Meeting of the Armed Forces Epidemiological Board, February 28–March 1, 1991, Ft. Detrick, Frederick, Maryland (USAMRIID Auditorium). 1st Row (Left to Right): Dr. Jordan, Dr. Johns, Dr. Mendez, Ms. Ward (AFEB Staff Assistant), Dr. Kurland, Dr. Dowdle, CAPT Parsons (AFEB Executive Secretary); 2nd Row (Left to Right): Dr. Benenson, BG Gleason, Dr. Legters, Dr. Thompson, Dr. Townsend, Dr. Engley; 3rd Row (Left to Right): CAPT Bina, COL Erdtmann, LTC Wright, Dr. Woodward (AFEB President), Dr. Halstead, Dr. Hornick

Bradley fighting vehicle and how to make this potent machine safe for its personnel, 3) health standards and population forecasting based on epidemiologic principles, and 4) acquired immune deficiency syndrome (AIDS), which is briefly discussed in the next section.

In the fall of each year, I arranged for the board to meet at a McCormick & Co. facility in the Chesapeake Bay, known as Parson's Island. This was an excellent meeting place, far off the beaten track, with fresh air, good Eastern Shore food, and an opportunity for civilians and military officers of all ranks to discuss problems of military medical interest. At one meeting we had the three Surgeons General and the Assistant Secretary of Defense for Health, all attending a three-day meeting. Meetings here promoted congeniality, open discussion, and the chance to get work done in a short time.

During this active period the board helped ensure fulfillment of the plan to build a Uniformed Health Services Medical School in Bethesda. The board directly intervened to help ensure stability of Overseas Research Laboratories which were under congressional attack. Such vital centers were located in Cairo, Bangkok, Manila, Jakarta, and Vietnam.

On another occasion, Maj. Gen. Gary Rapmund, head of the medical research and development command, was having serious

Meeting of the AFEB, Parsons Island, 1985

budgetary difficulties with Pentagon authorities. As President of the AFEB, I went with Gen. Rapmund to a budget meeting at the Pentagon and explained as a civilian how important medical research was for all the military services. As a civilian, anything could be said without any holds barred. As we left the meeting, a very high-ranking officer said to Gen. Rapmund, "O.K., we will work with you." Several days later Gen. Rapmund called me to say that not only were their funds restored, but additional funds were made available. This is a simple example of how a wonderful board of this character could work collaboratively with its military associates. Each member of the board was well indoctrinated and aware of military medical needs and at all times helped defend such important positions in their decision making.

About AIDS

After the close of the June 1985 meeting of the AFEB, the board was asked about its position on the AIDS issue. Never has the bureaucracy in Washington experienced such immediate action. The well-phrased request in the form of specific questions to the board appeared on the AFEB office desk within two days. This mandate was to occupy the whole summer and more. During this period, the Surgeon General's office and the Office of Health Affairs of the Department of Defense were being constantly bombarded by telephone calls with vitriolic statements from the press and angry comments by the general public. Practically all of the matters raised related to: confidentiality, informed consent, how to prevent spread of infection, and concern about contamination of the nation's blood supply for transfusion purposes.

The questions which the officers of the Office of Health Affairs and Preventive Medicine presented to the board were specific and broadly based. They dealt with policy and guidelines as to the following: 1) who should be tested for AIDS, 2) the safety and accuracy of various types of tests, 3) what to do to ensure a safe blood supply, 4) policy regarding new recruits for the military services who tested positively, 5) policy regarding those in the services who were detected to be positive, 6) should positive personnel be kept in the service, 7) should they be allowed to be deployed overseas, 8) how frequently should testing be repeated, 9) should those persons overseas be brought back to the United States, 10) policies regarding those test-positive persons who were in such sensitive positions as performance of surgical and dental procedures, and 11) policy regarding those persons in top-level, highly classified positions, or pilots of very high-speed aircraft. Also what should be done regarding prevention of AIDS, including barrier techniques and educational programs?

During this important period, the whole country was polarized because of obvious uncertainties and apprehension. Major risk groups at this time were those who abused drugs and homosexual men. This view was later shown to be incomplete. A special meeting of the board was called for August 9, 1985 at WRAIR for the purpose of helping defuse the unrest which was rapidly increasing.

Invitations were extended to several recognized authorities regarding laboratory, epidemiologic, clinical, and sociopsychological problems related to the AIDS issue. Happily, within the military services, there were ranking investigators such as Cols. Ed Tramont, Robert Redfield, and Don Burke, very capable officers, who had considerable experience and competence. Everyone was alerted. Since the AFEB is a public-type advisory committee, the meetings are open to the lay public and the scientific profession. Actually, the schedule of each meeting must be published.

The chief lawyer for the gay rights movement called from New York and various parts of the United States including Alaska. He requested agenda time at the meeting and free access for his interested associates who wished to attend.

The meeting room soon became jammed. Never had we had such a display of enthusiasm for any meeting, much less representatives from the press. The room was completely filled with chairs which were soon occupied, followed by standing attendees four rows deep, extending into the hallway.

After introductory remarks, I introduced all members of the board with their brief credentials to the audience. Ed Tramont was called as the first speaker and gave an excellent overview of the military situation, the incidence of cases, antibody positive numbers, demographic data, and a discussion of those steps being contemplated and taken to identify cases and control the spread. This was an excellent introductory statement and fully explained the military posture.

I then introduced Mr. Jeffrey Levi, legal counsel, for the National Gay Task Force. He made a few general comments and then proceeded to lecture the board and others present about ethical standards, confidentiality, and informed consent. I quickly and clearly assured him that the recommendations of the board to be formulated over the next several weeks would address the best interests of the military forces, the individual, and the public. His talk was followed by Dr. Mathalde Krim who spoke in general terms including comments about diagnostic procedures.

The presentations included the availability and accuracy of diagnostic tests, new contemplated tests, some data on how the AIDS virus was transmitted, and the relationship of incidence in ethnic groups and geographic locations. There was discussion of how AIDS patients are clinically classified, a very workable classification formulated by the WRAIR group of experts. There was little, if any, information on effective treatment or prevention by vaccine. At this time, there were many unknown factors and great emphasis was then placed on AIDS involving those who abuse drugs and men who engage in homosexual practices.

It was decided that a session would be held in September to formulate specific recommendations. We held a preliminary meeting of the subcommittee on AIDS in our cottage on Kent Island, Eastern Shore of Maryland, on Wednesday, September 11. Our country's leading experts on hepatitis and AIDS were all present. All numerous letter questions were addressed. A large and critical meeting of this type requires careful preparation and it is best to have carefully delineated answers to important and controversial questions before any open discussion on such a sensitive subject.

The fall meeting of the board was held during the two next days, September 12–13, 1985 on Parson's Island. This was planned as a closed meeting.

The first full-day meeting was open ended with complete discussion. All relevant points regarding problems related to AIDS and hepatitis were evaluated including clinical, laboratory, management, and preventive measures. Also matters related to sexually transmitted diseases were appraised and made possible by the input of respective authorities in these fields who attended.

As prearranged, at about 10 A.M. on September 13, the sound of a huge U.S. Army helicopter could be heard. The vehicle landed just outside the conference area. All members went to welcome Dr. William E. Mayer, Assistant Secretary of Defense for Health Affairs, and his Deputy, Dr. J. Jarrett Clinton. The recommendations that were derived from discussions during the subcommittee meeting and those of the past two days were presented to Dr. Mayer. Each question previously raised by the Office of Health Affairs was answered concisely and clearly. The recommendations made were clear-cut, precise, relevant, and fair with appropriate comments regarding the need for confidentiality.

One of our recommendations provided ample time for the military services to serially test all personnel for the presence of the AIDS antibody. Hon. Casper Weinberger, the Secretary of Defense, later changed that recommendation by designating that all personnel would be tested promptly. During the coming months the board addressed other important issues requested by the Office of Health Affairs. Also the board quickly responded to the request of this office by appointing a permanent standing committee on AIDS which was expected to immediately consider new

Presentation, Military Medal of Merit and Flag, May 14, 1992. M.G. Frederick N. Bussey, M.D. (left), T.E. Woodward, M.D. (center), and M.G.G. Enrique Mendez, Jr., M.D., Assistant Secretary of Defense for Health Affairs (right).

Arriving Vietnam, 1971

relevant information or issues as they developed. This total exercise was a truly cooperative effort of which our military forces and public can be rightfully proud.

When I retired as AFEB President in 1992, a special meeting of the board was held at the U.S. Naval Air Station, Norfolk, Virginia. We were privileged to tour the huge aircraft carrier USS Eisenhower, which was a truly exciting experience. This remarkably powerful ship and its officers and crew make one extremely proud to be an American. On May 14, a surprise reception and dinner were held in my honor. Hon. Enrique Mendez, Jr., M.D., Assistant Secretary of Defense for Health Affairs, presented me with the Military Medal of Merit and an American flag.

Agent (Herbicide) Orange and Vietnam

On a Friday during the autumn of 1970, Col. Robert T. Cutting, MC, Head of Preventive Medicine, Surgeon General's Office, U.S. Army called to ask if I could go to Saigon on the following Monday to help with a problem. Press releases were currently broadcasting accusations made by a professor at a prominent New England Medical Center and the World Health Organization that the U.S. military's use of herbicide Agent Orange as a defoliant in the jungles of Vietnam had caused serious and numerous birth defects in the babies of Vietnamese women. Not fully appreciated by me at the time was that in jungle warfare, it

Col. Robert T. Cutting

is necessary to destroy foliage of trees and underbrush to combat a virtually invisible enemy. Gen. Richard Taylor, MC, Commander of U.S. Medical Forces in Vietnam asked for AFEB help and specifically requested Dr. Colin MacLeod's assistance. Colin, then very busily occupied at the University of Pennsylvania in Philadelphia, had to decline and said "ask Woodward"!

I knew nothing about defoliants and knew only a few basic facts about genetics and birth abnormalities and did not regard myself as an epidemiologist. Nevertheless, the invitation was accepted under the name of the AFEB. I spent that weekend at USAMRIID (Ft. Detrick, Frederick, Maryland) learning everything possible about Agent Orange and was en route to Vietnam on Monday.

On arrival at Saigon, I had gathered some knowledge about Agent Orange, its indicated use, and possible health threat. General Richard (Dick) Taylor further informed me of the considerable public unrest present in Vietnam in addition to state-side reactions.

The next day, a major from the security services appeared. By that time, I had conceived a tentative plan including visits to regional health center areas where exposure to Agent Orange and birth defects were thought to have occurred. Also, I needed to visit jungle areas where defoliants had been used, in order to

Saigon Airport, 1971

evaluate water sources which could serve as a possible transmitting vehicle for the chemical. Finally, a careful survey of the large hospitals in Saigon was indicated, particularly involving the obstetrical and special clinical services. The latter evaluation was anticipated to provide data on the scope and impact of birth defects in infants and adolescents involving the current years and those well before the time that United States military forces had any contact or relationship with Vietnam.

Obviously, my mission required air transport since Vietnam is vast and rugged. The major indicated that I was entitled to use a helicopter, two armed squads, and two escorting fighter airplanes. This sounded like a whole invading army and I decided on the minimum support, a helicopter, its crew, and an armed sergeant.

Off we went to the Regional Hospital centers where I talked with Vietnamese physicians, nurses, and health personnel. They all informed me that birth defects were prevalent and had been common in the country for many years. We went to the hospital where a two-headed badly deformed infant had been born whose picture was distributed widely in American newspapers. These birth defects, they said, were not unusual in Vietnam.

The helicopter took me to jungle areas to see how the herbicides really cleared out a forested site. Actually, we were in the Cambodian Parrot's beak area at the time of the counter attack. Once, on asking the pilot if we could fly a little lower for better

Ted Woodward with M.G. Richard Taylor, MC, Saigon, 1971

vision, the response came back, "Tell the doctor this is low enough [1500 feet]; I am scheduled to return to the United States next week."

At the Saigon lying-in hospital, I never saw so many babies being delivered at one time. In one large delivery room (among many), there were 20 delivery tables, all occupied, arranged in a circle. Babies were being delivered by midwives. A physician was on hand and available in case of a difficult delivery or complication.

Records in the hospitals were excellent. They were complete, filed, and indexed with all relevant information including full names, dates, details of the delivery, complications, if any, and all key data including description of the newborn. It was simple to examine the records for the prior 10 to 20 years or more. I recorded all birth defects including hare lip, cleft plate, spina bifida, anencephaly, and others. Birth abnormalities were just as prevalent 10 to 20 years before America became involved in

Vietnam as they were during recent years in the late 1960s and 1970. There was no variance.

In order to convince the "doubters" I went to the adolescent clinics and confirmed the prevalence of congenital anomalies in children who visited these well-attended centers. There was no difference in the older versus recent records.

My final report was transmitted to appropriate military and Department of State authorities. I felt a humble sense of pride and satisfaction in having helped buffer an unfounded claim which questioned the integrity and ethics of our country. In our litigious society, it is easy to make a false claim and it is often difficult to prove it wrong!

Cooperation Between Government and Medicine

There are many problem issues—political, diplomatic, social, and medically oriented—which face any organized government. In most successful countries, there is a symbiotic relationship between governmental and public agencies which generally ensures a smooth working relationship and application of fundamental principles.

In addressing its medical science problems, the United States has been blessed with established governmental agencies such as the Medical Military Services, the National Institutes of Health, public academic institutions (the medical schools, research institutes), and The Rockefeller, Ford, Macy, Kellogg, and various religious and other foundations. Reliable, stable, and dependable close affiliation and mutual cooperation have been largely responsible for the scientific progress and understanding which has placed our country in a highly respected posture. One often wonders whether the public realizes why life expectancy in American citizens is as high as it is, in spite of problems that we knowingly face.

We are a favored group of people and I have always considered it a privilege to have contributed just a bit to help make a few things a little better. The Armed Forces Epidemiological Board is an example of cooperation between government agencies and academic medical centers, and exhibits cooperative spirit, mutual trust, and progress—all for the public good.

Chapter *17*

Veterans Administration Advisory Committee on Prisoners of War

$\int$ n 1980, the Veterans Administration, with stimulus from the White House during the early term of President Reagan, appointed an Advisory Committee to evaluate all aspects of health care and claims of former prisoners of war (POW) and to make recommendations for any indicated improvement, and assist in developing new legislation to ensure that full and fair restitution be made to any veteran when appropriately indicated. On receiving an invitation to become a member, I accepted with some reluctance since this was an entirely new venture for me about which I was relatively uninformed and ignorant. Nevertheless, I whole heartedly accepted the invitation to serve.

Much that I learned in the next several years was a sobering eye opener since I had no full insight or real information regarding the privation, depth of misery, and long continuing suffering that prisoners of war were made to endure. To be sure, the American Press had kept such information before the public. But I had not put into full perspective the horror of what had really happened behind those walls and barbed wire enclosures. My education came from former POWs who are all distinguished and courageous persons.

Imagine a daily diet of less than 600 calories which looked like slop, daily beatings for even a stare, being made to witness the beheading of one of your friends who stepped out of line knowing you might be next, no news from your loved ones, no news of the world, daily hard labor, inability to sleep, constant diarrhea, daily weight loss down to the bones, nothing but fear, panic, disbelief, depression.

The full committee was small, only 10 members with Lt. Gen. James L. Flynn, USAF, Chairman, who had suffered and experienced misery over three years as a former POW in Vietnam. One of the physician members, a former prisoner of war, was Dr. Joseph Nardini, a psychiatrist from Washington, D.C. who was one of the most sensible, intelligent, and erudite physicians whom I have ever known. He was a veteran of the Bataan Death March in the Philippines and suffered privation and imprisonment at the hands of the Japanese for over three and one-half years. Dr. Ralph Hibbs, Dr. William Shaddish, and Dr. Paul Galenti were members and former POWs. There were three non-POW physician members of the committee: Paul Beeson, Calvin Kunin, and me. It soon became very apparent during the early meetings that Gen. Flynn, Dr. Nardini, and other committee members were courageous men and dedicated citizens in every sense of the word.

When the Advisory Committee began its work in 1980, there were approximately 90,000 living former POWs from WWI, WWII, the Korean War, and the Vietnam War. Our initial meetings were held twice yearly at the VA Headquarters in Washington, practically within the shadow of the White House. Occasionally, smaller ad hoc meetings were held to consider special problems. The first several years were spent in fact-finding, and the sifting of medical problems into various grades of priority. The problems were enormous because the Veterans Administration had responsibilities for a huge health care system spread over all regions of the United States. In some of the centers, excellent practice standards prevailed, but in others this was not the case.

Obviously, as far as the POW problem is concerned, the major issues related to unanswered or unasked claims for disability. These matters naturally required sufficient funds for proper and justified compensation. This meant that the committee had to become fully aware of the claims process, the method of adjudication, standards of fairness in making claim decisions, and many other considerations. Throughout all of these earlier discussions, Joe Nardini was a beacon of enlightenment. Some of his scholarly publications on the subject had vividly described brutality, no available medicines, malnutrition, deprivation, fear, terror, depression, and their potential relationships to long-term disability. Dr. G.W. Beebe had worked on such problems including follow-up studies of former prisoners of war under National Academy of Sciences sponsorship. His information was invaluable and was later strengthened by similar follow-up data by Dr. William Page.

The committee carefully evaluated all issues and realized that decisions relied upon testimony of the former POW physician advisory members as well as relevant information from other countries. Data from the Armed Forces Institute of Pathology weighed heavily and importantly. Actually, a standard protocol of performing postmortem examinations of former POWs was developed.

On June 19, 1985, Gen. Flynn, Dr. Nardini, and I presented testimony to the House of Representatives Committee on Veterans Affairs. The meeting was well attended and the reception by the House Committee was most encouraging.

During the early years, the committee developed a comprehensive protocol for taking a history and performing a physical examination of former POWs. It was designed to fully inform and alert uninformed examining physicians regarding the many issues and problems which were equated with long-term incarceration, malnutrition, anxiety, and stress. The protocol became standard throughout the VA system. Symposia were held in key centers and brochures were prepared.

Much time and thought was devoted to the need to develop epidemiologic evidence regarding disabilities with the unanimous recommendation that, when in doubt, the decision should favor the claimant. Guidelines were developed to hasten the adjudication process. Dr. Howard Cohn and Dr. Carl Hughes, senior administrators of the VA, were most helpful. Social workers were made an important part of the decision and information examination procedures. Educational films were developed using professionals and experienced actors to highlight the POW problem and create a national awareness.

At other times when the more reliable and sufficiently documented data became available, other members of the committee testified before congressional committees. Capt. Richard A. Stratton (USN, chairman), Mr. Everett Alvarez, and Dr. William Shaddish were very impressive in fulfilling these roles, as was Ralph Levenberg, who served as secretary of the Advisory Committee.

This program was designed to change a situation which needed to be corrected and, in fairness, make restitution to those who well deserved it. The Veterans Administration authorities who actively worked with the committee could not have been more helpful, cooperative, or efficient. A hotline was established which allowed former POWs to receive immediate advice and guidance in how to proceed.

There are many difficult issues regarding the validity of claims such as musculoskeletal disorders, arthritis, heart attacks, chronic heart disease, chronic intestinal diseases, and all kinds of emotional problems. They all may bear a relationship to prolonged deprivation and malnutrition. These matters were placed in their proper perspective and carefully expressed, with considerate and fair guidelines established.

It was a great privilege for me to serve and continue to work with this committee. I have learned so much from these outstanding persons.

C h a p t e r 18

U.S.–JAPAN COOPERATIVE
MEDICAL SCIENCE PROGRAM

*I*n 1965 during a Rose Garden luncheon, President Lyndon Johnson and Prime Minister Sato of Japan toasted each other and made a pledge that their respective countries should join hands in helping improve the health of impoverished people in Southeast Asia. Our president then directed Colin MacLeod, executive director in the Office of Science and Technology (OST), to take the matter in hand and make appropriate recommendations. Colin and Dr. James (Jim) Shannon, director of the NIH, conferred and appointed a small delegation of American physicians and scientists who were to meet with their Japanese counterparts in Tokyo in 1965 and develop a plan. The U.S. Delegation consisted of Colin MacLeod (chairman), James Shannon, Thomas Francis, Stanley Bennett, Jack Weir, and me. At the time Celeste and I were in Lahore, West Pakistan, working with our ICMRT unit there. I made a long trip from Lahore via Karachi, New Delhi, Bangkok, and Hong Kong to Tokyo. These were stormy days in Tokyo for the United States because of the very unpopular war in which we had become involved in Vietnam. Indeed, several days before arrival, belligerent Japanese students and agitators had stormed the U.S. Embassy there, and had personally confronted Ambassador Rieschaur.

The small delegation met first with the ambassador and his medical advisors. The next day we met with our Japanese counterparts at their Ministry of Health sitting across the table from Dr. Kurokawa, the Japanese chairman, and his few associates who appeared stiff-looking, nonsmiling, and very straight. In his opening remarks, Dr. Kurokawa commented, "Things have changed considerably since your President and our Prime Minister talked in Washington." Things did not look promising.

To the great credit of our two countries and the inspired leadership of Drs. MacLeod and Kurokawa, the three-day meeting was successfully held, guidelines for planning and organization were formulated, and the first meeting ended on a positive note. Full confidence and trust were significantly established at that first meeting which was crucial.

Plans were put on the table for development of four or five panels on research which would be comprised of the best qualified scientists from Japan and the United States. Panel research was expected to be relevant, new, and aimed at improvement of health in Asian people. The five categories for study chosen initially were: cholera, tuberculosis, leprosy, parasitic diseases, and malnutrition. A panel on viral diseases was discussed early but had to wait a year or two until administrative and strategic details could be solved.

The governments of Japan and the United States were expected to contribute the necessary funds (yen and dollars), equally, which were sufficient to ensure that research programs would be adequately funded and the costs of travel and meetings would be provided. Each country would appoint a separate panel for each category of study with a well-qualified chairman and several recognized experts in each field of work. The joint delegation was expected to meet annually, alternately in Japan and the United States. A small planning committee was expected to meet at mid-winter. Symposia were expected to be held on various panel projects at varying times and when possible before the joint delegation meetings. Panel meetings were expected to be held in either the United States or Japan with full collaboration by each side. Critical review of each panel's program was expected, every five years, to determine whether a panel should continue, be re-oriented, or dissolved. In the event that new panels were to be developed, each delegation should reach full consensus and hold a scientific symposium on the new subject several days prior to the joint annual meeting. At that time it would be determined by the joint delegation regarding the advisability of initiating a new program. Since 1965, five new panels have been established, including one on AIDS, and guidelines and organization within existing panels have been altered based on new needs and indicated changes.

Our respective governments now consider the U.S.–Japan Program as the best example of a bi-national program which exists anywhere. The United States has had three separate delegation chairmen, Dr. MacLeod, Dr. Ivan L. Bennett, Jr., and Dr. Charles Carpenter. Chuck Carpenter, an accomplished clinician and investigator, is a product of the Hopkins System. He had extensive experience working with cholera in Asia and later effectively chaired the Department of Medicine at Case Western Reserve in Cleveland. His leadership of the American delegation of the U.S./Japan Program has been commendable. I have served as acting chairman on two occasions. The Japanese delegation has been very ably led by Drs. Kurokawa, Suwa, Someya, and Shimao. The Ministry of Health and Education in Japan, the

Ivan Bennett

Celeste Woodward, Ted Woodward, Foreign Minister Nakayama.
Presentation of the Order of Sacred Treasure, Tokyo, July 17, 1990

Department of State, and Institute of Allergy and Infectious Diseases of the NIH serve as administrative agents for the respective countries.

After each five-year period, a published report of progress is produced. In 1990, the 25th Silver Anniversary of the program was celebrated in Tokyo. This occasion became one of the sad experiences in my life. Just prior to the joint delegation meeting in July 1990, Ivan and I were privileged to meet with the Minister of Health and each of us received a high citation from his Highness, the Emperor. Celeste and Martha Bennett were with us. After this pleasant occasion, our wives returned to the hotel and Ivan and I had a light lunch before a scheduled meeting of our subcommittee. On leaving the luncheon room, Ivan felt faint and collapsed in my arms. Initially, he attributed this to a GI attack which unfortunately was not true. He slowly developed an extensive blood clot of the basilar artery which soon paralyzed the lower part of his body. Our Japanese medical associates could not have been more prompt and efficient in their care of Ivan, who was taken to the Red Cross Hospital in Tokyo by ambulance. The very best neurologists in Japan immediately responded, as did the entire intensive-care group. The care which he received could not have been better anywhere.

It fell to my lot to represent him, as chairman, at a large public meeting scheduled for the next day which was to be attended by the young Prince and her Highness. Before leaving the bedside a phenomenal thing occurred. On speaking to him I indicated my intention to attend the meeting in his behalf. Since he could not speak because of an intratracheal tube, he took his fingers and made a sweeping motion like a half moon. On my lack of understanding, he wrote "Smile" on a piece of paper. When speaking for him at the General Assembly, his greetings and warm sentiments were expressed. I relate this little vignette which occurred at the bedside as a lesson of remarkable courage. Later other family members arrived from the United States just briefly, before he experienced cardiac and respiratory arrests. His death was quiet and merciful. America lost one of its finest productive physicians of the late twentieth century.

Chapter 19

ON MEDICAL EDUCATION

Medical School Admissions Committee

For a dozen or more years, I was privileged to serve on the committee which determined the eligibility and made the final offers to the entering medical school class. Prior to the computer-oriented concept of determining the suitability of a college senior to become a physician, the process was simple and the ground rules were clear. This was when personal qualities were equated with scholarly attainments and each kept in balance. With the advent of the computer and the relative ease of reading printouts, guidelines have changed. It may be accurately assumed that a computer will not perform a rectal examination during the remainder of the twentieth century without some discomfort. Nor will the computer accurately describe the character traits, sensitivity, attitudes, empathy, and motivation of young men or women who aspire to become physicians. I have always doubted whether a grade point average is a true measure of scholarship or whether the MCAT (Medical College Aptitude Test) picks out the gifted from the average candidate. Happily, I served during the early period and escaped the inaccuracies of the current method. Privately endowed medical schools had, and still have, some freedom of choice, much more than state-supported institutions. Yet, there are exceptions to each and it is refreshing to observe a partial return to the old and more thoughtful system.

Interviewing techniques are a useful guide to seek out desired traits, albeit with some limitations. Letters of recommendation from a college mentor and premedical committee are vitally important, provided that the referring institution has a record of reliability in supporting its worthy candidates and taking measured care to describe the total candidate. This includes scholarship, desires, ability to communicate, interest in college, and community activities, aside from book or didactic knowledge per se.

Once we carefully evaluated a candidate from Franklin and Marshall College, my alma mater. On paper, the candidate looked quite suitable to us in spite of a negative recommendation from the premedical committee. We knew that F&M takes its screening responsibilities seriously. In working with the college committee, we found clear evidence that this was not the type of candidate whom we desired. Our offer to enter the freshman class was denied. If all schools and all involved persons took seriously the writing of letters of endorsement for any purpose, society would be better served.

One day, I introduced myself to a new candidate who was seated next to a middle-aged woman. The young man was asked to enter the office and the lady rose to join us. "Madam, who are you?" "Why I am the boy's mother!" After this rather surprising experience, I asked in a friendly manner, "Just who is going to medical school?" She responded, "Why my son is." I then politely asked her to wait outside so that we could discuss personal matters. She was taken aback but inside the office, the boy thanked me. I can well imagine his apprehension in facing this interview under the contemplated circumstances. All came out well and hopefully I had helped cut the umbilical cord.

Another lad (the spoiled son of wealthy parents) from upstate New York afforded me a surprise. He had participated in no college activities, had few, if any, friends and absolutely no interests, had wasted his summers in Europe, and had no insight into where he had been or what he had seen. After an hour or more of an attempt to find a spark, I shook his hand and wished him well. About three minutes later, he rushed back down the hall, through the door into my office. He loudly remarked, "They told me you would ask about motivation, you didn't ask about that." I said, "Young man, we have been discussing that for the last hour and a half."

These anecdotes will close on a pleasant theme. One young man, who had always aspired to be a physician, had a very difficult time in college, particularly with science courses. The best grades he could muster in organic chemistry, physics, and general biology were C's. Yet, he was into everything—student council, college activities, and sports, in addition to working summers and winters to pay for his tuition and keep. Also, he had been a Boy Scout who found his way into many community activities. His father was dead, yet he had helped in the care of his mother. John Krantz and I knew of his background and his desirable traits and swayed the committee who admitted him. This young man had rough sailing for the first two years and received a failing grade and one or two conditional grades in major subjects. Yet, he routinely came early to school, left later than others, and literally pushed his hardworking brain to its peak. The Advancement Committee was ready to dismiss him. John and I again went into the breach and urged the necessary support to retain him. During the clinical years, he received top grades in internal medicine and surgery in his group, and he sailed through. In the small community where he settled, everyone had a warm word to say about their physician. Moreover, I know that often he would take time to stop by the home of physically disabled patients, place them in his car, and take them into the country while he made house calls to relieve their boredom. John and I had foreseen that this young man had what it took to be a good doctor—it is doubtful whether a computer will ever detect such traits.

A passing grade of 70 always troubled me. Once Celeste's father asked her, "What is passing in medical school?" She remarked, "70." Mr. Lauve then remarked, "What if the patient has the other 30 percent of the illnesses." My father-in-law combined wisdom with practical sense.

On Continuing Education

Departmental members accepted invitations to speak to various county medical societies throughout the State of Maryland. These served to acquaint referring physicians with the resources of the medical center in Baltimore. It became clear that continued medical education (CME) for the practicing physician was an essential step toward keeping abreast of new technologic and diagnostic developments in a rapidly changing field. To this end, the department organized and presented the First Postgraduate Conference in Medicine on January 20–22, 1959, at the University Hospital. It was held under the sponsorship of the Committee on Postgraduate Studies and the Medical Alumni Association of the university. The intensive course embraced the fields of endocrine-metabolic diseases, infectious diseases, hematology-oncology, and general medicine. Guest faculty were Dr. John F. Enders, Ph.D. (Nobel Laureate, Medicine, 1956, Harvard), Dr. Claude J. Mijcon, M.D. (Johns Hopkins), Dr. Lawson Wilkins, M.D. (Johns Hopkins), and Dr. Joseph E. Smadel, M.D. (National Institutes of Health). University of Maryland faculty participants were Drs. Thomas B. Connor, Harlan I. Firminger (pathology), Sheldon E. Greisman, Arthur L. Haskins (obstetrics-gynecology), Fred R. McCrumb, Jr., Maurice C. Pincoffs, Milton S. Sacks, Merrill J. Snyder, Carroll L. Spruling, Charles L. Wisseman, Jr. (Microbiology), John G. Wiswell, Joseph B. Workman, and myself. In addition to specific lectures, there were case presentations by house officers which illustrated specific clinical and diagnostic points and a clinical pathologic conference by Drs. Pincoffs and Harlan Firminger.

Chapter 20

NO SUBSTITUTE FOR EXCELLENCE
Unpaid Debts to Special Persons

*L*ife as a teacher of medical students and young physicians, practitioner for patients, and investigator of clinical problems has repaid me much beyond what I have
contributed. In searching through a depth of memories and experiences, my mind uncovered a number of I.O.U.s to several
persons who, by virtue of their stature, professional example,
and teachings, unwittingly allowed me to borrow from them.
It is impossible to make full reparation, but there is some solace
in realizing that others, too, have borrowed heavily from
these special persons whose help and encouragement to me
are incalculable.

Maurice C. Pincoffs

Marurice C. Pincoffs was a gifted clinician. Two driving forces
sustained him: to teach the best in medicine and to serve the patient. Older concepts were carefully blended with modern views,
and he had the uncanny ability to relate each to the patient, to
the problem, and to the students. Each patient was a case study,

a careful exercise in clinical evaluation. His skill in unraveling a problem had few equals. Older associates in Baltimore confirm that his bedside acumen equaled that of William Osler. From Maurice C. Pincoffs, I learned thoroughness at the bed-side combined with a fundamental interest in the laboratory sciences.

From 1922 to 1954, Dr. Pincoffs chaired the Department of Medicine at the University of Maryland. It was my privilege to succeed him.

Marcel Baltazard

Often, because of human conflicts, America's physicians have found themselves deposited in foreign countries and confronted by microbial diseases for which they possess but superficial knowledge. In December 1942, as a young medical officer in Morocco, I was forced to become instantly knowledgeable in problems relating to plague, typhus, and relapsing fevers, diseases that were not household disorders in the United States.

My first foreign medical friend was Marcel Baltazard, acting director of the Pasteur Institute in Morocco. He spoke no English and my French was awkward. However, our friendship struck up immediately, and he eagerly let me teach the Pasteur staff the technique of complement fixation, a new diagnostic aid for the rickettsial diseases and a technique which comprised about 50% of my laboratory competence.

Balta gave me much beyond friendship. From him came a comprehension of the need to relate nature's patterns of illness to the type of studies that should be performed in the laboratory. He and his mentor, Georges Blanc, fully understood the phenom-enon of microbial persistence. The rickettsiae responsible for both epidemic and murine typhus were shown to remain viable for five years or more in dried louse and flea feces. The same type of persistence held for the soft tick, *Ornithodoros moubata*, and for the agent of spirochetal relapsing fever.

Balta felt all along that the rat was not the proprietor of plague but perhaps only its administrator. He demonstrated clearly and taught me that, under natural conditions and in labo-ratory experiments, plague bacilli remained viable in the detritus and soil of deep burrows where rodents had died of plague. This mechanism, which he called "peste endogee," explained how the disease persists in plague foci for prolonged periods. America owes him much, as I do.

Leon A. Fox

As field director of the U.S.A. Typhus Fever Commission during World War II, Leon Fox showed everyone under him how to act and react; he directed by doing and not by issuing memoranda. When he had confidence in anyone, he expressed his wishes succinctly and kept out of their way as long as the issue appeared to be reaching a solution. Leon Fox was a field epidemiologist, a mover of people, and a persuasive teacher of preventive medicine.

Stanhope Bayne-Jones

Everyone who knew Stanhope Bayne-Jones respected him. "B-J" accomplished almost everything: chairmanship of a department of bacteriology, dean, chancellor, writer, army general, epidemiologist, administrator. He was recognized as a wise man of integrity. During World War II, despite preoccupation as deputy director of preventative medicine and director of the U.S.A. Typhus Fever Commission, B-J went once after midnight to the Washington National Airport for special hyperimmune pertussis serum for an infant of a junior officer working under him. Most would have sent an aide; he went himself. The infant was our son, Craig.

Joseph E. Smadel

My greatest debt is to Joe Smadel. When we first met in 1942 at Walter Reed, our paths and interests were divergent. Having just made notable contributions to virology at the Rockefeller Institute under Thomas Rivers, Joe joined the U.S. Army to straighten out certain affairs of the medical corps, then heavily engaged in war. Meanwhile, at Walter Reed Army Institute of Research, I was learning all about rickettsiae: how to separate them from yolk sacs and diagnose their diseases by the technique of complement fixation, all rather distant from the stethoscope.

Joe's achievements made him one of the outstanding and versatile scientists of the mid-twentieth century. He tackled everything with gusto and expected no reward. He did research because he liked it, and his brand of enthusiasm often sparked others through example. Honors he received, yet he was the silent partner in many other endeavors and cared little for the credit. He was uncanny in his ability to grasp a point, and his gift for vivid expression (often splashed with a dash of profanity) made his stand unmistakably clear. On Joe's resignation from the National Foundation for Infantile Paralysis, his associates placed in their minutes: "The resignation of our lovable bastard is accepted with regret."

Joe taught me much about science that helped me sort out difficult medical problems. He clarified for me the importance of the bridge between the bench and the patient and proved that bench and field work, rather than armchair philosophy, were essential. When I was a young departmental chairman, he helped me formulate criteria for selecting staff. Good training, teaching, ability, interest in teaching, and creativity were not enough. The creative person must present documented evidence of that creativity by publishing something decent and readable. This type of person is always a wise investment. Joe is affectionately remembered for his friendship, encouragement, and the opportunities he helped provide me for finding adventure in medicine.

Raymond Lewthwaite

Raymond Lewthwaite was a great friend of the United States; in his quiet but effective way, he contributed much to scientific progress. During World War II, all one needed to do to learn of scrub typhus was to ask him. Had more questions been asked, our losses in the Pacific Theater from typhus might have been much less.

Equanimity as a scientist best characterizes this humble man. His knowledge was broad, his approach to problems, his facility to take the pressure off pressing matters and make persons of diverse interests and temperaments perform as a cohesive unit made him an unusual man. Culture, dignity, and wry wit all made him an attractive companion. Whether engaged in directing British Colonial medical research or watching Joe DiMaggio, he was content. From him, one could not help but learn perspective, a lesson for which I am grateful.

Kenneth Goodner

Perhaps my most irascible, unpredictable, and sensitive friend, for whom much more was borrowed than given, was Kenneth

Goodner. Known as K.G. by more than two decades of students of microbiology at Jefferson Medical College, he ranks as one of the most proud and effective medical school teachers of the group. Born in McCune, Kansas, and a doctoral candidate under Hans Zinsser at Harvard, K.G. was a contributing member of the cadre of young, brilliant men at the Rockefeller Institute for Medical Research over his sixteen years' tenure there.

K.G. was really unsung locally, yet recognized universally for his scientific contributions to immunology, for helping to develop a yellow fever vaccine, and for studies of pneumococcal pneumonia, plague, and cholera.

He must be given considerable credit for his perceptive observation of the significance of *Escherichia coli* as a causative agent of human diarrheas. But K.G.'s greatest job and legacy were his contact and personal concern for students. He was not soft, sentimental, patronizing, or scornful of them, but rather a father to everyone. He wished young men and women to achieve their potential as fine physicians and never ceased to impart the glow of enthusiasm fed always by the rich tradition of medical history, one of his constant preoccupations. Thanks are due K.G. for his tireless search for medical knowledge and his unique ability as a superb teacher.

Colin M. MacLeod and Thomas Francis, Jr.

My rich memories of Colin M. MacLeod and Thomas Francis, Jr. stem from more than two decades of association with the Armed Forces Epidemiological Board, the Public Health Service, and the U.S.–Japan Cooperative Medical Science Program. The two, as close friends, had much in common: versatility, wisdom, absolute insistence on scientific accuracy, intolerance for stupidity, and cultural interests. Their lives were marked by notable scientific work, chairmanship of top departments of microbiology and preventive medicine, and exemplary public service. Their respective work on the pneumococcus and influenza will endure with time.

Karl F. Meyer

Much is owed to Karl Meyer for his insistence that clarification of the pathogenesis of pestilential diseases, coupled with the study of their environmental and epidemiological features, is the key to control and treatment. The need for thorough postmortem examination possessed him. Encephalitis, plague, brucellosis, psittacosis, leptospirosis, poliomyelitis, and others were some of his models. The ability of microbes to persist in animal or human tissues was one of his favorite subjects. He tackled everything with excitement and enthusiasm. Unrivaled as a raconteur, his vivid expression and remarkable sense of history made him an indefatigable teacher. Once he spoke vividly of the "traffic of saliva at a Mexican funeral" to make the point of the direct human spread of *Yersinia pestis* that followed the kissing of the dead. Once he remarked that a New Mexico man did not die of plague but of "too many antibiotics." Another time, when discussing an early problem with polio vaccine, he remarked, "All the others slopped in enough formalin to kill the virus but also the antigenicity." When delivering an invitational lecture on plague in Baltimore in 1961, after an hour, K.F. said, "With that introduction, I will now begin my talk."

K.F. Meyer's career as a field scientist, coupled with his gift for picturesque expression gave me, a neophyte, a clearer view of why a problem is a problem and which route to take to solve it.

John Holmes Dingle

John Holmes Dingle was the epitome of the complete physician, a man without a jealous bone in his body and one whose life was full of accomplishment and help for others. The son of a North Dakota minister, a member of a large family, he had to become educated the hard way by working to pay tuition. A high honors graduate of Harvard Medical School who worked with Hans Zinsser, his military record was also one of excellence. He never ceased his public service while organizing and directing one of the best departments of preventive medicine in the country. His versatility was so great and his clinical interest and competence so outstanding that he could just as easily have developed a good department of internal medicine. I know well my indebtedness to John and without doubt many feel the same way. Every honor received by John was earned and bestowed by its donors with pride.

These men strove for and achieved excellence in their lives and chosen fields. By the conduct of their lives, the examples they

Top, left to right: Maurice C. Pincoffs, Marcel Baltazard, Leon A. Fox, and Stanhope Bayne-Jones. Center, left to right: Joseph E. Smadel, Raymond Lewthwaite, Kenneth Goodner, and Colin M. MacLeod. Bottom, left to right: Thomas Francis, Jr., Karl F. Meyer, and John H. Dingle.

set, and their wise counsel, they enhanced our profession and inspired so many. Along with the need for solid foundations in the basic and clinical sciences, the opportunity to associate closely with such informed professionals was an advantage of immeasurable value. It is not possible to adequately express the extent of this indebtedness since they gave me so much advice, help, and friendship.

Chapter 21

ABOUT FRIENDS

*T*hroughout my life, I have been blessed with many special friends. Gordy Power ranked among the top of my best friends, perhaps reinforced in large part by our heritage as Carroll County boys. Added to this was our second cousin kinship. Never one to show displeasure or express unkind words, Gordy was a man well liked by everyone. He lost his left arm as a result of an injury followed by a serious gas gangrene infection which forced an amputation at age 10. Yet, he never complained nor showed much evidence of disability. He was the first one-armed Eagle Scout in America. His ability to play tennis, catch and throw a baseball, hit a golf ball, and swim attested to his determination and fortitude. Successful in politics, he was elected to the position of Chief Executive in Baltimore County. To my mind, he was too sincere and painfully honest to be a good politician. Happily, he left politics and returned to an active law practice and a warm family life.

Slim Chalmers has an equal ranking in spite of the wide geographic space between us. He has excelled in many endeavors: a star athlete at Franklin and Marshall College, a 1932 Olympic

Celeste Woodward and Slim and Mary Chalmers

swimmer, a great success as head coach of swimming at Lafayette and West Point, Senior Assistant Athletic Director at the Military Academy, and Athletic Director at Iowa State and Indiana. He

Green Spring Valley Hunt Club: Erwin Huber, Van Rand, Henry Beeler, Ted Woodward

has had a happy life with his lovely wife Mary and their six children. Among my friends, he is the one who thinks that he is still in college and, until recently, found time to coach the YMCA team in swimming in Hendersonville, North Carolina.

Leonard Getschel, my banking friend, tried very hard to become a duck hunter. Whether Leonard ever hit a duck or goose is unknown to me. Yet, I know of no one who was more good company and one who could interest women and men alike with his stories rendered in dialect. His wife Libby always knew how to keep him in line.

Just up the hill in Northwood were Van and Connie Rand whose friendship has faithfully extended for many years. As one of the few physicians practicing in our small community, I was called to see Van's father and render a bit of help.

Van Rand played golf exceptionally well. Never one to show emotion, he kept things to himself. But when he blew a foot-long putt, his thoughts should never be put into words. He had the best swing in the Elkridge Club. Van quietly worked for the good of things, such as his insurance company, his church, and his family and friends. Van and Larry Perin very graciously accepted me as a perennial duffer. His wife Connie is more like a member of the family than a friend. Often we have enjoyed the company of Frances and Erwin Huber. She is the daughter of my wartime boss General Leon Fox.

Leonard and Libby Getschel

Van and Connie Rand

Frances and Erwin Huber

Larry Perin had a dry, poignant sense of humor. Not only did he reach his mark as a successful lawyer, but he stood up and legislated for good sensible rules of human behavior. His interest in public affairs ran deep and he was a staunch supporter of orderly processes. Margaret, also a dear friend, and Larry had a happy life together and were justly proud of their family.

Larry and Margaret Perin

Ivan Bennett was a sincere, good friend for many years. He had one of the sharpest minds in American medicine and was not afraid to express it at any level of sophisticated conversation. His sense of timing and ability to choose the right words at the right time was matched by only a few. Ivan accomplished much and contributed significantly to clinical medicine and to experimental pathology, particularly in relation to infectious diseases. Not only was he a remarkable medical administrator, but a happy and warm husband and father.

My friendship with Roy Galloway, which began initially at Camp Conoy, the Baltimore YMCA camp located previously on the South River near Annapolis, has extended over many years. He became a top executive of the Union Carbide Company with the responsibility for handling their products in Asia. Our adult friendship became consolidated when Lee, his attractive wife, and children returned from Calcutta; most of the family were ill with amoebic dysentery. Somehow they ended up in my office in Baltimore, instead of one in New York, because someone had recommended me as a physician who knew about tropical diseases. The friendship was immediately renewed and medical treatment was effective. Our children joined the circle and we have remained close. The Galloways are sailors; they settled at

Roy Galloway

Celeste, Puddin #3, Gordy Power, and Jim Gear

Wye Landing and adapted themselves as established Eastern Shoremen.

James H.S. Gear was my friend who most closely personified "Mr. Chips." This moniker refers to his calm demeanor. For him, time was not nearly as important as accomplishment. When Jim Gear spoke of medicinal science, one never realized that many key advances in knowledge were made by him. Humility and gracious behavior, being a "gentleman," were his trademarks.

After early education in Scotland, Jim's family migrated to South Africa where he forged an international reputation in tropical medicine. In this vast country, he became an expert on scientific virology, rickettsiology, and tropical disease and was the distinguished head of the South African Institute for Medical Research and the Poliomyelitis Institute for many years.

His side interests included anthropology, ornithology, and European, South African, and American history. Jim and his equally gracious wife, Josephine, "Jo," were the epitome of southern hospitality. The Gears' favorite treat was to take their guests to Kruger Park, a vast game preserve larger in space than Maryland and Delaware put together. All animals, large and small, live in a protected natural state in this huge forest.

Jim only considered the trip successful when the King of Beasts, the lion, was spotted and watched. He thought like a lion and could sense their presence by smell, character of terrain, spoor, time of day, etc. On a memorable trip, Ken Goodner, Joe Smadel, Boetha Demillon, Jim, and I finished the Kruger Park visit and started the long trek by car to Johannesburg. Jim asked whether we would like to hear some of the history of South Africa. For the next four hours, he spoke continuously step by step beginning with the first Cape settlement, the trek northward, the conflicts between the European settlers and the native Bantu, including the warlike Zulus and other tribes. Jim blended in the English intrusion and the bloody conflicts among the Boers, Bantu, and British military forces. He so perfectly timed his historical sketch that when we reached the Orange River, he remarked, "This is the river which Winston Churchill swam after his escape from Boer imprisonment." Blended into his account was the influence of Rhodes, the builder and diamond czar, and the discovery of gold in South Africa and its impact on the history of that country. In the account, he included many strange diseases which were closely connected to the terrain, animals and insects, diamond and gold mining, and the intrusion of foreigners.

This remarkable account held our intense interest and shortened the long ride. When he finished, he said, "Now, would you like to hear something about American history?" None doubted that he could deliver. The early problems and struggles of the two countries, South Africa and the United States, have similarities with similar heroes and adversaries.

Dan Ellis, a Virginian reared in Richmond before being transplanted to Boston, became one of the best clinical gastroenterologists at the Massachusetts General Hospital or anywhere. We met and became friends in Morocco after I ventured into the Sixth General Hospital. We then performed some investigative studies of typhus fever in collaboration with Edward F. Bland, a distinguished cardiologist. On return to Boston after the war, Dan entered practice with Dr. Chester Jones, his chief and great friend.

Dan believes in an orderly life, whether it involves medical practice or teaching medical students and house officers, and insists upon maintaining the highest ethical values in the medical

Dan Ellis   *Tim and Marnie Babylon*

profession. He is as honest as he is forthright when he confronts an issue. No one ever catches him failing to do his homework. The Board of Regents of the American College of Physicians and the Joint Commission on Hospital Accreditation know this so well. Each has been enriched by his wise counsel. He is a star with many friends.

Dan and Eloise have a happy family. They are fun to be with whether it involves lobster, oysters, bourbon, hunting, bridge, or good conversation.

It was through Dan and Eloise that we met Midge and Travers Nelson, not in Baltimore which is their home, but at Isle Au Haut, a delightful island off the coast of Maine. This is a great summer place for Boston and Baltimore people. Midge and Travers are simply lovely persons, gracious in conversation, skilled on the tennis court, and devastating at bridge.

Perry Culver is another accomplished woodsman and is one of my busiest and most enthusiastic friends. Perry gets involved in countless activities which relate to good medicine, good teaching, or good fellowship. In addition to his prior important role as Director of the Harvard Medical Alumni Association, his wise advice was sought by numerous high-level health agencies. Sandwiched in between his scurrying around, he served a large and

Dock at Isle Au Haut: Kits, Eloise, Midge, Celeste, Dan, Perry, Bisty, Travers

Perry, Mason, Dan, Travers

Perry Culver

faithful clientele of patients who sometimes waited hours for him to appear. This they did willingly and admired him even more for his expert and devoted care. Yet, Perry never seems to show any sense of harassment and turns out the light only after satisfactorily completing the day's work. Kits has been a perfect wife for Perry; she is considerate of everyone and everything.

Postwar Friends

As a country boy who regarded Baltimore as a huge, great city, it took me some time to think and converse in such a sophisticated setting. Early on, I decided to just act natural, keep my own shop in order, and say it the way it is. Baltimore is full of such people and it was a treat for me to meet and live with many of them. They have become a part of me.

John Winslow lived next door. Nancy and John helped shape Craig's life and equally loved the others. Across the street was Will Murray, a special, wholesome type of fellow. Even when things were tough, you would never know it. Will died early in life, but his loving Kitty and four sons are a testimony to his high standards. Just a little east of us in Northwood were Charlie and Ann Orth, who raised Ched and Ann, who were childhood friends of our kids. Charlie played golf as intensely as he practiced law; his talents took him to the Maryland Court of Special

Nancy and John Winslow

Kitty and Will Murray, 1954

Charles and Ann Orth and Henry and Ann Beeler

Appeals. Just next door in Northwood was Tal Graham, who was considerate, warm, and sincere.

Soon after the war, I came onto a more raucous group of athletes. Henry Beeler was a top athlete at Johns Hopkins, particularly in football and lacrosse. Henry, along with Moke Merriken, were very formidable lacrosse players and played in the Olympics in 1932.

John Corckran fit into a special mold; he was another of that loyal Hopkins crowd. Thoroughly likeable, John developed a small manufacturing plant into a most successful one. He was a good golfer who told me a hundred times what ailed my game. Ceil, his wife, misses him very much, as do his sons, John and Jimmy. Jimmy keeps John's memory very fresh for me.

Our friendship with Phil Mackowiak extends back to Sherwood Forest days when he, Craig, and Sis were practically in diapers. Now he is a professor and academic chairman of medicine, accomplished as a teacher and clinical investigator. Phil and Connie, his lovely wife, are great company. Frank Calia and Liz fit the same mold. Their fellowship has enriched our lives. Now Frank is a busy dean and wisely finds time for teachng medical students and house officers. He is an excellent role model like

Jimmy Corckran's wedding: John Corckran, Ceil, Jeannie, Jimmy

Phil. The Mackowiaks and Calias know so well the warm affection and love of family.

Bob Kent and Bob Poole were as different as night and day. Together, they developed a company which installed a lot of air conditioning units in Baltimore and over the east coast. An indeterminate number of years ago, Bob Kent concluded that it was sinful and downright distasteful to grow older. In his mind, he

Philip Mackowiak, M.D.

Bob Kent, 1983

succeeded. Yet, the aches, creaks, and muscle pains which he tells me about are not due to the aging process but, in his mind, to very special diseases. Frankly, I have run out of names of diseases. Somehow, Bob still believes in me in spite of my ineptness. He can handle a rigorous schedule, a lot of medical terms, and my insults. Bob is a special friend and a very tolerant patient. Bob Poole was very different. Bob and Pete, his loving wife, made a popular couple. Bob always said how it was, or should be. Pete usually adjudicated the matter.

Among my McCormick friends, Paul Frisch and John Doub, and their wives Miriam and Margaret, fit in the same mold. They think only nice things and carry them out. Margaret and John have many interests, of which sailing is one. Margaret is first-mate, cook, and captain. Their three sons are Eagle Scouts.

Big Ernie Issel functioned in a special world which involves "get the job done, don't fiddle around, and show me." This trait never hurt him or anyone. Among my special legal patients is Ed Weant of Westminster. He has been a very effective lawyer and judge of the Court of Appeals.

John Sipple and I knew each other very casually as boys. During and after World War II, our paths crossed. John made frequent voyages as a naval officer to North Africa and the Mediterranean. When we met there, we were able to console each other. John became a successful banker. He and I played about the same

Charles and Anne McCormick

caliber of poor bridge but enjoyed each other's company, along with Ruth who usually beat us at the bridge table.

Celeste and I visited Aunt Grace in Frederick which occasionally brought us in contact with Dr. Charlie Conley, Mrs. Theresa Mathias, and Mac and Sue McCardell, who are all good company.

Margaret and John Doub

Paul and Miriam Frisch

When Sis and Mark were married in 1971, we began a warm relationship with Willard and Bernice Applefeld, which has provided many lasting memories.

Somehow a long line of college educators found their way into my office. The first was Dr. Wilson H. Elkins, President of the University of Maryland from 1954 to 1978. Never ruffled, he had the uncanny ability to keep a great number of jointed and disjointed persons in line. The state of Maryland is in his debt for his contributions in developing a top-class university. His successor, Dr. John Toll, had even a larger responsibility with greatly expanded campus centers in Baltimore, Catonsville, College Park, and the Eastern Shore of Maryland. He, too, has ridden well with the punches and commanded the respect of legislators in Annapolis.

A large university needs chancellors and it has been my privilege to help keep a few of these fine persons fit medically, not that they really needed much help. Among them was Ray Ehrensberger, the senior member of this group, who missed little, enjoyed life, and greatly expanded the frontiers of the University of Maryland in the education of others overseas. The University's Foreign Educational program developed by him became a model of its kind. His fitting successor and productive educator was Stanley Drazek. He was a most dedicated and effective man. Dr. Ben Massey now carries on this great overseas program. A quiet, most sincere, broadly educated and cultured member of the College Park campus was Dr. Lee Hornbake. He complained little, served humbly and efficiently, and conducted himself as a most effective gentleman. All of these persons were appropriately chosen and appointed to fulfill their keys roles.

Among our friends, Tim Baker showed an easy facility to endure hardship, without complaint, and come out smiling. Highly successful in developing a major Baltimore enterprise, he suffered a few health setbacks in perfect balance; with him Grace was poised and always wore a ready smile. They beat us in bridge consistently as did the Murphys. Pat Murphy was never ruffled, always ready with a wry comment, a quizzical question, or a helpful hand. His wife Fran is a very friendly and a most gracious lady.

Charlie and Anne McCormick had a great and happy time through many years until his premature death.

Sonny Almond and I came to know each other when he and Anne McCormick became involved and were married, which pleased everyone.

Pop Siegel, a product of Georgia Tech, lived in Baltimore for a while, and later he and Marian and their family of boys moved to Atlanta. Pop was a straightforward man, so proud of his sons, who had a very keen business sense, a sharp wit, and a warm capacity for friendship. Never boastful of his own accomplishments, he was warmly pleased over the good luck of others.

Tim and Grace Baker, Jean and Moke Merriken

Peg and John Reifsnider, Grace Baker, Celeste Woodward

Warm friendly relationships such as these have helped make me a happier person, and through them came a certain realization that society is composed of rainbows of colorful persons, all of whom helped make things more fresh and mellow.

The United States–Japan Cooperative Medical Science Program, which began in 1965, brought me in contact with many extremely qualified professionals among whom special warm relationships developed. Earl Beck, an established citizen of Frederick, Maryland, provided the cement which was instrumental in keeping Japanese and American scientists working collaboratively and effectively on serious problems such as leprosy, tuberculosis, cholera, virus infections, parasitic disorders, and other pestilential diseases. Never one to become unhinged, Earl arranged and produced the grease and oil which helped ensure a smooth running system. Often we worked together to prepare detailed reports and communiqués which were objective, accurate, and readable. Jane Kinsell became the Administrator of the U.S.–Japan program after Earl, and brought to it a keen sense of prompt efficiency and welcome collaboration.

Bill Jordan is a scientist for all seasons who contributed very importantly to the U.S.–Japan Medical Science Program and similarly to the Armed Forces Epidemiological Board, each of which he served with distinction for many years. His incisive and broad capability throughout the field of microbiology are assets which have greatly benefited America and global science. Earl and Bill are valued friends, as is John La Montagne, whose wide capabilities brought added strength to the U.S.–Japan program. There have been many other refreshing associations during my years of service with the U.S.–Japan and AFEB programs.

Col. Dan Crozier was the type of military medical officer who has helped ensure stability of purpose and advance knowledge in many areas of science. Gen. Bill Tigertt had one of the best minds in the Army Medical Service, particularly in the context of historical events. Bud Benenson has Bill Jordan's similar qualities and has never shirked in serving his country in and out of uniform for many years. Bud and Bill have helped put all kinds of biological vaccine problems into proper order. The public has greatly benefited from their contribution.

Paul Densen, was chairman of Harvard's program in community planning. No one in my experience could look more squarely at a statistical or sociologic problem involving population groups and human dynamics. His incisive mind and ability to communicate ideas in words or in writing about difficult problems made him a very valuable national resource. Everyone benefited from knowing him, and how fortunate I am to have been enriched by him through the activities of the AFEB.

Of all of the executive secretaries of the AFEB with whom I have been privileged to serve, Col. Robert (Nick) Nikolewski

Col. Dan Crozier　　　*Gen. Bill Tigertt*　　　*Bud Benenson, M.D.*

Paul Densen and M.G. Mendez

leads the list. As a dedicated and talented medical officer, he left nothing to chance and took nothing for granted. Nick had the uncanny ability to smell trouble before it occurred and knew what steps to take in order to avoid catastrophe, which can easily occur in Washington. Col. Adam Rapalski, another talented U.S. Army Officer of Polish extraction, served the Armed Forces as a superbly efficient officer and as executive secretary of the AFEB. My contact with him in the latter capacity was limited. Also, my medical school classmate, Col. John Rizzolo, was a most able executive secretary of the AFEB during his service in the United States Air Force. Actually, practically all of the executive secretaries who have served the AFEB have contributed importantly to their country. Among them are Col. Bob Hughes and Capt. Mike Parsons, USN. Our citizens must somehow be informed of the remarkable way that hardworking, dedicated, highly talented, and well-qualified medical officers and specialists in the discipline of Preventive Medicine have contributed importantly to the welfare of the United States, including the public and the military services. It is not possible for me to go through the list of those special professional persons known to me. This is a distinguished

Col. Robert (Nick) Nikolewski

Col. Adam Rapalski

Col. John Rizzolo

list. Somehow all of this information could be assembled by a historian who, through his or her efforts, would produce a document of inestimable value.

Fond Memories of a Special Friend

None of my friends can quite match Joe Usilton who is among that amicable and special breed of Eastern Shoremen whom James Michener so vividly described in his classic *Chesapeake*. Joe was born in Rock Hall and spent most of his adult life on Kent Island where he managed and cared for Parson's Island, a farm and recreation site for McCormick and Company. In terms of schooling, Joe had little and yet he was one of the most intelligent, highly respected, and sensitive men whom I have ever met. His intelligence came not from the classroom or books, but from his perceptive ability to observe nature and become a part of its mysteries. A deep understanding of animals, birds, fish, tides, character of people, children's desires and needs, were all second nature to him. He had a second sense as to what might happen and what to do before it does. Somehow he knew about the wind, tides, and weather and how and when to be cautious. Habits of wild fowl, fish, crabs, clams, and predators such as fox, raccoons, hawks, and owls were imbued in him. Also, he knew how to outsmart them by lure and trapping. Above all, he taught by talking, not about himself, but about his endless store of knowledge from observing nature's wonders.

In a duck blind, he could tell the species and sex of a duck, while others saw only a speck in the air. He knew where to build a cottage, house, barn, or shed and how to construct it. Everyone respected his wisdom in such things and listened to him.

Boats were his natural habitat and he could tell a good one from a dud as easily as he judged people. He navigated the entire course of the inland waterway for well-to-do friends with large boats, though he never had lessons on navigation. I never heard him say an unkind word about anyone. Never one to complain,

Joe Usilton

he had much reason to, particularly because of bad hips and knees from overuse.

Just to have him shuck oysters in the kitchen for some of my city friends and tell stories outmatched anything on television or from Hollywood. The best among many anecdotes about him involves a group of physicians, lawyers, and other educated professionals who had the treat of seeing Joe in action. My dear friend, Eph Lisansky, held a special wild fowl dinner in his lovely home a number of years ago. Joe was one of Eph's guests and came to the city from the Eastern Shore. The meal, long to be remembered, boasted all types of fowl, including a few illegal types not to be discussed. After the scrumptious dinner, with Port, the conversation lagged a bit. For years, I had saved the breast bones (clavicle to doctors) of every type of two-legged birds known to me: chicken, turkey, guinea, snipe, partridge, most species of duck, brant, goose, and swan. All neatly cleaned, shining, numbered, and in a bag, I had waited for the proper occasion. These bones were placed on the table and each of these intrepid and intelligent hunters was asked to separate them. Naturally, while all of this mass of intelligence looked bewildered, Joe stepped in. Never had he looked at a wishbone. The true Eastern Shoreman in preparing a duck or goose merely plucks its breast feathers, cuts out the breast for a filet, and forgets the rest.

Based entirely on his innate intelligence, Joe quickly separated the land birds, such as chicken, turkey, or guinea, from the wild birds by size and bulk of bone. Then he came down to the ducks of which there are many species with differing habits. We kept urging him to tell us how he was making such decisions: "This is a mallard or wood duck because it is not as strong as a diving duck." "This is a canvas-back rather than a widgeon because the 'Can' flies higher, dives deeper, as much as thirty feet, and is a stronger bird; the widgeon does not dive as far and often feeds in the wake of a 'Can.' Marsh ducks have a less dense bone structure." Joe did not miss one duck or bird, though he had probably not seen another wishbone! That is native intelligence!

Always, when we or our children were in Joe's careful hands, we felt calm, confident, and secure. Men and women, such as ourselves, felt a warm and wholesome affection for him which simply set him aside as someone special. There were no dissentions; everyone loved and respected him.

Perhaps these comments have been too long but it has been with the hope that the words would comfort a bit while we pay a tribute to our friend. His death really signaled an end to an amazing era. This has been said before about others, many times in the past. Yet, this was our time, these were our feelings, this was our dear Joe, a companion to whom we bid goodbye. How fortunate for us to have lived with him. The heritage which he left is one of excellence: a loving family to whom we convey our warm sentiments and a richness in friends. Our memories of Joe will always be fresh, pure, and green.

Morale Builders

During a long life, everyone has memorable experiences in addition to those nice letters or words from former students or associates who take the time to communicate a cordial expression. Several special nice memories beyond the confines of the family and close friends have helped make me feel that much of it all was worthwhile. My purpose in relating a few is simply to stress that the values and real fiber of life are not the material gains or advantages, but rather the warm satisfaction which comes from human feelings and sensitivity.

During the several months before my retirement as departmental chairman, there were many memorable experiences. My friends had some nice things to say which always bolsters ego. Yet, the nicest part of these festivities was the action of the medical student body which commissioned a portrait to be painted. Portraits are rather dull things, but the sentiment which prompted the medical students to do this has lasting value for me. After all, medical schools should be for students, and school teachers should serve those being taught and not themselves. That is what the gift meant to me, an appreciation of a school teacher who tried.

A few years ago, during the commencement festivities for all of the University of Maryland Professional Schools, I received a surprising and unanticipated tribute from Dr. Michael F. Pratt, President of the 1980 Senior Class, who was privileged to address the entire assemblage in the Civic Center. He spoke of the physicians' responsibilities and kindly remarked:

> First and foremost we must guard against complacency as Emerson once said, 'Most of the shadows of this life are caused by standing

in our own sunshine,' our past accomplishments and our present jubilation must not eclipse our future efforts. An example of this type of continuing dedication can be taken from the professional life of Dr. Theodore E. Woodward, who will retire in 1981, after twenty-seven years of brilliant leadership as Chairman of Medicine at the University. The vitality of his intellectual energy has been felt by many of his colleagues and students over the years, through his unique commitment to medical education. As exemplified by Dr. Woodward, we have a responsibility to society and to ourselves which requires that we continue our endeavors with the same energy and purpose that have made the commencement ceremony possible for each one of us.

Not to be forgotten is a lovely dinner given for my wife and me by the secretaries and classified personnel of the Department of Medicine. They perform so much important work, mostly behind the scenes, which is essential for any smoothly operated activity. For their work, they receive such little credit.

For about four decades, the University of Maryland had an orderly who was among the finest of men known to me. His daily assignment was the ancillary care of many ill patients on the private patient floors. Every patient received his same caring personal care and attention which involved many activities such as taking them from bed to various hospital units or from bed to chair, making the bed, giving a bath, a back rub, or an enema, helping with a more comfortable position, and so many other things. Mr. Robert McLeod retired after thirty-eight years of devoted service. Everyone—nurse, physician, administrator, or associate—knew, loved, and respected Robert. Once I mentioned to him, "Robert, if we had three more like you, we could really make this a model hospital." In his quiet way, he responded with a smile, "Dr. Woodward, they don't make them like that any more." Robert was given a retirement dinner which was enthusiastically attended. Later, a news reporter published an interview with him. On being asked what he considered a stimulus for him, he responded, "Dr. Theodore E. Woodward, Professor and Head of Medicine (at the University of Maryland Hospital), has been my biggest inspiration. He is what a doctor ought to be." This is about the finest tribute I have ever had.

When Robert died at home, it was my privilege as his physician and friend to be with him. This is the role which physicians have traditionally filled which was largely instrumental in making medicine such a respected profession. For all physicians, the

Robert McLeod

communication between them and their patients can be intimate and rewarding. Life can be much happier and its problems often softened if time is taken for a touch of sentiment.

Family group

Chapter 22

THINKING IT OVER

Remarks to Pre-Medical Honor Society, Franklin & Marshall
College, September 23, 1995

he Lord Buddha, who lived in the sixth century, B.C.,
preached that "Freedom from disease is the first blessing."
One has only to travel to not so remote undeveloped envi-
ronments to witness life as it existed in ancient and biblical times.
Village life today in the Asian subcontinent, the Middle East,
Africa, and the Far East has changed little since the active lives of
Confucius or of Christ. In these rural settings, infant mortality is
excessive, death in children is commonly caused by common
childhood illnesses, respiratory infections, cholera, and other diarrheal diseases. We should not forget that anemia and malnutrition are prevalent in children within several blocks of the two
Baltimore medical schools.

In these settings, infants nurse at breast well after teeth erupt
since cow's milk is scarce. Yet, mother's milk is thin because she
is undernourished. It is lacking in total calories, in protein, and in
essential fatty acids, all of which are necessary for proper growth

and development of the child. Studies have shown that the human brain is 80 percent developed by the time of weaning. Protein and certain amino acid deficiencies in mother and child can seriously influence intellect permanently.

It is commonplace to see barefooted, inadequately clothed children making cakes of the droppings of domestic animals to be dried for fuel. Such droppings should be returned to the soil as fertilizer, yet, there is no wood or coal for fuel to cook with or provide warmth in cold weather. Naturally, children contract a multitude of parasitic diseases, including hookworm infestation, which adds to their undernutrition, anemia, and poor development.

It is sobering to realize that a decade ago, it was crudely estimated that 54 percent of the world's people lived in twelve countries on about 9 percent of the world's income, while the 7 percent of the world's population who lived in the United States and Canada consumed about 43 percent of the world's income. This gap has changed some with the rapid industrialization of Western Europe and Japan in which America played a key role. Yet, the western nations cannot feed the large populations in underdeveloped countries by merely sending them surpluses. Rather, we can provide the knowledge to receptive people through teaching better methods of irrigation, crop enrichment, better poultry, and animal husbandry. They must be motivated to want to do something. This involves leadership on their part with the secondary assistance of affluent nations. These are the factors which will alleviate human suffering more than just sending a new vaccine or a supply of antibiotics. Some economists argue that these medical advances and anti-insecticides have compounded the world's nutritional problems by reducing the death rate. Unfortunately, progress must come from providing a very necessary and expensive commodity—education. Incidentally, this is sorely needed to gain an inroad to the world population pandemic.

Let me cite several personal experiences which exemplify how health is contagious for people: an addiction to health.

In 1943, with another medical officer, I crossed the desert in Aden Protectorate to Yemen. Scores had died of an epidemic thought to be typhus fever. Early in the morning, after a midnight arrival by Lorry, we asked a lad of 10 to take us to the house of someone recently deceased. The boy said, "You ask for the dead when the graveyards are full." We soon confirmed the presence of a sizeable epidemic of typhus fever and proceeded to delouse members of households, house by house, block by block, using DDT. Soon these backward, uneducated villagers literally drove us into the secluded back rooms to help the Muslim women as well as the men. This was contrary to custom for a man to minister to a woman. Yet, they quickly observed that the powder effectively killed lice and something constructive was being accomplished. Up to that point, they had no concept that the disease was louse transmitted. People are *not* basically ignorant and are receptive to all aids to better health.

Desire for health was so contagious in Naples, Italy, during the World War II typhus epidemic that we had to command police officers to keep order during our delousing procedures. Mothers became hysterical lest their bambino not be given DDT powder first.

Not long ago in Dacca, children and adults with cholera died like flies from diarrhea loss—as much as twelve quarts of body water lost daily. Barges were organized as first aid stations adjacent to a bazaar or market area along the Bramanhaputra River. People flocked, young and old, including women and infants, to be given saltwater by vein. In this same setting, inspired young American physicians later developed the oral rehydration technique which revolutionized the treatment of cholera. Health knows no barriers, political or religious. We can be proud that our country, indeed, our medical school and hospital, engaged actively in such international health programs. The University of Maryland had a research center in West Pakistan which was engaged actively in studying the health problems peculiar to this country. Sophisticated studies were conducted in the laboratory and field work conducted in remote villages and in mountain terrain within the shadow of China.

David Livingston would never have accomplished his adventurous journey through Africa without his acquaintance with the *healing heart*. The various savage tribes whose territories he traversed were *deaf* to the voice of the missionary but were capable of appreciating the good services of the medical man—a high testimony to the benevolent and all powerful character of the nursing and medical professions.

Was medicine always trusted and honored? Few realize that George Washington, in his final illness, was hastened to his death by excessive blood-letting for treatment of a streptococcal sore throat. Reflect back in America to the beginning of the 20th century, and before, when public opinion and regard for the medical profession was low. Life expectancy was about age 45 which, unfortunately, is the current level for those born and now destined to live in impoverished countries. In the United States in the late 19th and early 20th century, there was a plethora of medical schools with ten in Baltimore at one time. Without preliminary educational requirements, they were little more than diploma mills with a certificate awarded in two years. The two years involved hearing lectures during two-month sessions in the fall and spring. Public regard for the average graduate was low. Many were looked upon as quacks. Often, promising graduates studied abroad or entered the military or public health services. In the early 1900s, the public contributed less than 1 million dollars for medical research when religious denominations enthusiastically received an excess of 18 million. Now, in the late 20th century, the public contribution to medical research and education is astronomical. The National Institutes of Health alone receives 1.5 billion dollars annually.

We have come a long way. Life expectancy is in the late seventies, and we have effective prevention for diphtheria, measles, pertussis, rabies, tetanus, anthrax, poliomyelitis, smallpox, influenza, and rheumatic fever. Cures have been developed for such ravages as pneumonia, tuberculosis, plague, typhus, typhoid, meningitis, sepsis, endocarditis, cholera, dysentery, and syphilis. Also, there are important partial answers for diabetes, pernicious anemia, Hodgkin's disease, some forms of leukemia, cancer, and mental illness. Maternal mortality is low.

This new posture of **"trust"** and **"respect"** gained by the medical profession was not bought by dollars alone, but by phenomenal advances contributed by the minds and work of men and women.

Now, the public is restive. In the first place, medical care costs too much in spite of the fact that America is regarded as the Mecca for scientific medicine and education.

The public now expects answers for the ravages of arteriosclerosis, organ cancers, infertility, Alzheimer's disease, and AIDS. They want a way to slow down getting old, and a dignified death. Some of you will help clarify basic problems and many others will play important roles in applying these new advances to the care of your patients. The way is tedious, the horizon is bright, and the objectives are obtainable. If the profession works in collaboration with society as a whole, there is no question that proper guidelines will evolve for some of the ethical questions faced now, and in the future.

Now that you want to be a physician there are probably many uncertainties and concerns which enter your mind, such as: "Am I smart enough?"; "Do I possess enough facts?"; "What about my past successes or failures, my being gifted or skilled?"; "What will I do, where will I settle, will I be successful, trusted, respected?"

The patient does not grade us according to A's, B's, or C's, but rather on such attributes as: are we cultured persons; do we respond to their needs; do we listen understandingly to their problems with sincerity, unhurried and interested; are we thoroughly grounded in the fundamentals of medicine; are we thorough in our examinations of them; and do we guide their problems purely based on technical procedures or our evaluation of them as whole persons? Expressed differently, are we people-oriented physicians? There are significant differences. Patients can easily discern the difference and practically always give their confidence and trust to the sincere physician, properly trained, who is oriented to their individual problems.

What factors will determine your future? Naturally, you will need to seek and achieve a certain scholastic background at an appropriate educational level. This is necessary to ensure that you can cope with the problems presented by the fundamental or basic sciences in medical school which can be difficult. This basic knowledge is not a roadblock in your career development but a fundamental stepping stone to the understanding of clinical medicine, that is, the proper care of the patient.

What determines the outcome and impacts upon most of these high values is really our attitude, our motivation. This is really more important than facts; it is more important than appearance, special gifts, or skills. Attitude can make or break a government, a company, a church, a college, or a home. We cannot change the past or the way certain people act strangely or inappropriately, yet, our attitude toward how we embrace each day, our association with others, and how we react to life's problems is a very balancing influence. Every one of us is responsible for and can change our attitude, and with it can come the shape of our character and career.

Society will always trust and honor you as a physician, if you respond to its needs intelligently, sensitively, and sincerely. Honor is not an inherited attribute; everyone has an equal chance. It shines in the less fortunate as well as in the privileged. Honor really is an inner sense, difficult to define. It is simply a wholesome feeling that one senses within, something fresh and pure. It is a guiding inner principle that spontaneously urges us to embody those attributes which favor others more than self. To think and practice it is its own reward. It cannot be purchased.

Sixty-two years ago, I was in your same position as a starting senior student at Franklin & Marshall. Our country was bewildered and in the throes of its greatest depression. To make matters worse, dark clouds were collecting over Europe because of a man who had written his creed, *Mein Kampf.* At the time, I was a chemistry major and a little confused because there was uncertainty everywhere.

Although reared in a physician's family, there was no persuasion to study medicine because of the current social and economic unrest. Bread lines were long, banks literally closed, the stock market crashed, and unemployment was never higher.

Yet the healing art was in my blood. My brother was then a junior medical student and my application to medical school was not made until May of the senior year.

The very stimulating and positive forces here at F&M were teachers like Professors Foster, Kresge, Murray, Noss, Klein, Kunkle, Beck, and Weisberger. Inspiring, in their manner, they inculcated the need to study, to think and not cram. Also, hats are off to the athletic program with stimulating models like Uncle Charley Mayser and Shober Barr who worked closely with us.

There may be such a phenomenon as serendipity, but don't bank on it. Yes, there will be many opportunities and chances. Through your diligence and the guidance which you have received, you will be well prepared to recognize the roads to be taken and the blind ends to avoid. Already, many of you have chosen the health care road you wish to take. Keep an open mind at this stage; it is all exciting. There are no easy gratuities, but all will work out well because of you and *your* desire to achieve. Good luck!

(*Note:* I was very pleased that our grandson Mathew was in the audience as a freshman pre-medical student.)

Remarks to Medical Graduates of The University of Maryland School of Medicine and Hospital, 1979

Being a physician has given me a lifetime of opportunities—as well as a lifetime of observations. At times I have been called upon to speak to various medical school graduating classes. Perhaps some of the thoughts I have expressed on those occasions will serve others in our profession as well.

Medical school serves only to provide you the foundation needed to become a good doctor. But what really matters is your attitude and whether you will devote the time and effort to do the job well.

• *Maintain a sense of humor.* Communicate with your patients at a level they understand. Establish a friendly relationship with patients both old and young. A ready smile when appropriate or a well-chosen anecdote often help win over a recalcitrant patient and make your association with others much more rewarding.

• *Maintain high standards mixed with graceful humility.* There will be difficult problems which are normal parts of our profession and our lives. When those uncertainties arise, don't be so certain that you have all the answers or the correct diagnoses. Each problem resembles a coin which has two sides; be willing to turn the coin over. The Japanese consider the bamboo a much wiser tree than the oak. "During a storm it bends with the wind and when the wind subsides it springs back to its normal position. But the oak tries to show its strength, to stand up to the wind and for its pains usually ends torn up by the roots." This is not an admonition to abandon a view or sacrifice a principle, but rather to weigh problems objectively and accept the premise that another person's viewpoint may be correct.

• *Don't underestimate success; define it for yourself now.* Success is not difficult to achieve if you clearly understand and define it for yourself early in life. It matters not whether you become the top physician in your community, the president of the local or national society, or a Nobel Laureate. These are unessential, although such outward recognition is granted a fortunate few. The values which you adopt for life will shape your success. Set your sights first on becoming good husbands, wives, and parents. In whatever phase of medicine we choose, all that society can ask of us is that we perform the best we can. Equally rewarding for a physician is the satisfaction that in the process of performing service, someone else has been helped along the way. A physician in either the community or academic center has a unique opportunity to teach others if only by precept.

• *Cultivate friendship.* Friends are among humanity's most priceless treasures. One must be a friend in order to have a friend. Friends lend comfort at times of difficulty and solace in times of sadness. True friendship requires time for nurturing, patience, hard work, and ceaseless concern for the person you call a friend. Focus on quality and not numbers. When this type of relationship has been established, you will be richly blessed and rewarded with a lasting treasure.

• *Stay young: youth does not necessarily cease at a set age.* Age has no boundaries. Youthful ideas are not a monopoly of youth. During your career, don't aspire just to become a good doctor but rather a special one who might be regarded as that physician who knew all about a special clinical sign, who perfected a needed technique or procedure, or found time to work with the Boy Scouts or raise six good kids or grew the best holly trees in the county. Anyone who develops a hobby, within or outside medicine, will experience special gratification and fulfillment.

• *Serve the community.* Make time to join civic and church groups, school boards, Boy and Girl Scout troops, art museums, etc. After you establish yourselves as physicians in the environment of your choice, then seek an outlet which will make the community respect you even more.

• *Continue your education.* Medicine progresses so rapidly that we hardly appreciate its advances. They match those of earlier decades when diabetes, pernicious anemia, infectious diseases, cardiac abnormalities, hypertension, and others succumbed to progress. Now medicine is on the verge of control of cancer, greater understanding of chromosomes, and genetic manipulation and refinements in diagnostic techniques which would stagger our forefathers. Just think of it! Pace yourself to keep learning in spite of being busy. Develop a system for storing and seeking new knowledge. Take advantage of any particular opportunity which chance or nature presents to you. Recognize it when it happens.

   • *Be a family person.* Marry when you are sure of the right person and raise a family. In so doing, be good husbands and wives. This responsibility comes before medicine. Be good parents, the one who taught the kids how to throw a ball, ride a bike, swim, play with dolls, camp, fish.

Remember this prayer by an anonymous author:

Slow me down. Break the tension of my nerves and muscles with soothing music of the singing streams that live in my memory. Help me know the restorative power of sleep. Teach me the art of taking mini-vacations, of slowing down to look at a flower, to chat with a friend, to pat a dog, to read a few lines from a good book. Remind me each day of the fable of the hare and the tortoise, that I may know that the race is not always to the swift, that there is more to life than increasing speed. Let me look upward to the branches of the towering oak and know that it grew because it grew slowly and well. Slow me down, Lord, and inspire me to send my roots deep into the soil of life's endearing values, that I may grow toward the stars of my greater destiny.

   • *Be aware of others.* In so doing, evaluate through judgment and understanding before giving advice too freely. Others will give you their confidence when your beliefs are sincere, fair, and conveyed in an articulate manner.

   Finally, in closing, let us all continue to nurture our aspirations and values so that they can serve us well whether the road is rough, or smooth, or even too quick for our own good. In the conduct of our lives, rely on the principles of love and affection for family, the enjoyment and warm fellowship of friends, devoted service for the welfare of others, and a touch of sentiment. Fulfillment of these ideals will return one of life's most precious rewards, the respect of our fellow man.

FOND MEMORIES OF A
LARGE MEDICAL FAMILY

*T*hroughout these many years, I have had the privilege and opportunity to meet frequently with medical students and house officers, associate with them, and in a small way help contribute to their career development. It has been gratifying to watch them mature into competent physicians, and to grow in their wisdom and judgment to ultimately assume important roles in our profession as practitioners, educators, investigators, or an amalgamation of each. Equally rewarding has been the opportunity to occasionally have a friendly dialogue with them, exchange greetings, and learn of their medical experiences and family life. Space permits only a brief word or two about this large family collection of physicians. Mention of others has been made elsewhere.

David Kipnis was appointed to the Distinguished Chair of Medicine at Washington University, St. Louis, and fashioned a remarkable career for himself as an endocrinologist and as an authority in the field of carbohydrate metabolism. Bill Spicer completed his fellowship in pulmonary diseases at the University of

Pennsylvania and after his chief residency in medicine developed our innovative program in primary care as well as a training program in medicine for nurses. Other able contributors to this unique and effective program were Herb Kushner, Jim Quinlan, Tony Riley—all who remain active as able clinicians in Baltimore. Charley Hoesch and Ray Liu were among that effective group of physicians in Baltimore. T. Kenney Gray became Director of the Division of Endocrinology and the Clinical Study Center at the University of North Carolina, where he also served as Deputy Director of the Department of Medicine. Richard P. Wenzel accepted an appointment at the University of Virgina School of Medicine and Hospital; there he was elevated to the rank of Professor of Medicine and became recognized as one of the nation's authorities in the field of nosocomial infections. Now Dick is Chairman of Medicine at the Medical College of Virginia, Richmond. Jean Jackson, after her chief medical residency and work as head of the Division of Rheumatology at the University Maryland, returned to Boston as staff physician of the Robert Brett Brigham Hospital and Assistant Professor of Medicine of the Harvard Medical School. Michael Weinblatt, after completion of his training in medicine, joined the staff of the Robert Brett Brigham Hospital and became one of the outstanding staff members there under Dr. Frank Austen. Another Boston standout is Lou Caplan, now leading neurologist and Professor and Chairman of Neurology at the New England Medical Center.

Other medical residents established important careers for themselves, such as Jim Cerda, Professor of Medicine and Deputy Director of the Department at the University of Florida. Philip Toskes became Professor of Medicine in University of Florida and head of the Division of Gastroenterology. After her fellowship in endocrinology at the Massachusetts General Hospital, Jane McHaffey was appointed there as staff physician and Assistant Professor of Medicine at the Harvard Medical School. Philip Mackowiak became Associate Professor of Medicine at Southwestern Texas Medical School and assistant head of the Division of Infectious Diseases of the Veterans Administration Medical Center in Dallas. In 1988 he returned to Maryland as Chairman of Medicine at the Baltimore Veterans Administration Medical Center and Vice Chairman of the Department of Medicine. His work on fever is historic. Herbert DuPont served first as a fellow and later Assistant Professor of Medicine at Maryland in the Division of Infectious Diseases. He was then appointed head of the Division of Infectious Diseases and of Microbiology and is now Professor and Director, Center for Infectious Diseases at the University of Texas, Houston. Stephen Greenberg moved to Baylor in Houston and contributed so importantly in virology and teaching and is now Vice Chairman of Medicine and a most effective academician.

Zalman Agus was appointed full Professor of Medicine at the University of Pennsylvania and head of the Renal and Electrolyte Division. Jonas Shulman was appointed Professor of Medicine at Emory University School of Medicine and Chairman of the Department of Community Medicine at Emory in Atlanta. After his formal training in medicine at Maryland and at Boston, Allan Myers became head of the Division of Rheumatology at the University of Pennsylvania. Following this appointment, he became Professor of Medicine and Deputy Chairman of the Department at Temple University where he is now Dean of the School of Medicine. Eric Bergquist served as Fellow in Infectious Diseases at Maryland and was then appointed as head of the Division of Infectious Diseases at Thomas Jefferson Hospital. Philip Russell, who trained for several years in medicine and in infectious diseases, was later appointed Commandant of the Walter Reed Medical Center and Commandant of the Fitzsimmons General Hospital. Allan Ronald, who served as assistant resident in medicine and Fellow in Medicine, became Director of the Division of Infectious Diseases at the University of Manitoba and later Chairman of the Department of Medicine there.

David Charkes, trained in medicine and nuclear medicine; he became Professor of Medicine and of Radiology and head of the Division of Nuclear Medicine at the Temple University School of Medicine. Jules Puschett joined the University of Pittsburgh School of Medicine, and was appointed as Professor of Medicine and head of the Division of Nephrology. He made important contributions to the curriculum of that school. After his training in medicine at Maryland, Zaheer-Ud-Din returned to his native Pakistan as a military officer and later was appointed to the rank of Brigadier and Surgeon General. Robert Myerburg left Maryland following his medical training to become Professor of Medicine and head of the Division of Cardiology at the University of Miami. Arthur Schmale, who received training in medicine, joined the faculty of the University of Rochester as Professor of Medicine and Psychiatry.

Following his training in medicine, Jay S. Goodman trained at Vanderbilt in infectious diseases and joined the faculty of that medical school and returned to Baltimore as head of the Department of Medicine at the Mercy Hospital. Bill Dear also joined the Mercy Hospital faculty and developed an efficient unit in nuclear medicine. Richard Cash trained in medicine and infectious diseases at Maryland, performed work in cholera at Dacca, and later became Associate Professor of Public Health and Hygiene at Harvard University. Ronica Kluge trained in medicine and infectious diseases at Maryland, joined the faculty of the University of West Virginia, and later became Professor of Medicine and head of the Division of Infectious Diseases at the University of Texas, Galveston. Marcia Schmidt came from the University of Florida, with Ronica, for training in medicine. She served as chief medical resident from 1971 to 1972. Rheumatology became her special interest and she joined the strong group at the Good Samaritan Hospital under Dr. Mary Betty Stevens. Michael Friedman completed his training in medicine and in infectious diseases at Maryland, joined the faculty of the University of Pennsylvania, and became Professor of Microbiology. After his training in medicine at the University of Maryland, Dr. Giraud Foster became Associate Professor of Physiology at the Johns Hopkins Medical Institutions.

Elijah Saunders became head of Cardiology at the Provident Hospital in Baltimore and later Associate Professor of Medicine and head of the Division of Hypertension at Maryland, where he is a recognized leader in stressing the significance of high blood pressure in African Americans. Richard Reba, who trained in medicine and in nuclear medicine at Maryland, was appointed to the faculty of George Washington University as Professor of Medicine and head of the Division of Nuclear Medicine. After his chief residency in medicine, John Rogers joined the faculty of the University of North Carolina in clinical pharmacology and later was appointed Chairman of Medicine at the Good Samaritan Hospital in Baltimore. Dave Levy, a former chief resident joined the School of Public Health at Hopkins and became an authority in mechanisms of allergic reactions. William Fishbein completed his training in medicine and has served as a senior staff member in pathology at the Armed Forces Institute of Pathology.

Susan Howard completed her training in medicine at Maryland, joined the Veterans Administration, and was appointed as head of infectious diseases programs for the Central Veterans Administration. John Mather trained in medicine and pulmonary diseases at Maryland, later joined the Veterans Administration, and became a senior staff physician of the VA in Washington. After his training in medicine at Maryland, Kurt Sligar joined the faculty of Cornell Medical College in neurology in New York City. Brian Baldwin trained in medicine and in cardiology at Maryland and ultimately entered the private practice of medicine and cardiology in Dallas. Always he has continued strong ties with his alma mater.

Ed Frohlich, who trained with us in medicine, is now Alton Ochsner, Distinguished Scientist and Vice President for Academic Affairs at the Ochsner Medical Foundation, New Orleans. Ed has made notable contributions to the field of hypertension.

Further north, at the Mayo Rochester Minnesota, Len Kurland settled where he organized and developed one of the best epidemiologic and statistical collection systems in the country. He was senior consultant and Professor of Epidemiology at the Mayo Clinic and remains very active now as an emeritus contributor.

Mike Oldstone, a trainee with us in medicine, neurology and infectious disease, joined the Department of Immunology, Scripps Clinic and Research Foundation, La Jolla, California. His work in the immunochemical field has clarified the mechanism and pathogenesis of encephalitis and many viral diseases. He is a recognized authority in the field.

After Jan Geiseler completed his chief residency at Maryland, he trained in infectious diseases at Chicago and moved west to Los Angeles. There he is a Director of the Infectious Diseases Service and their large AIDS Unit at USC University Hospital.

Worchester, Massachusetts became the home of Leonard Morse. There he became a fixture as an able practicing clinician, yet he found time to conduct practical and important studies on community medicine and sporadic outbreaks of transmittable diseases. In 1996, he was President of the Massachusetts Medical Society; he has always stressed the need for quality control and high ethical standards.

Before his untimely death as a young man, Joe Fitzgerald contributed significantly to the high level of medical practice and teaching activities at the Hospital Center in Salisbury, Maryland.

Yash Togo came to us from the University of Tokyo in 1956 for training in infectious diseases and virology. His contemplated stay was for two years. Happily, he did not return and contributed importantly to our research program and vaccine activities for several decades. A few years later, he became Merck's senior representative for Japan, but Baltimore is Kay's and Yash's home.

Two old salts, Milton Miller and Bill Stodgehill, came from Kentucky for training in medicine. They returned to Louisville and became leading physicians there. Recently, Milton has published an interesting, very readable, and sensitive book about his experiences as a combat infantry man in Germany during the later stages of World War II.

Many reliable friends and associates enjoyed their teaching and performed so well. Among them are John Sadler, Emilio Ramos, Paul Light, Bob Singleton, Nathan Carliner, Gary Plotnick, Mark Applefeld, Bill Valente, and Joan Raskin. A little earlier was Tom Connor, John Wiswell, Jim Allen, Dan Schubert and Shelley Greisman. Hal Standiford, a busy man who makes himself always available, is now Governor of the American College of Physicians for Maryland. Don Dembo keeps busy and serves so effectively in cardiology at the Sinai Hospital and contributes importantly to local medical society activities. George Lawrence keeps very active at St. Agnes Hospital and finds time to affiliate with the Maryland Endocrine Group. Emile (Mickey) Mohler, a former house officer and an outstanding clinician, contributes so importantly to many local medical activities. At Harbor General Hospital, Chris Papadopoulos ably directs the cardiology program.

Westminster and Carroll County have been blessed with the medical talents of Jack Harshey, Vincent Fiocco, Dan Welliver, and Alva Baker—all excellent physicians active in civic affairs as well. In Easton, on the Eastern Shore, Donald T. (Ted) Lewers, an internist-nephrologist first developed a creditable nephrology program at Maryland General Hospital before moving there. Ted is now a trustee of the American Medical Association. Bill Wood contributes to the high standards of medical practice in Easton as did Skip Dawkins before his untimely death.

Terry McGuire, a very busy practitioner in Seat Pleasant, Maryland, has found time to carefully evaluate patients' problems and publish important data on community-oriented infections.

In Frederick, there is a long line of solid alumni and house officers who found a happy home; Harry Chase, now retired, my classmate, Bernard Thomas, George Smith, Casper Klein, and Ali Afrookteh are all fine physicians who have greatly strengthened the excellent medical staff at the Memorial Hospital.

York, Pennsylvania has well profited with the teaching and medical practices of Francine Camitta Butler and Wolfe Blotzer, each a fine clinician with special talents in endocrinology and rheumatology, respectively.

Several old friends who left internal medicine to become leaders in other fields are Karl Weaver in pediatrics and Paul Meyer in neurosurgery. John Eckholt has made a fine career in neurology; all are in Baltimore.

Norton Spritz is Professor of Medicine and a leading educator and investigator at Cornell, New York University; he is a recognized authority on the ravages of arteriosclerosis.

Larry Tierney, now on the academic faculty in San Diego, makes the teaching of medicine and infectious diseases interesting for medical students and house officers.

Gregg Elliott at the University of Colorado, Denver keeps active in medicine and pulmonary medicine. His contributions relate to primary pulmonary hypertension and associated lung disorders.

Bill Marshall, class of 1958, is a busy clinician in Dayton, Ohio and active in academic affairs at Wayne State University as Vice-Dean. He has served as President of the Ohio Medical Society.

Bill Gillen was one of the first house officers to train in our general practice Family Medicine Program in the early 1950s. He is an active practitioner in Kansas and maintains frequent contact with us. Gene Gangarosa and Michael Gregg became senior members and most effective contributors at the Center for Disease Control in Atlanta. They worked in Lahore, Pakistan during the early days of the Tropical Disease Medical Center there. Gene became Dean of the American University in Beirut and Mike, among many things, helped clarify the relationship between Pontiac fever and legionella.

Of some interest, a number of medical school and department alumni have returned to present the annual Maurice C. Pincoff's Lecture in Davidge Hall. They are:

David M. Kipnis, 1974
Michael B.A. Oldstone, 1984
Leonard T. Kurland, 1990
Edward D. Frohlich, 1991
Louis R. Caplan, 1992
Richard P. Wenzel, 1993
Arlie Mansberger, 1996
Philip Toskes, 1998